THE ADVANCE THROUGH NORTH AFRICA

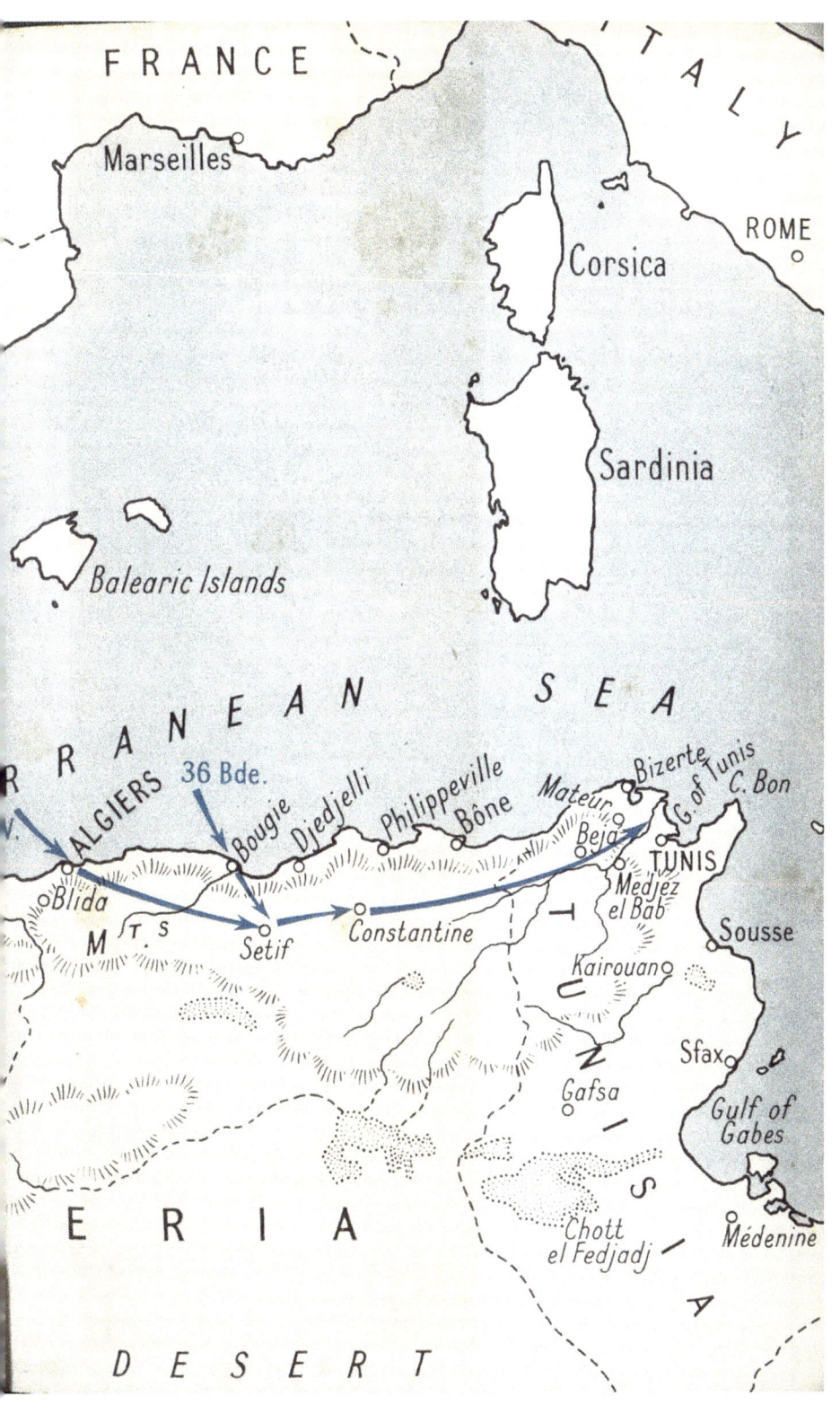

ALGIERS TO AUSTRIA

This history of the campaigns of 78 Division and its journey from Algiers to Austria is dedicated to those officers and men of the Division who were killed in action or died through wounds, accidents or illness incurred whilst serving in the Division and thus did not live to see the Dawn of Victory.

> "Take thou the splendour, carry it out of sight
> Into the great new age I must not know,
> Into the great new realm I must not tread."
>
> ALFRED NOYES.

CYRIL RAY

ALGIERS TO AUSTRIA

A History of 78 Division
in the Second World War

The Naval & Military Press Ltd

Published by

The Naval & Military Press Ltd
Unit 10 Ridgewood Industrial Park,
Uckfield, East Sussex,
TN22 5QE England

Tel: +44 (0) 1825 749494
Fax: +44 (0) 1825 765701

www.naval-military-press.com
www.military-genealogy.com

In reprinting in facsimile from the original, any imperfections are inevitably reproduced and the quality may fall short of modern type and cartographic standards.

ACKNOWLEDGMENTS

THIS history of 78 Division has been based as far as possible on the divisional war diaries, kindly made available by the War Office, and on unit accounts of various phases of the campaigns. I have also consulted, for the strategic background, General Sir Kenneth Anderson's and General Sir Henry Maitland Wilson's official reports and Field-Marshal Lord Alexander's official despatches, published as supplements to the *London Gazette*.

Much of the detail, however, comes from personal diaries kept by officers who served in the Division, from accounts given me verbally, and from books on the North African, Sicilian, and Italian campaigns written by newspaper correspondents each of whom saw something of the Division's achievements.

My thanks are due, therefore, to the following officers for material lent to me during the writing of this account:

Lt. S. D. Bowles
Major G. R. Brocklebank, D.S.O., M.C.
Major D. Carey
Lt.-Col. D. G. Collins
Brigadier V. Copland Griffiths
Captain J. F. Dawson
Major the Hon. R. E. Denison-Pender
Major T. Dixon, M.C.
Colonel J. C. Gilroy, O.B.E.
Major M. S. Hancock
Major D. A. Harris, M.B.E., M.C.
Major K. C. Hind
Major H. M. A. Hunter, D.S.O., M.B.E.

Captain I. McKee
Captain Nigel Nicolson
Captain R. M. Porter
Captain A. D. Paterson
Captain H. F. Payne
Captain J. A. Pike
Major N. C. Pollock, M.B.E.
Captain D. A. M. Pring, M.C.
Brigadier F. S. Reid, C.B.E., D.S.O.
Brigadier N. Russell, D.S.O., M.C.
Brigadier T. P. D. Scott, C.B.E., D.S.O.
Major S. Stewart, M.C.
The Officers of 17 Field Regiment, R.A.

I have also consulted the following published works, to the

ACKNOWLEDGMENTS

authors and publishers of which I wish to express my thanks:
Birth of an Army, by the late A. B. Austin, of the *Daily Herald*,
Road to Rome, by the late Christopher Buckley, of the *Daily Telegraph*,
Tunisian Battle, by the late John d'Arcy-Dawson, of Kemsley Newspapers,
The Monastery, by Major Fred Majdalany, M.C.,
History of the 8th Argylls, by Lt.-Col. A. D. Malcolm, O.B.E.,
and *African Trilogy*, by Alan Moorehead, of the *Daily Express*.

In addition, the editor of the *Manchester Guardian* kindly allowed me to use despatches written for that newspaper by the late E. A. Montague from North Africa and by myself from Italy.

Throughout the writing of this account I have been guided and corrected, with the greatest patience and kindness, by Brigadiers J. Wedderburn-Maxwell, D.S.O., M.C., and D. A. S. Browne, C.B.E., and Lt.-Cols. G. Ashmore, O.B.E. and A. D. Malcolm, O.B.E., and others whom they themselves consulted, together with three former commanders of the Division, Lt.-Gen. Sir Charles Keightley, K.B.E., C.B., D.S.O., and Major-Generals V. Evelegh, C.B., D.S.O., M.C., and R. K. Arbuthnott, C.B., C.B.E., D.S.O., M.C.

In expressing my gratitude to these officers I must make it plain that such inaccuracies as may have escaped their notice are my own, as are any judgments expressed on strategy and tactics.

Finally I must thank my secretary, Miss Diana Hunter, who has typed, retyped, and typed again my crabbed and much-corrected manuscript, and who has marshalled maps and material with a generalship worthy of the Division to which they referred.

CONTENTS

	page
Foreword	xiii
Prologue	xvii

BOOK I. NORTH AFRICA

I. The Team Takes the Field	3
II. The Two Pronged Thrust for Tunis	10
III. A Plan that Failed	24
IV. The Nine Attacks of Von Arnim and the Ten Day Battle of the Ten Peaks	32
V. Into the Straight	48

BOOK II. SICILY

I. Introduction	59
II. Fortnight of Fighting	61

BOOK III. ITALY

I. Introduction	81
II. From the Toe to Termoli	83
III. Rivers to Cross	93

CONTENTS

IV. The Mountains and the Monastery	107
V. The Road to Rome	122
VI. Hannibal's Battlefield	141
VII. Egyptian Interlude	153
VIII. The Northern Apennines	159
IX. Winter in the Mountains	176
X. Spring in the Valley	191
XI. The Argenta Gap	199
XII. The End in Italy	214
The Occupation of Austria	227
Appendix A. Order of Battle	235
Appendix B. Commanders and Staff	236
Glossary	241
Index	

ILLUSTRATIONS

facing page

5 Northamptons on patrol	18
Point 667, near Medjez-el-Bab	18
View towards Chaouach from 5 Northamptons' positions	19
237 Field Company R.E. clearing mines	19
A patrol of 2 Lancashire Fusiliers near Chaouach	34
Gen. Sir Harold Alexander and Maj. Gen. Evelegh at an O.P. near Heidous	35
Mule Harbour near Bettiour	35
Mule train on the path to Tanngoucha	50
Tanngoucha	50
Maj. Gen. Evelegh and Brig. Wedderburn-Maxwell preparing the attack on Longstop, April 22, 1943	50
8 Argylls advancing to attack Longstop, April 23, 1943	50
Looking towards Tunis	51
Entering Tunis	51
Gen. Sir Kenneth Anderson presenting decorations after the capture of Tunis	51
Entering Centuripe	98
Centuripe	98
Looking north across the Sangro	99
The Sangro Escarpment	99

ILLUSTRATIONS

Rest Camp at Portocannone	114
Winter; line of communication	114
Maj. Gen. C. F. Keightley	115
Cassino Castle and Town	122
Beyond the Rapido. 214 Field Company R.E. making a bridge	122
Advancing in the Liri valley	123
38 (Irish) Brigade Pipes and Drums in Rome	123
Bailey Bridge at Valsalva near Castel del Rio	162
Bridge near Castel del Rio	162
Maj. Gen. R. K. Arbuthnott	163
Path near San Apollinare	178
Transport in the mountains	178
Making the road from Cuviolo to San Apollinare	179
The road to San Apollinare completed	179
The ford at San Clemente	186
Jeep service station at Castel del Rio	186
Rear H.Q. 78 Division in Castel del Rio	187
Damaged trucks at Rear H.Q. after shelling	187
Gen. Mark Clark, G.O.C. Fifth Army; Maj. Gen. R. K. Arbuthnott; Lt. Gen. S. C. Kirkman, G.O.C. XIII Corps	194
The Senio bank	195
Crossing the Santerno	195

MAPS

The landings at Algiers

Tunisia

Advance of 36 Brigade, November 1942

Advance of 11 Brigade, December 1942

The Medjerda Valley and the Ten Peaks

Sicily

The Battle of Centuripe

Route of Advance—Taranto to the Sangro

The Battle of Termoli—the advance

The Battle of Termoli—positions after the Battle

The Crossing of the Trigno

The Battle of the Sangro

Route of Advance—Naples to Rome

Cassino and the Liri Valley

Route of Advance—Rome to Lake Trasimene

The Mountain Battleground. Winter 1944-45

The Advance to the Winter Line

The Advance to the Po

Austria

THE LANDINGS AT ALGIERS

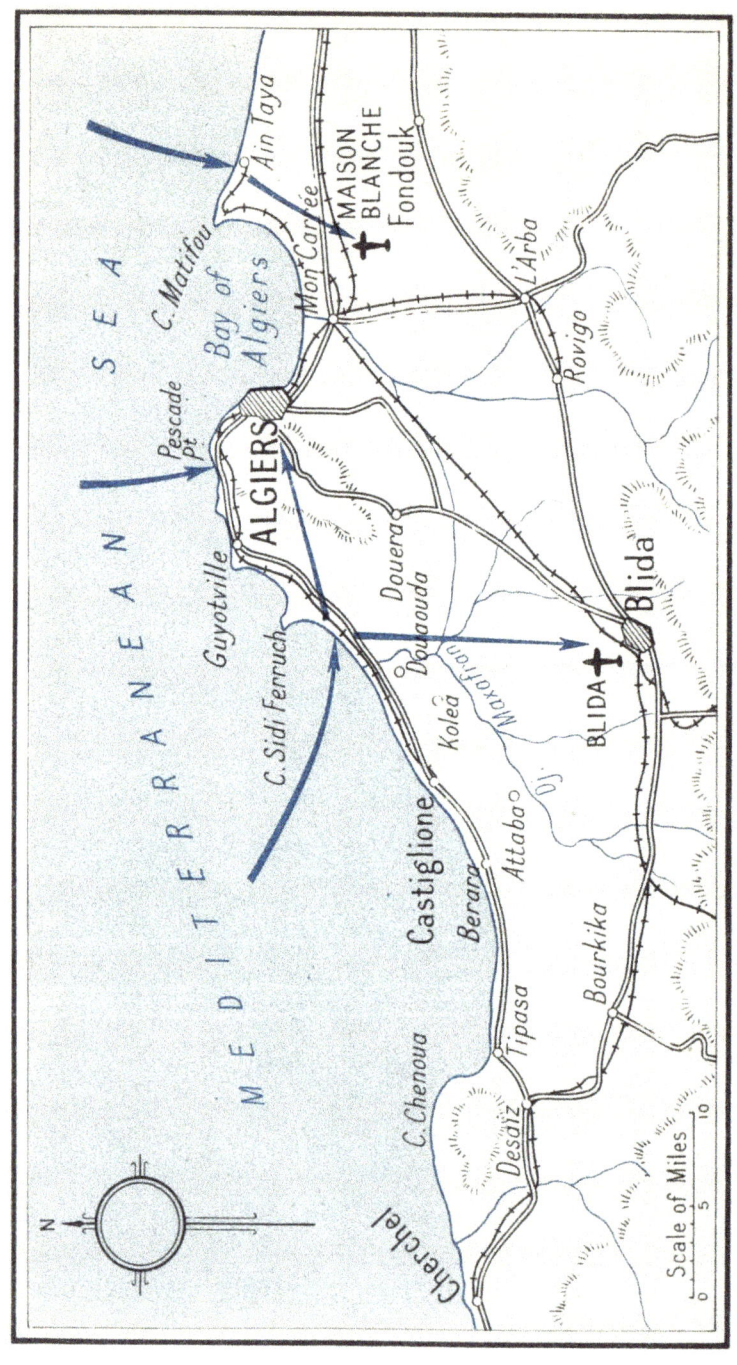

TUNISIA

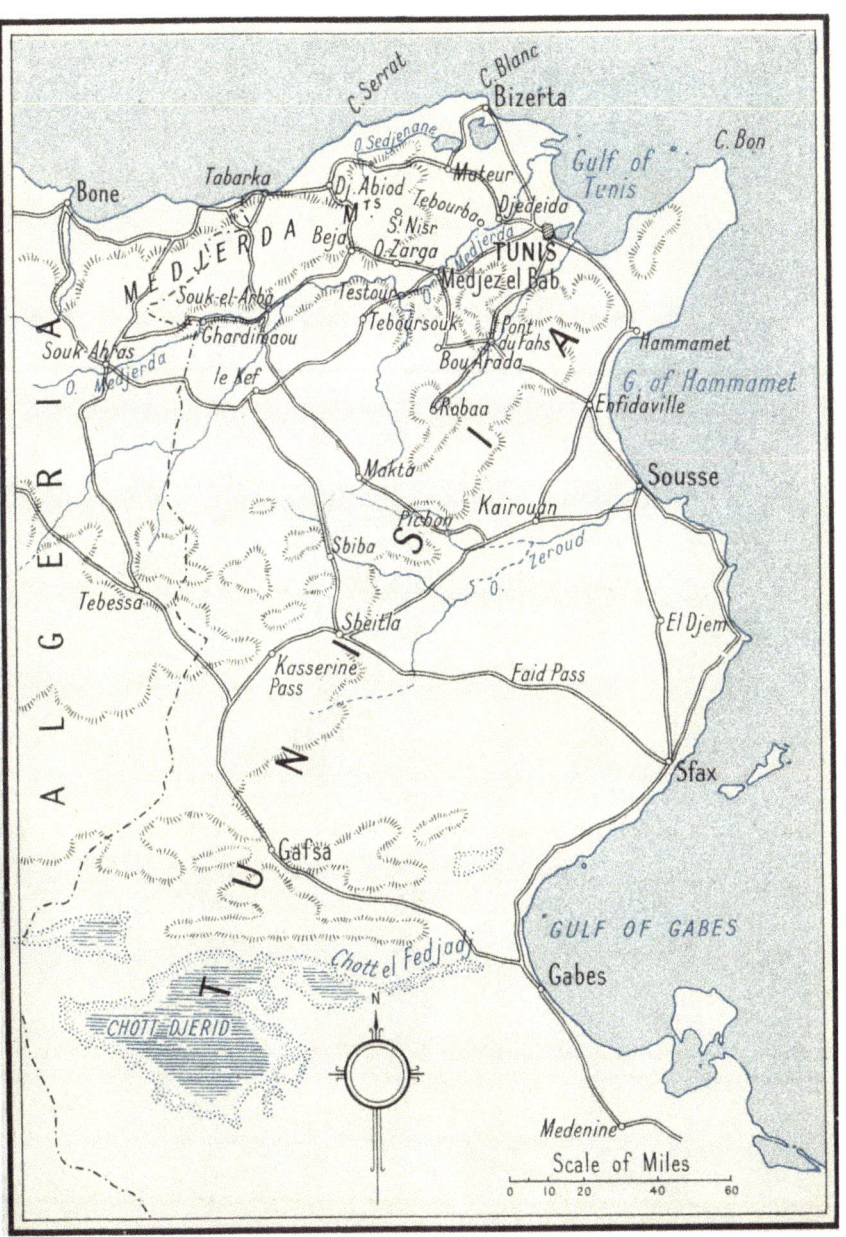

ADVANCE OF 36 BRIGADE, NOVEMBER 1942

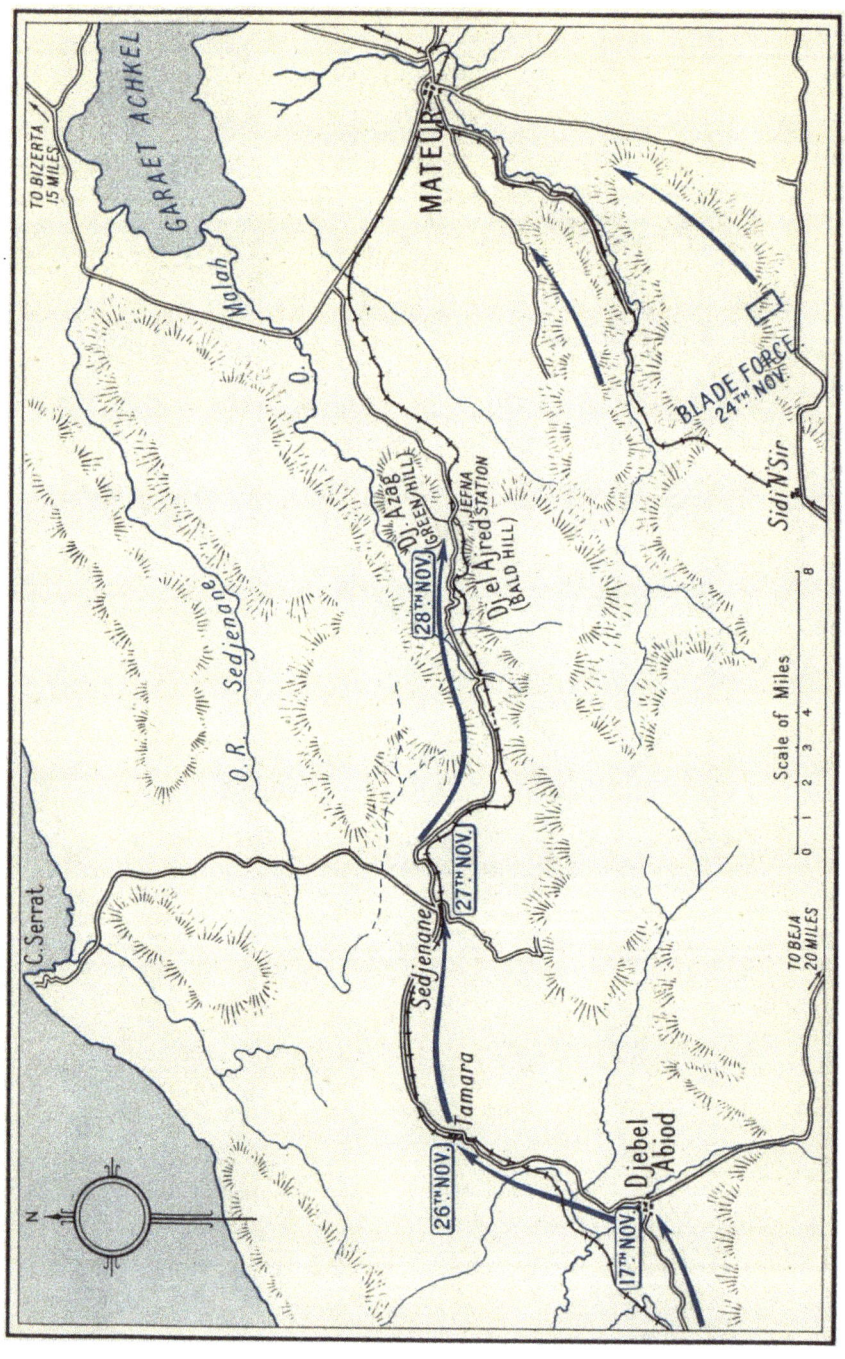

ADVANCE OF 11 BRIGADE, DECEMBER 1942

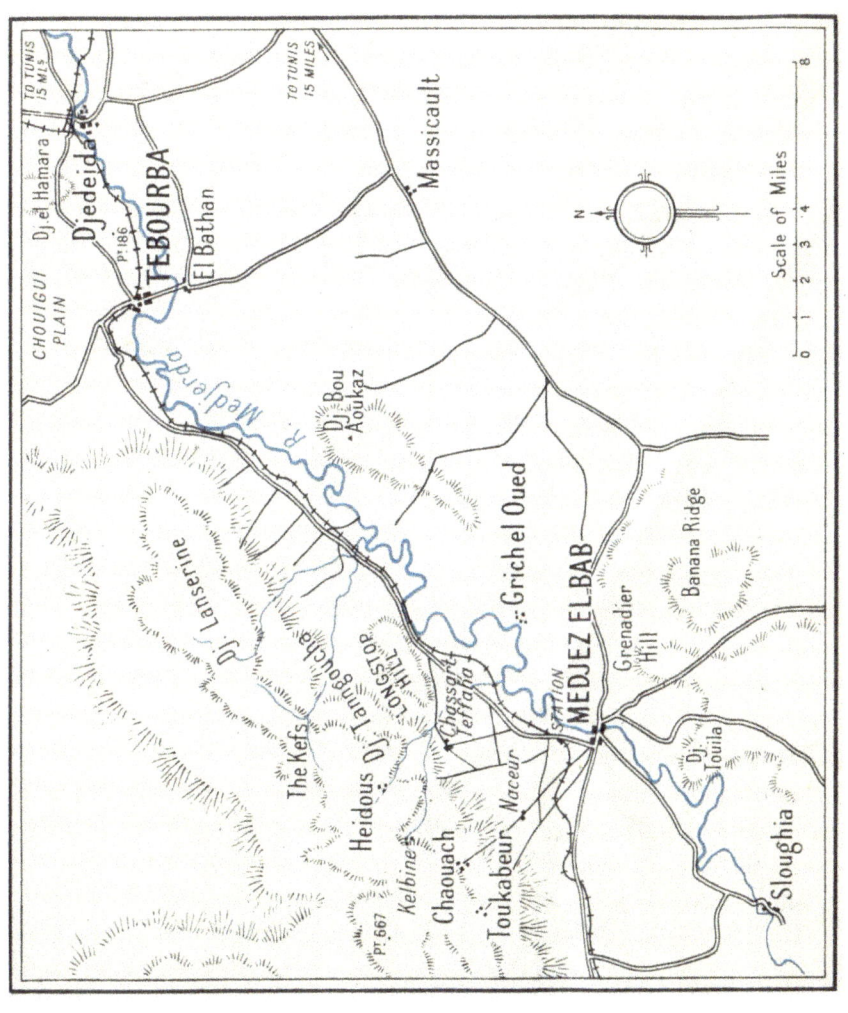

THE MEDJERDA VALLEY AND THE BATTLE OF THE TEN PEAKS

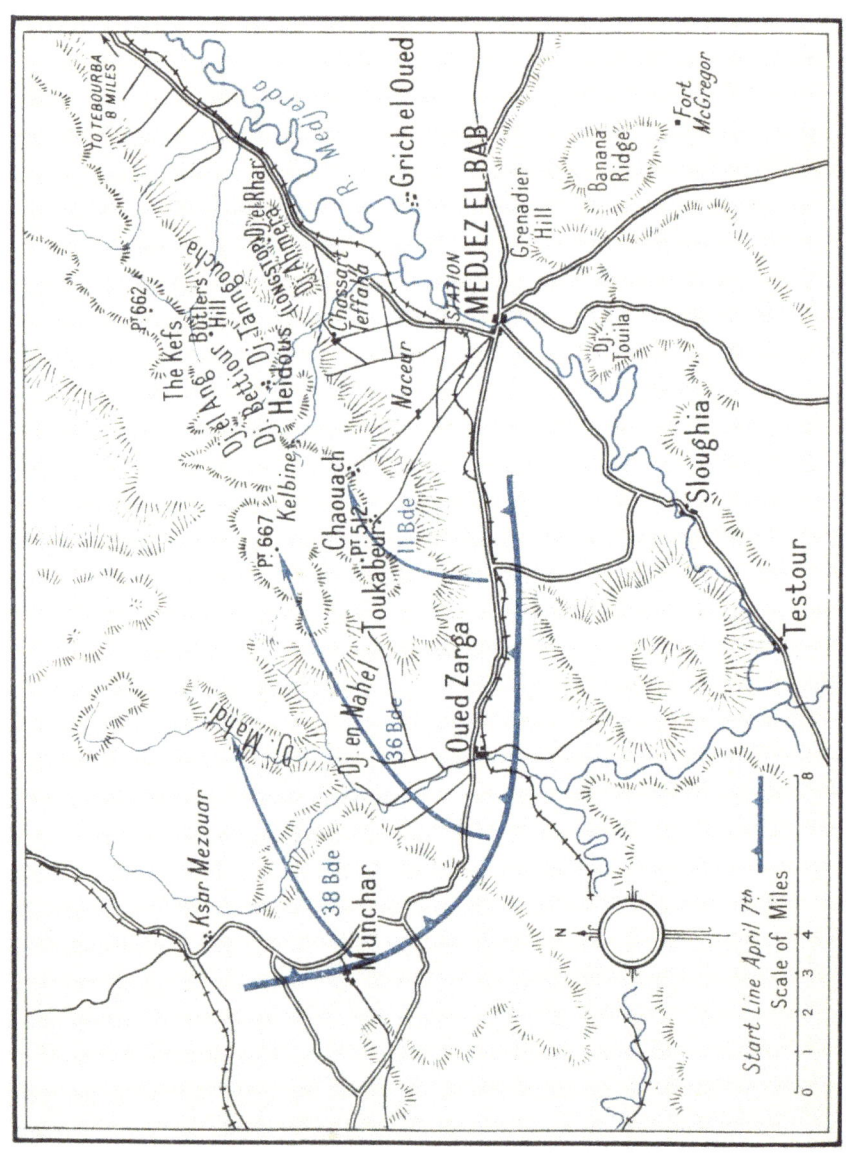

SICILY

THE BATTLE OF CENTURIPE

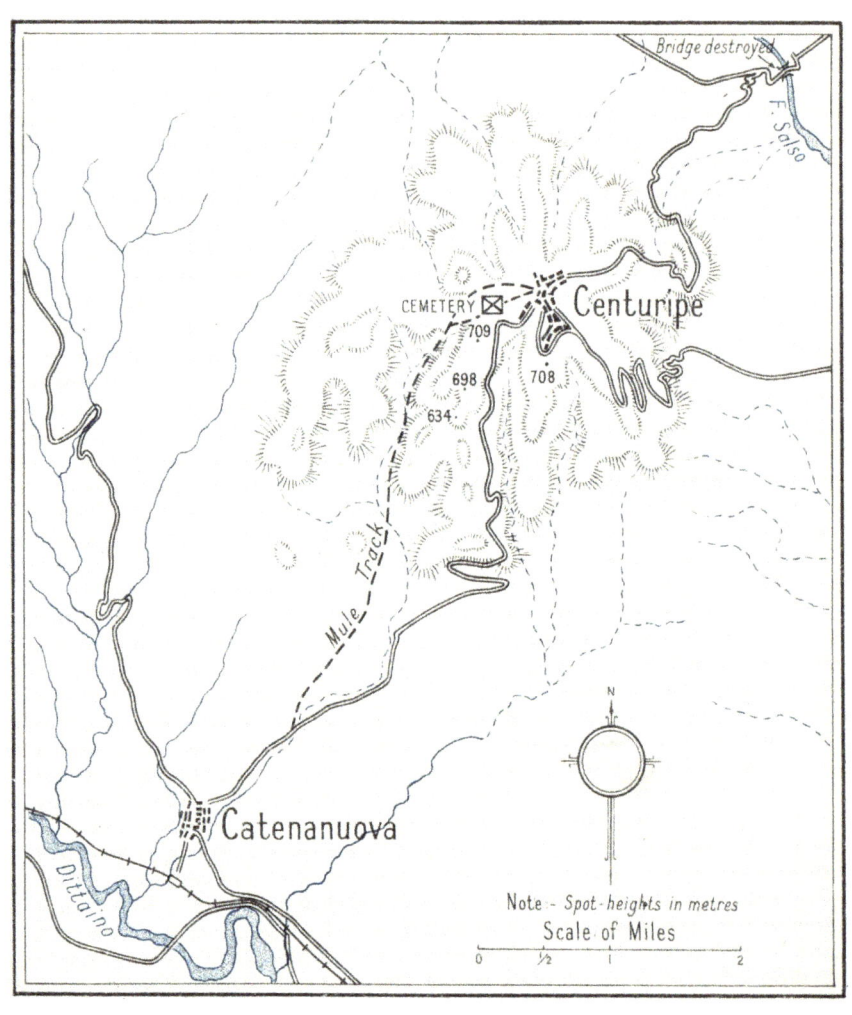

ROUTE OF ADVANCE—TARANTO TO THE SANGRO

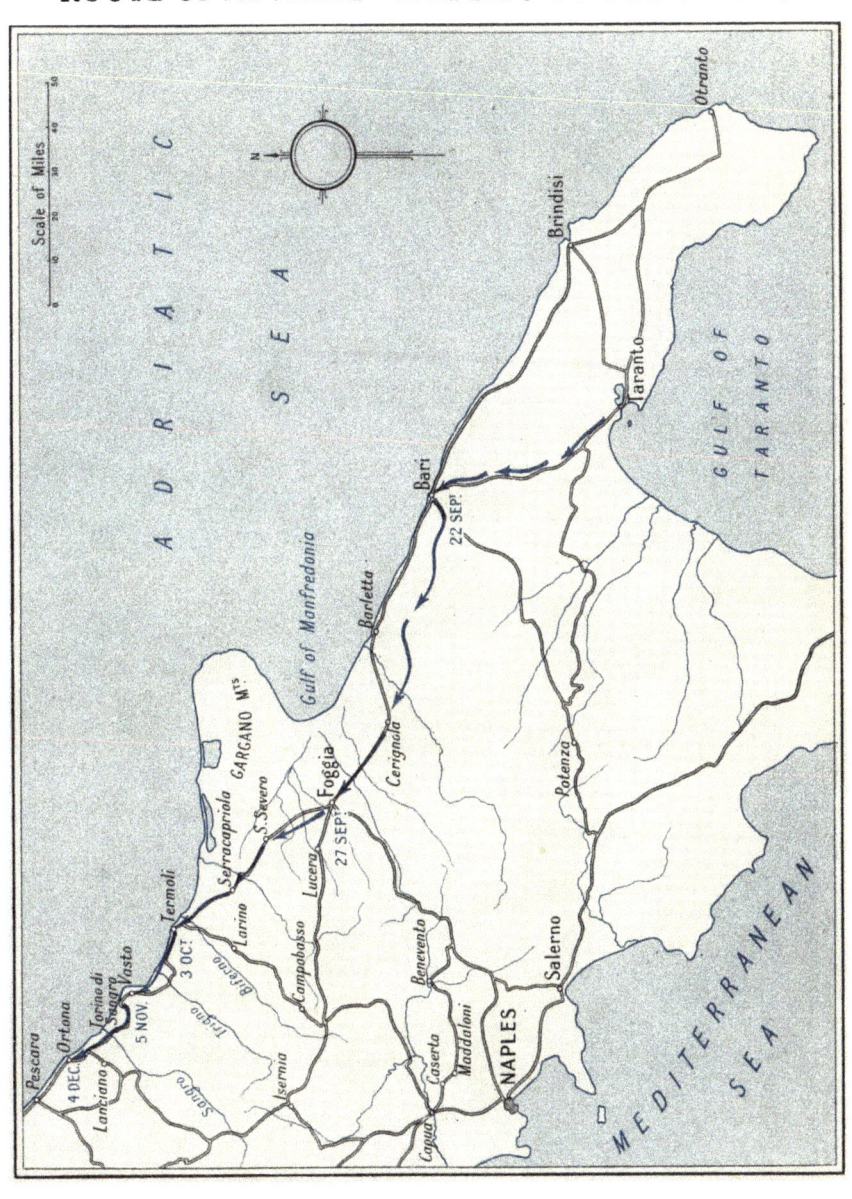

THE BATTLE OF TERMOLI—THE ADVANCE

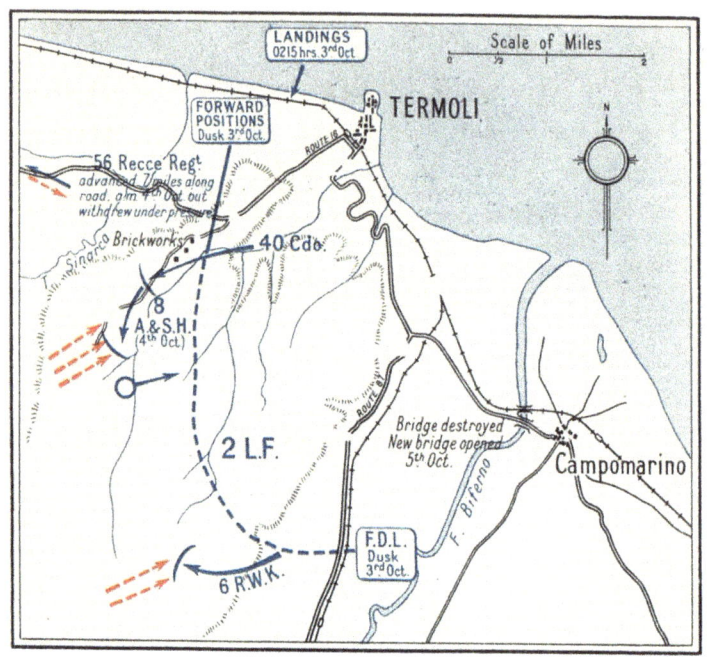

POSITIONS AFTER THE BATTLE

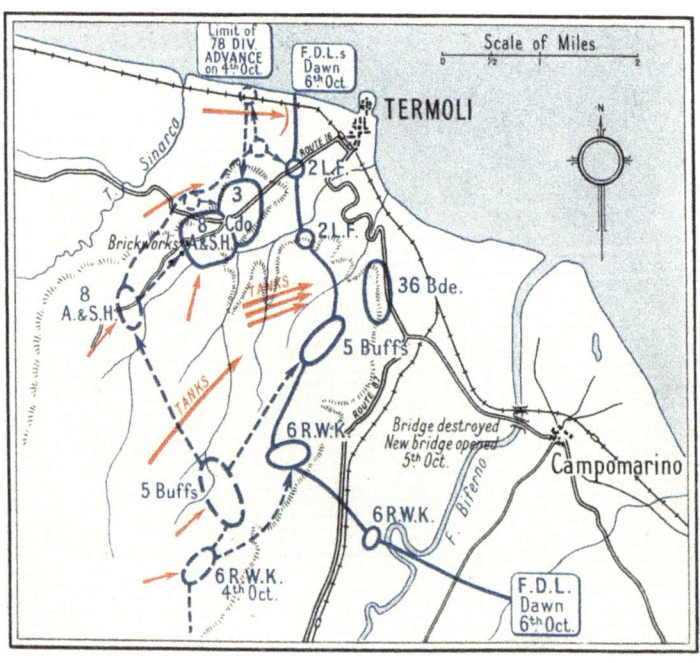

THE CROSSING OF THE TRIGNO

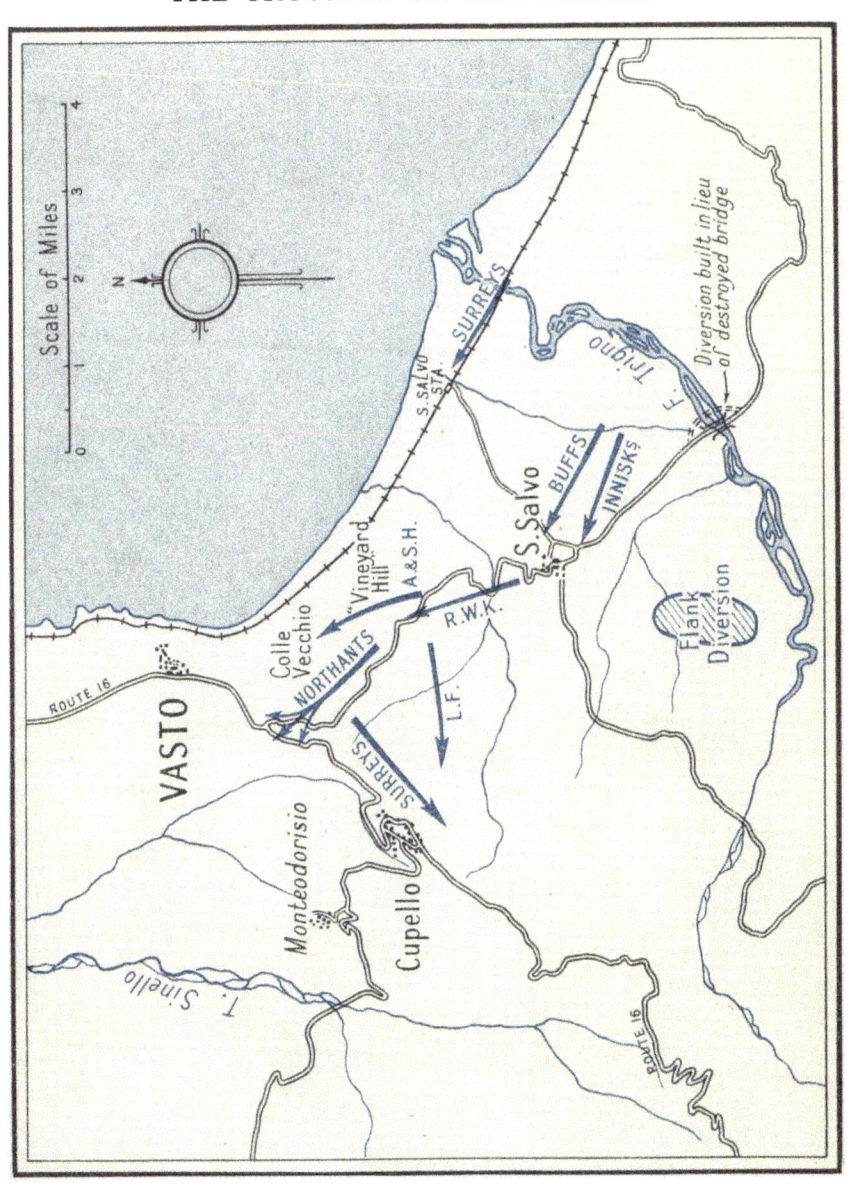

THE BATTLE OF THE SANGRO

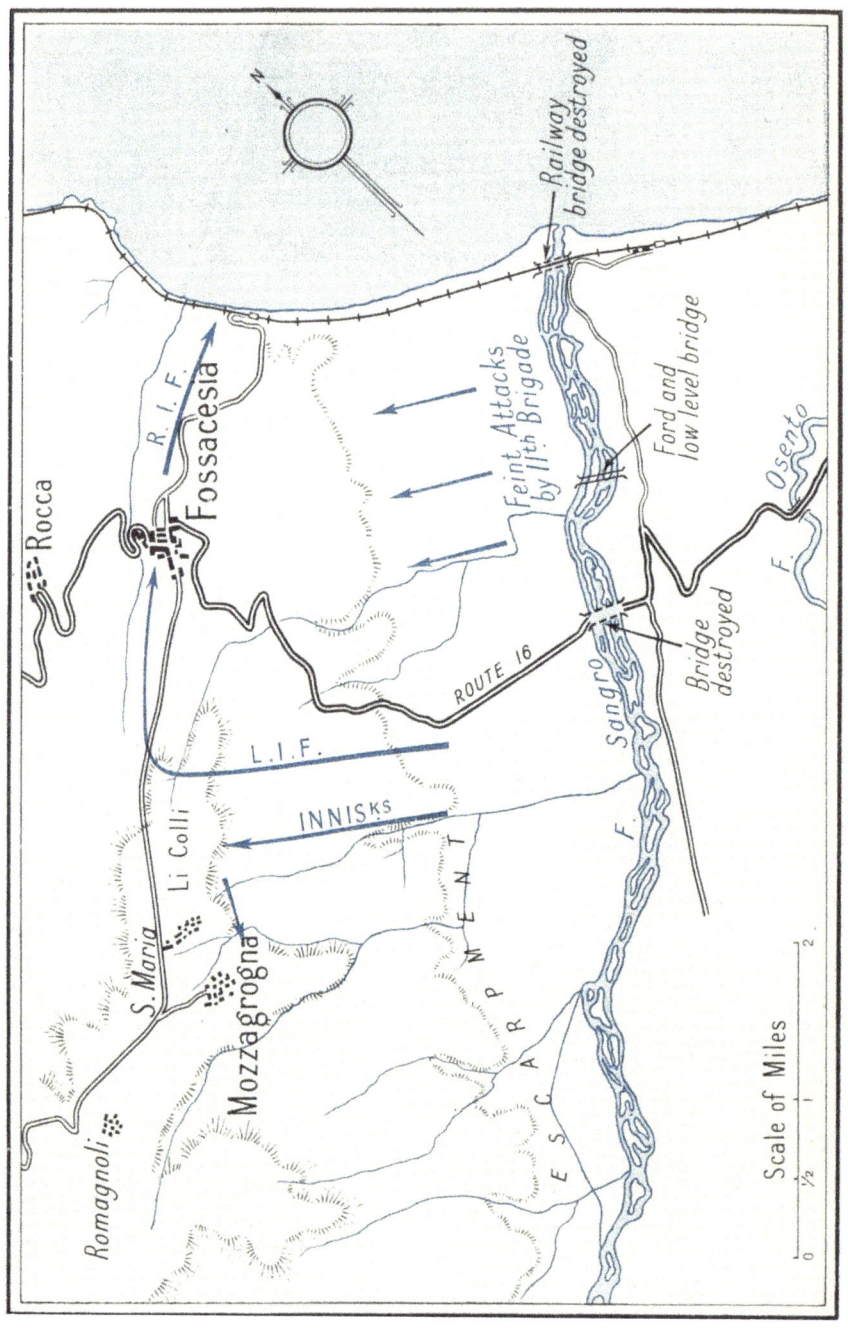

NAPLES TO ROME

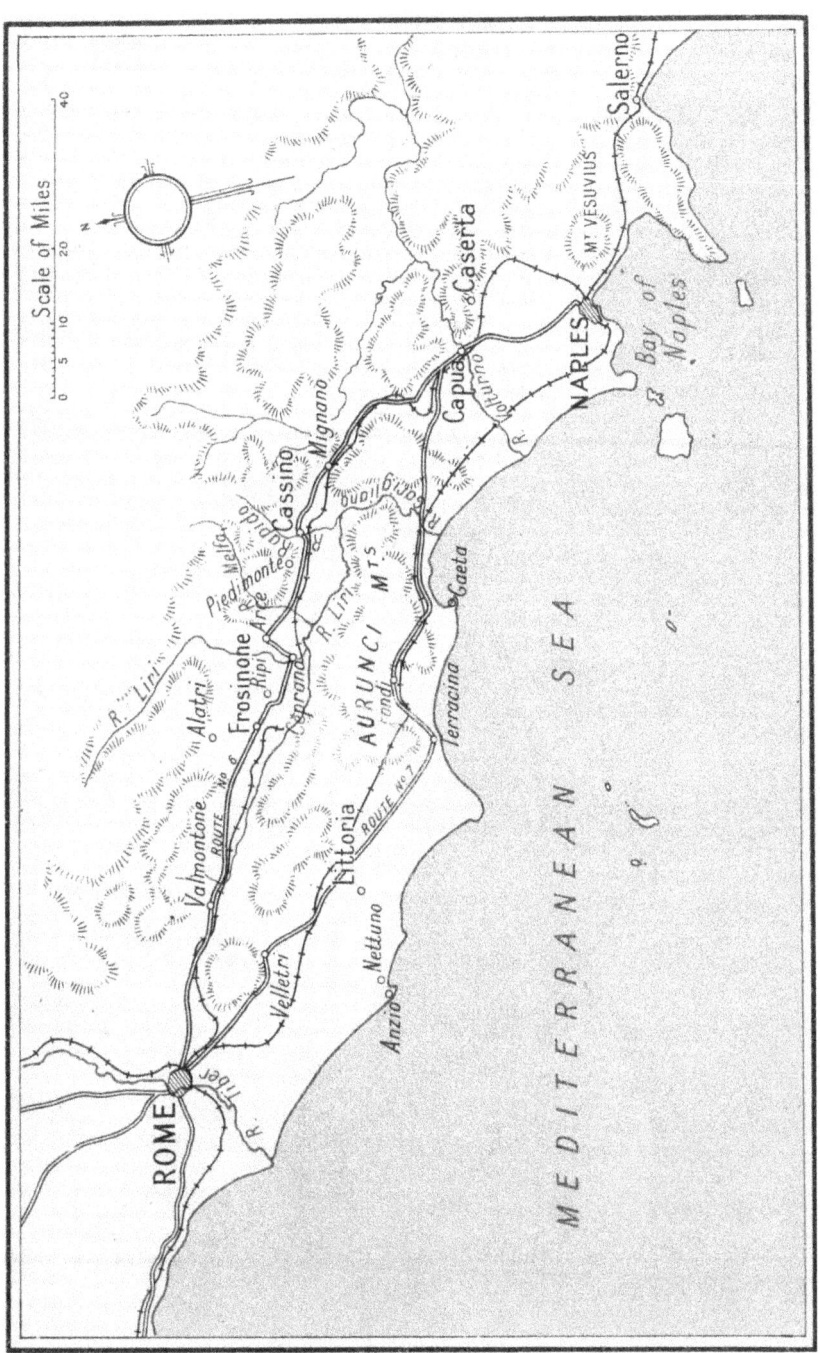

CASSINO AND THE LIRI VALLEY

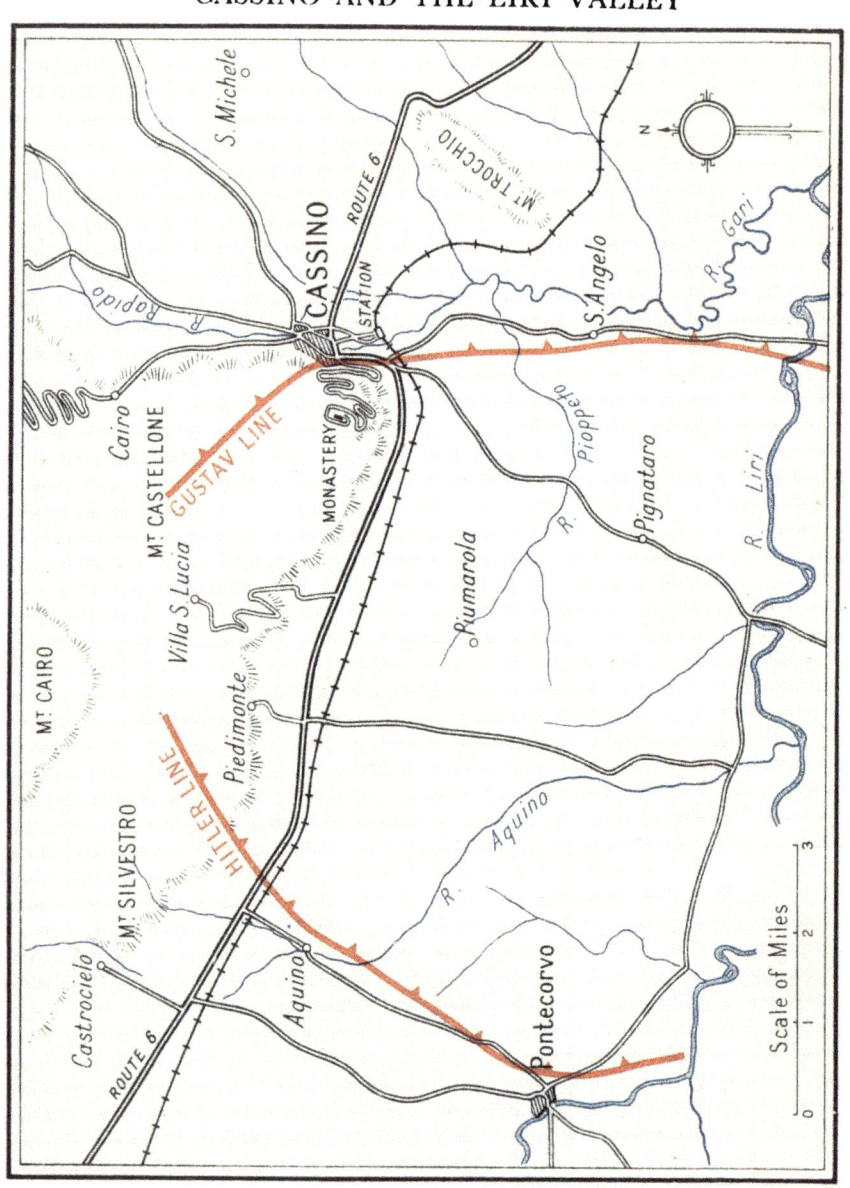

ROME TO LAKE TRASIMENE

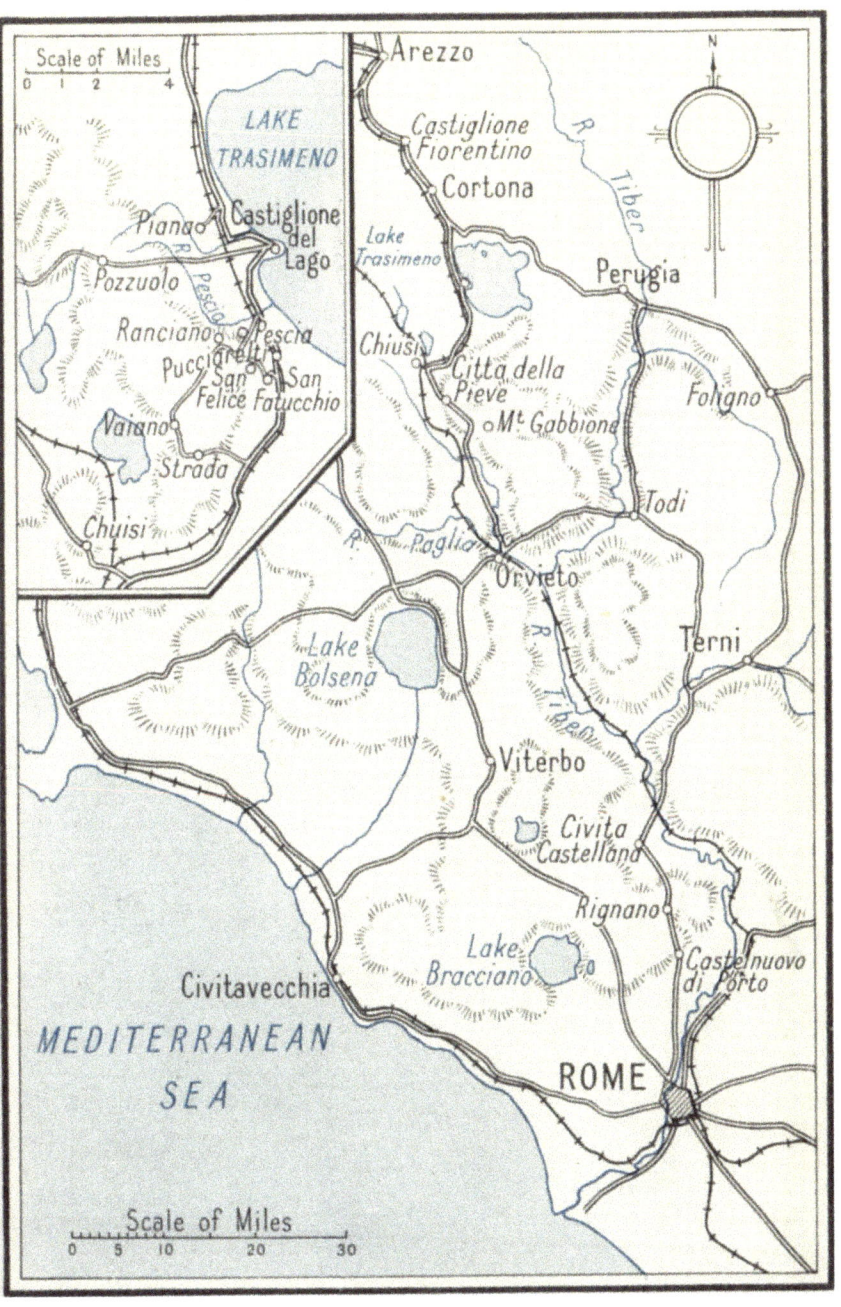

THE MOUNTAIN BATTLEGROUND. WINTER 1944/45

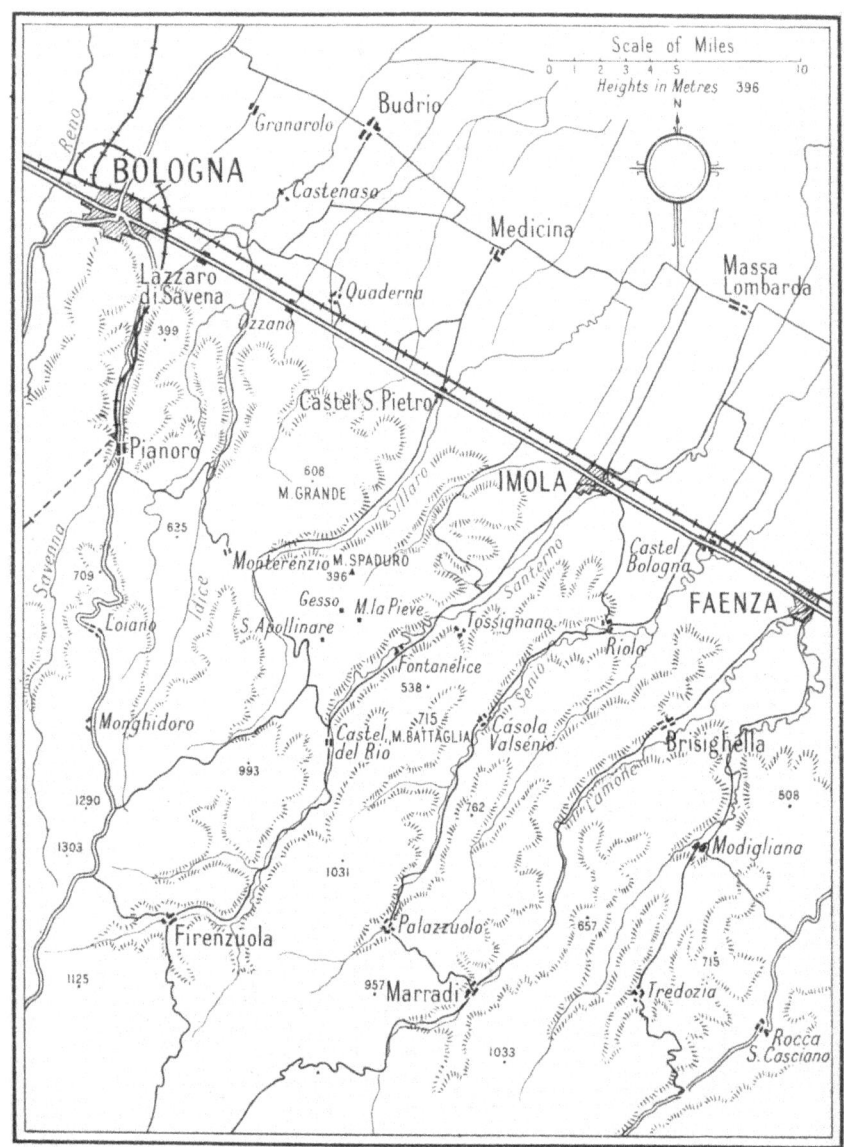

THE WINTER LINE

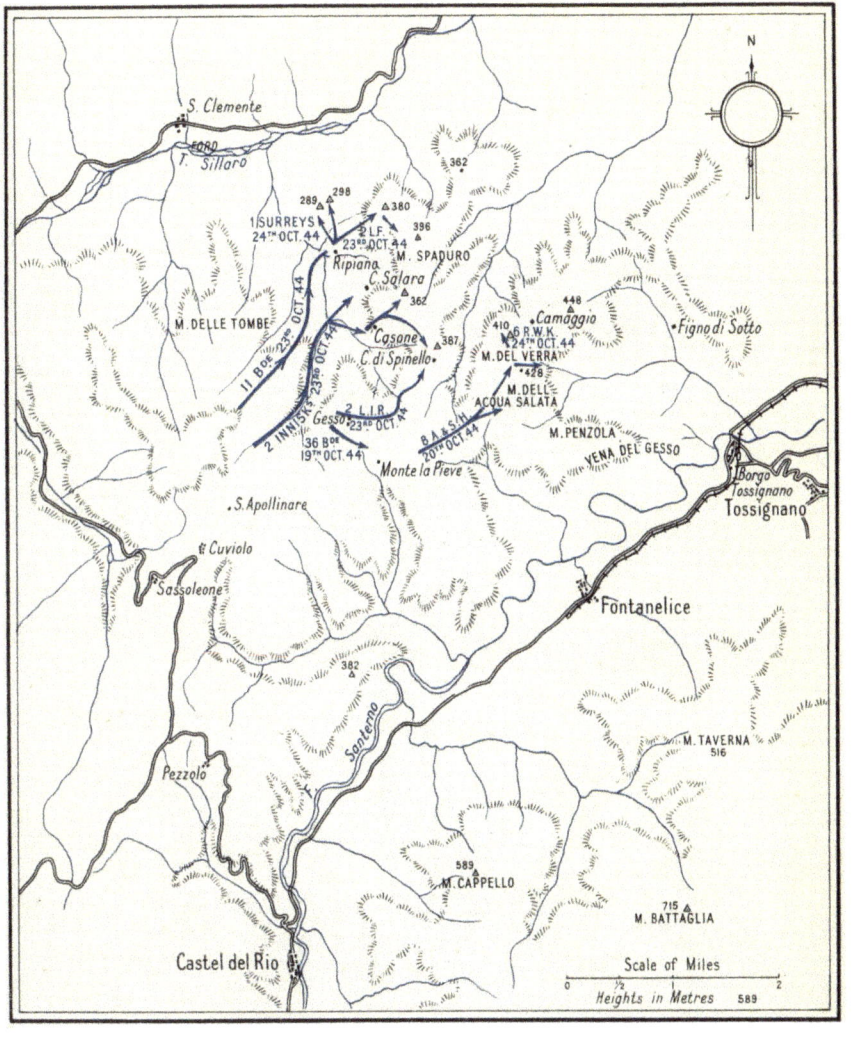

THE ADVANCE TO THE PO

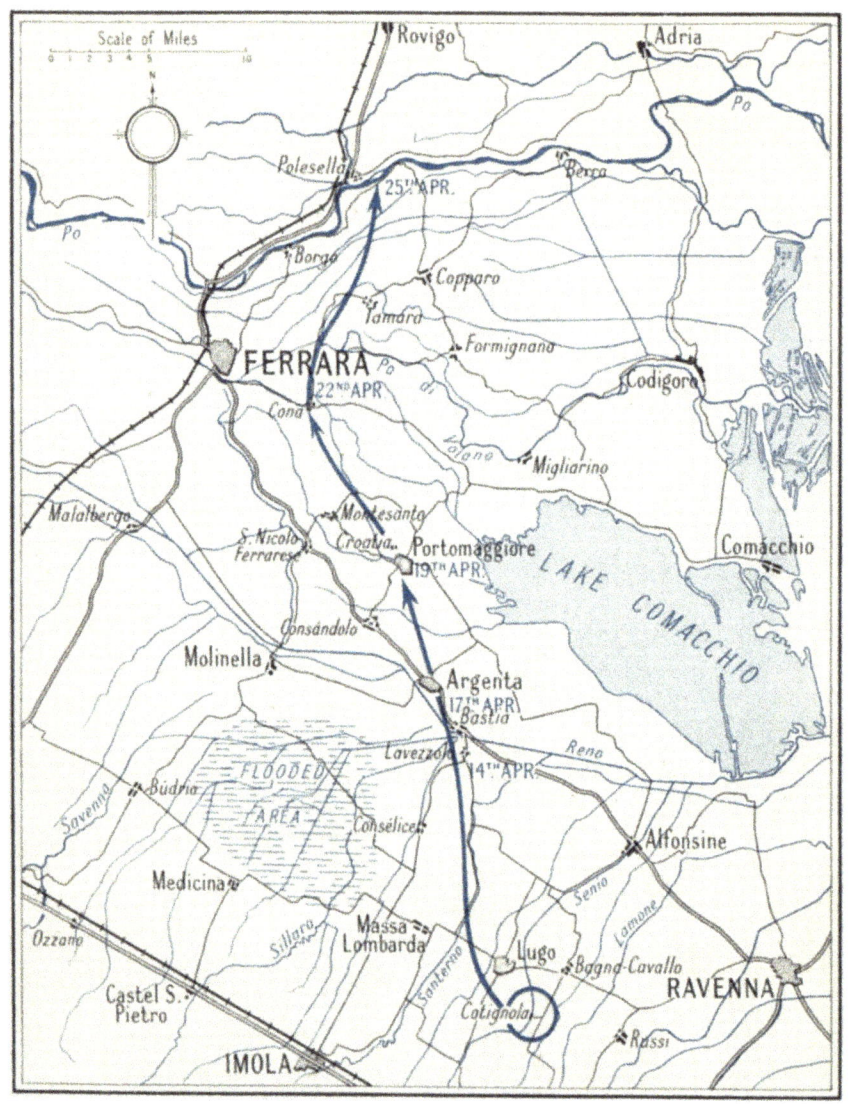

AUSTRIA

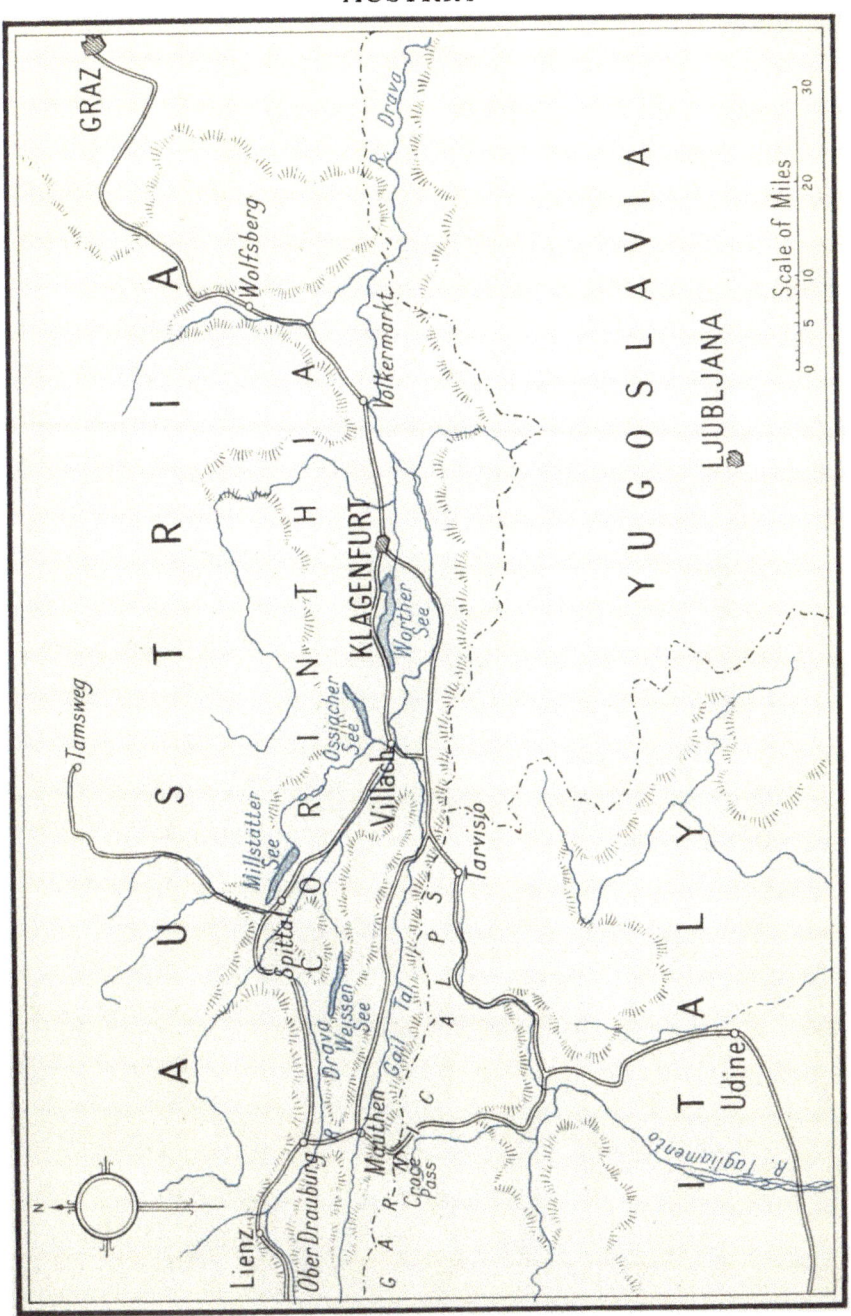

FOREWORD

by Lt.-Gen. Sir CHARLES ALLFREY, K.B.E., C.B., D.S.O., M.C.

I CONSIDER it a great honour to be asked to write a short foreword to this Divisional history as, in my opinion, the 78 Division was the finest fighting division of any that I had the privilege to have in V Corps.

It was formed in Scotland in 1942 with the object of landing in North Africa that same year. It was given one brigade from a regular division and all the troops were carefully selected. Six months were available to knit these fine troops into a cohesive fighting force. All ranks got down to it with a will with the result that, by the time the landing in North Africa was made, the Division had the "feel" of an experienced division. But most of the troops were as yet untried in battle. Every effort was made by the Divisional Commander to ensure that they got the best possible launch in the initial stages. That this was done at a time when an all-out drive on Tunis was being made reflects the greatest credit on all commanders.

The original attempt to drive straight through to Tunis, a distance of 500 miles, was not successful mainly because the Germans brought in strong reinforcements by air. During this period 78 Division fought with skill and great dash. No one could have done more. They were faced by first-class troops, experienced in battle, and they fought magnificently. Inevitably hard knocks were taken, and when it became clear that the capture of Tunis was not possible, the Division was badly over-extended. In addition it was 500 miles from where it had landed, and its lines of communication were strained to the utmost.

It succeeded in reorganising itself and occupied a defensive position in order to build up for another effort. This second effort, timed for Christmas, had to be abandoned owing to

FOREWORD

torrential rain, and 78 Division settled down to a grim winter. Everything possible was done to help them materially, but for the bulk of the winter they were stretched to the limit and opposed by a first-class enemy. They acquitted themselves magnificently gaining experience all the time. Very soon it was clear that our men had the measure of the enemy, and the initiative in no-man's-land passed into the hands of 78 Division.

The winter was an anxious one with many attempts by the enemy to pierce our positions on other parts of the British and American fronts. This made it impossible to relieve 78 Division in order to give them a rest, or to reduce the extended frontages they were holding. Probing attacks, raids and actions by strong fighting patrols were almost nightly affairs with the result that little rest was possible.

In the spring fresh divisions began to arrive from England and preparations were made for an advance on Tunis. Much preliminary fighting was necessary in order to clear the enemy from strong positions overlooking our proposed line of advance. This entailed a lot of very hard fighting in extremely difficult country, much of it being done at night. The bulk of this fell to 78 Division who mounted attack after attack clearing the ring of hills overlooking Medjez-el-Bab, and finishing with the epic attack which captured Longstop Hill. Not only had they fought continuously throughout the winter but they had also done the bulk of the fighting which so successfully opened out the way for the final assault. No wonder therefore that when they were brought up to take over Tunis after its capture, and received an hysterical welcome from the French, *The Times* correspondent reported: "Though the French may not have known it, they were thanking the right men". During the fighting of the last six months they had suffered very heavy casualties and had been fighting continuously under severe winter conditions. Their morale throughout had been beyond praise and everyone recognised that the Battleaxe Division was second to none.

It is interesting to look deeper into the reasons why this fine division found its feet so soon and established itself as a first-class fighting division. The infantry would be the first to acknowledge the wonderful support they received, not only

FOREWORD

from their own Divisional Artillery but also from Corps and other supporting artillery. The Divisional Staff used their artillery in the best possible way and the liaison between infantry and gunner was such that the infantryman came to expect and knew he would receive first-class support. And so he did. In addition in the hill fighting the support the Division got from their tanks—especially the Churchill tanks—was outstanding. The crews got their tanks to many places which the Germans considered tank proof. The care taken in the original launch of the Division into battle had a great deal to do with its subsequent success. In the actions which followed, it was extremely skilfully put into battle and given the best possible chance of success by its commander. Finally it would be fair to say that the Administrative Staff can claim their full share of the success attained. The troops were splendidly served by the Administrative Staffs at all levels from Unit to Corps, and it certainly produced its results on morale.

I have dealt at some length with the initial launch into battle and the North African campaign as that is where I had the closest contact with 78 Division. It was, however, only the start of a great war record. The Division went on to Sicily and fought just as everyone expected it would.

There was little rest before it was committed to battle again in Italy, where, pushing up the East Coast it found itself faced by a succession of river lines. Here again the Division acquitted itself beyond all praise finishing with the battle of the Sangro which was a classic in its own way. After this it was pulled out, in December, 1943, for a rest which it had more than earned.

The part taken by 78 Division in the Cassino battle and the fighting up to the end of hostilities are well described in this book. I am happy to think that a division with such a splendid war record has now had its achievements put on permanent record.

C. W. ALLFREY,
Lt.-Gen. (Retired).

July, 1951.

PROLOGUE

by Brig. J. WEDDERBURN MAXWELL, D.S.O., M.C.

SEVENTY-EIGHT DIVISION was born in June 1942. Many of its formations and units had been training together for some time and, with the expansion of the Amphibious Force 110 into First Army, it was obviously sound to organise this élite spearhead of our new armies as a normal formation. Its components came from many sources. 36 Independent Brigade had replaced 29 Brigade when the latter sailed to capture Madagascar earlier in the year, an operation that more than confirmed the excellence of the training—tactical and administrative—directed by the Combined Training Centre from Largs, whose training grounds and beaches sprawled up the bays, lochs and headlands of the west coast of Scotland. 11 Brigade came from the short-lived "new model" 4 Division. 1 Guards Brigade had joined the force a year earlier when, under the code-name "Pilgrim" an expedition was embarked, ready to provide an alternative should Franco—or Hitler—neutralise Gibraltar.

The artillery was drawn from similarly varied sources. 17 Field Regiment had worked first with 29 and later with 36 Independent Brigade Groups. 132 Field were sturdy Welsh Territorials, and 138 came from 47 (London) Division. 64 Anti-Tank, Q.O. Glasgow Yeomanry, and 49 Light A.A. completed the gunners.

56 Recce arrived from their parent division and the Royal Engineers from other sources.

The staff and services came from existing units or were formed from scratch.

A collection of first-class formations and units does not create a division. Two things were needed, and by good fortune they were to hand; a Commander of the highest leadership, ability and determination; and a Divisional Spirit.

PROLOGUE

Vivian Evelegh was the first, and he produced the second, setting the seal on it by a brain-wave of sheer genius. He chose as the Divisional sign a battle axe.

Many units and individuals had already experienced the excitement of imminent action, ranging from a possible second Dakar in September 1940, through Italy, Norway, Sicily, France and Africa, always to be disappointed, so that a slight cynicism was at times noticeable when any new "specialised mobilisation" was ordered.

Now, in August 1942, with their first and only divisional exercise "Dryshod", barely over, and the troops settling back into billets and camps conveniently close to the Clyde, the Division's planning staff was suddenly ordered to London.

"Torch" was the code word, and, on learning the objective and outline plan, commanders and staffs were galvanised into the urgency of realism. For this was *it*, no question of that, success awarding the highest prizes on sea, on land and in the air.

The reopening of the Mediterranean was valued at 3,000,000 tons of merchant ships. The eviction of the Axis from Africa would add the magnificent Army of the Nile to our rapidly increasing offensive strength. Lastly the new air bases would vitally assist the restoration to the great maritime democracies of that flexibility of power which hitherto had been afforded mainly by their navies.

By now the decisive importance of secrecy was universally understood. This involved G and Q staffs in the most trying and detailed complications, working to two plans, the real and the "cover". They succeeded brilliantly, though elsewhere there were some narrow shaves. In late August the wife of a junior staff officer, meeting her husband in London, asked "What's all this about First Army going off?" She had heard from the wife of one of the heads of the Army staff that the Army was sailing, and she knew its destination. General Evelegh reported this immediately to the Army Commander.

A tray of maps was seen by the Division's C.R.A. leaving the planning centre in London, Norfolk House. The top map, spread flat, was headed "Algiers" in the largest letters. "Security" went into a frenzy.

Originally destined to sail in September, the expedition

PROLOGUE

was delayed one month. All October troops poured up to the Clyde and into the ships. Stores were loaded, and K.M.S. (1) (convoy Mediterranean slow No. 1) sailed a week or more before K.M.F. (1) (fast) carrying the assault force.

On October 26 all was ready, and the final conference was held on board H.M.S. *Bulolo*, the specially fitted command ship, where Navy, Army and Air Force gave their final orders. Immediately afterwards Admiral Burroughs, in sole command for the next phase, visited every ship, speaking briefly but inspiringly to troops and crews, and giving them the famous motto of his former command, 10 Cruiser Squadron, "It all depends on me!"

There was a fair lop on the Clyde, and a drab autumn drizzle as the ships left their anchorage at the Tail o' the Bank and filed steadily between the guard-ships into the open sea. The Division must have felt to a man that they were at last committed. Training, leave, letters even, were over. They were the spearhead of Britain's new armies and their selection for this task could mean only one thing—they were Britain's Best. Natural excitement was to be expected, but this was fanned to the deepest intensity by events which, though thousands of miles away, concerned them intimately. For at midday on Saturday, October 24, the news-boys of Glasgow had gone suddenly wild with the first news of the attack by the British Eighth Army at El Alamein, and by evening the whole fleet knew.

Dawn on the 27th showed the forty-nine ships of K.M.F. (1) steaming fast to the west, with Islay and the Mull of Kintyre immediately to the north. Keeping station on *Bulolo*, the convoy was formed up eight abreast in six deep lines. Destroyers circled in front and on the flanks; a carrier lay out on the port side with the cruiser *Sheffield* close by. Coastal Command watched over us for days, far out into the Atlantic, Fleet Air Arm from the carrier maintaining a ceaseless patrol close in. Somewhere, hundreds of miles to the east, steamed Force H, the Battle Fleet, guarding against any possible interference from surface ships. U-boat areas were plotted on ships' charts and a certain tension ensued from time to time among those who "knew the form".

PROLOGUE

The British troops were kept hard at it. P.T., dummy R/T, scramble nets and even gun drill. The U.S. troops looked on, and gradually followed suit.

In due course, to the relief of all, secrecy was progressively "broken down", so that junior commanders and even individual soldiers got their orders and made their plans.

The convoy turned south and, near the Azores, swung again eastwards. Approaching Gibraltar, it passed through K.M.S. (1) and went through the Straits in the dark, with dawn giving a wonderful view of the Sierra Nevada capped with early snow.

Again relief, for not only were we still unnoticed, but another possible complication lay behind. The possibility of opposition from Franco's Spanish Morocco and Tangier had been taken into account, and a plan, rough but necessary, made for the capture of the south side of this gateway of the Mediterranean.

That day a hostile long-range patrol, flying at great height, located the two fleets, Force "H" and K.M.F. (1), the former twenty to thirty miles to the north, masking the Vichy fleet at Toulon and the southern French ports. The enemy reacted quickly but, strangely, selected the warships for their attack, instead of the vital, irreplaceable and highly vulnerable assault force. The grey dusk that evening became a giant fireworks display, the twinkling of guns at ships' level forming the base of a great area of bursting A.A. shells, as a muffled grumble came across the water clearly audible above the engines of the troopships.

November 7 came, the troops prepared for the night ahead and at 00.30 hours on November 8 the landings commenced.

The general plan was as follows.

The assault on the North African coast was to be focused at three points; Algiers, Oran and Casablanca. British and American troops were to co-operate at Algiers, while the Americans dealt with the two western landings.

The operation was conducted as all-American, by which it was hoped to obtain the maximum co-operation from the local French administration and forces. It was realised that bitterness towards Britain was strong in many French quarters.

So Major-General Ryder, commanding 34 U.S. Division was responsible for the easternmost operation—the landings

PROLOGUE

around and the capture of Algiers and its airfields, and the consolidation, militarily and politically, of this area as an Allied base. He had for this operation his own 34 Division; our 78 Division less one brigade group; Blade, an armoured regimental group from 6 Armoured Division; U.S. Rangers, and British Commandos.

Thereafter, and dependent on the opposition encountered and the political situation generally, First Army (British) consisting of 78 Division and Blade, with 1 Parachute Brigade was to strike east with all speed—objective Tunis. This plan gave the line Constantine-Philippeville on D+15, i.e., November 23. In the event, the Division was on the line Oued Zarga-Djebel Abiod far to the east by that day, and fighting was in full swing on a wide front, against first-class German troops, with Blade under Colonel Hull even further east between Tunis and Mateur, and one mobile column from 11 Brigade having penetrated to the outskirts of Bizerta.

Such then, was the background of 78 Division. It had the honour and the fortune to be out in the lead when the two great democracies at last seized the strategic initiative. Few troops could have equalled, none surpassed their performance. Their choice was fully justified.

BOOK I

NORTH AFRICA

CHAPTER I

THE TEAM TAKES THE FIELD

ALGIERS was lit up, and its lighthouse flashing. There was no moon, but enough light from the town and from the stars for the ships to show as black silhouettes against the grey of the sea and sky. The Americans (parts of their 34 Infantry Division) were well away before midnight, and by a minute to twelve the Northamptons and the East Surreys, awkward and clumsy under their full packs, had climbed down the scramble nets into the landing craft. The long, low boats were pitching in a heavy swell. Men were singing on the troop decks, comfortable in the warm air, happy at the news they had heard on the wireless of Eighth Army's advance, speculating about their own future.

Then the Lancashire Fusiliers got away, to find the same anti-climax on the beaches that the Northamptons had found, when they touched down on the beach at two in the morning. There was no opposition: only an occasional crackle of fire in the distance. The *Manchester Guardian* correspondent, wading ashore with the infantry as day broke, found little Arab boys grinning and saluting on the beach, and noted that "the first act of many a British soldier on reaching Africa was to sit down on it and change his wet socks".

The Lancashire Fusiliers, marching into Douaouda in the mild early morning, fifteen miles from their landing place, passed a French family in its gig trotting off to church. (November 8 was a Sunday.) The French did not even nod, but the Arabs in the streets of the village were cheering.

It was at Sidi Ferruch, fifteen miles west of Algiers, that the brigade's guns and vehicles were still being landed. The landings and unloadings went on till late afternoon, when it was so clear that there was little or no opposition that it was no longer worth while to tackle the difficulties of an open beach and a sea getting steadily rougher. The infantry had reached the heights above the town without the aid of vehicles and "B" troop, 321 Battery, of 132 Field Regiment, was already in position to cover Blida airfield, twenty-five miles inland, so it was clear that the rest of the vehicles and stores could be landed, in the proper shelter and with the proper equipment, at the Algiers quays.

The French troops at Blida airfield, who had surrendered once, early in the morning of November 8, to a Fleet Air Arm pilot and taken a receipt from him, seemed still uncertain whether to resist. For some days "B" troop and the French pitched camp 200 yards apart, with their guns turned on each other, before matters were arranged.

Generally speaking, though, the uncertainty as to French reaction in North Africa did not last long. There was a day of intermittent fighting here and there; a certain amount of confusion among the allied troops, due to lack of telephone or wireless communication between units and to shortage of transport while the landings were going on; a few French tanks and cavalry, themselves equally confused, were loose in the neighbourhood; and then Darlan surrendered the city of Algiers.

That there was so little bloodshed and so little damage to future relations with the French was due, partly at any rate, to the care with which the British and American troops had been briefed and the tact with which they carried out their orders. The American combat team, for instance, which reached Maison Blanche airfield at 5.45 on the morning of November 8 made no reply to the few shots with which the French greeted them; the airfield was surrendered at 6.20. One company of Lancashire Fusiliers, marching towards Blida in sections, saw riflemen lurking in the hedges on either side of the road. The company commander ordered his men to march on and take no notice. As the company commander reached the rear of the French positions he met and saluted his French opposite number, who was clearly delighted that he had had no need to take action. It was equally clear that he would have fought if the Fusiliers had fired.

On November 9, General Anderson, with a small skeleton staff, arrived at Maison Blanche airfield by air from Gibraltar.

The landing itself, of 11 Brigade, two British commandos, and part of the American 34 Division, had been under American command for operations. The maintenance and supply, on the other hand, of both American and British forces landed in the area of Algiers was a wholly British responsibility, which for the first four days after landing devolved on the Q staff of the Division. It entailed getting the port of Algiers working as rapidly as possible so that all the ships of the assault convoy could be unloaded and the port made ready to receive the second convoy on D plus five, when the responsibility for the port was taken over by First Army.

Now the troops of 78 Division, with the commandos, reverted to their own G.O.C., Major-General Evelegh—other British troops being temporarily under the command of the American division, charged with the security of Algiers and the airfields at Maison Blanche and Blida. Taking over the command of the Eastern Task Force, under General Eisenhower as Commander-in-Chief, General Anderson directed Major-General Evelegh to carry out the pre-arranged plan for the capture from the sea of the port of Bougie and Djidjelli airfield with 36 Infantry Brigade Group, assisted by the Navy.

The last sporadic opposition from the French ended on November 10, and 36 Brigade landed unopposed at Bougie on the following day. The Buffs, however, who were meant to seize the airfield at Djidjelli and stock it with petrol, were prevented from landing there by the heavy swell; they had to go on to Bougie by road, and did not reach the airfield until November 13. Meanwhile on November 11, it became known at divisional headquarters that aircraft at Djidjelli would be grounded next day for lack of petrol. Six six-ton lorries, some of the few that had been landed for use in the port of Algiers, were hastily loaded with petrol and an escort provided from some sappers no longer required on the beaches. At this time it was unknown whether the road to Bougie was open and clear of possible resistance by isolated French posts. The party drove all night and completed the 170-mile journey by first light on November 12. It was while this petrol was being transferred to the tanks of our aircraft that the morning's first hostile air attack began. Although this effort failed to save some of the ships in Bougie harbour, it did prevent the loss of grounded aircraft.

In the course of one of the attacks, an aerial torpedo destroyed the first batch of home mail for the British First Army in North Africa—chiefly, in fact, for the Division. Our losses in men were light, but they were heavy in equipment: for some time to come the infantrymen of 78 Division had only the clothes on their backs and the equipment they could carry. The loss of the men's greatcoats, which could not be immediately replaced, was one of the greater hardships that the men had to face, as the nights were already cold and soon wet into the bargain.

Meanwhile, although French resistance in Algiers had been negligible (just long enough, however, according to General Anderson, to cause delay and doubt), events in Tunisia were taking a different turn. At the moment of the landings there were no Axis garrison troops there—only the handful of officers composing the Armistice Commission—and the German and Italian High Commands were taken completely by surprise. But Axis reaction was swift, and effectively assisted by the conduct of Admiral Esteva, the French Resident-General.

The first German troops arrived by air at El Aouana airfield, near Tunis, on November 9, only a day after the allied landings. Esteva offered no opposition to the Germans—not even as much as had delayed us so slightly in Algeria. There was a ready-made force in Sicily and Southern Italy, which was being held in readiness in case of an allied landing at Dakar; its troops began to pour in to Tunis and Bizerta, by air and by sea. They seized the key points of the two cities; they executed or imprisoned the known and suspected Allied sympathisers; they took over the ports of Sousse, Sfax and Gabes and the inland town of Kairouan; they built runways for aircraft, dug weapon-pits and anti-tank ditches, laid mines and mounted guns. Within a week there were 5,000 front-line troops in and around Tunis and Bizerta; they had tanks; and they were still flying Messerschmitt and Focke-Wulf fighters. They had occupied Mateur and pushed out south and west, and they were in contact with the advanced troops of 36 Brigade west of Tabarka (about twenty-five miles west of Djebel Abiod) and with the French at Sidi Nsir and Medjez.

By the end of November the Axis had some 20,000 men, with armour, in Tunisia. The Luftwaffe, with its ground staff, was followed by anti-aircraft and anti-tank units. Then came echelons of the German 10 Panzer Division and 334 Infantry Division, and men of the Italian 1 Division, all forming General von Arnim's Fifth Panzer Army. Our own forces consisted of two brigade groups, each of 4,500 strong; Blade Force, 1,800; and 1,500 divisional troops—a total of 12,300.

Why had we not forestalled the Axis occupation of Tunisia by landing there ourselves? The War Office's explanation—given in a footnote to General Anderson's despatch—is that the small force we could spare for the landing had to be concentrated, and it was dangerous to venture without air cover into ports that the German bombers (based on Sicily) could reach. The reality of the danger was proved, the War Office points out, by the shipping losses incurred as far to the west as Bougie; they would have been heavier still, and with worse results, at the Tunisian ports.

It was for this reason that an early intention to land the Division's remaining brigade, 1 Guards Brigade, at Bone had to be abandoned. It was not merely that shipping was short, once it was decided to augment the American share in the landing at Algiers, but that Bone was within reach of fighter-escorted German bombers. The losses at Bone from air attack would have been far heavier than those at Bougie.

However, action was taken to seize Bone as early as possible, and to make it safe for shipping. As each sub-unit landed at Algiers with its transport complete they pushed forward to the concentration area there—the drivers "driving like hell all day", as the G.O.C. put it, to cover 300 miles in just over twenty-four hours, "the first sign of the great spirit in 78 Division".

Meanwhile, in the early hours of November 13, two destroyers from Algiers slipped into Bone and landed No. 6 Commando, with a platoon of anti-tank guns from 11 Brigade. The port and the aerodrome were seized, but bombed so heavily and consistently, day and night, that when six coasters put in on November 17 there was no Arab labour left in the town to unload the ammunition, petrol and supplies. By an improvisation typical of those early days the Division's C.R.A. lent the men of one of his light batteries to serve as stevedores.

* * * * *

The whole purpose of the North African landings was to occupy Tunisia as soon as possible, and General Eisenhower decided not to wait until First Army could be built up, but to advance immediately with the forces he had, and with improvised lines of communication. There still seemed to be a chance, at the time, of securing advanced positions near Tunis, or even Tunis itself, before the enemy had consolidated his own forces there.

Once it had been realised that there was to be no opposition from the French, divisional headquarters, with the divisional troops, mustered what transport they could and pushed forward over the four hundred miles of mountainous tableland to Souk-el-Arba. Only about half of the Division's second-line transport was available and the journey called for an untiring effort from the R.A.S.C. drivers, over bad roads and usually with overloaded vehicles.

(There were drivers who drove divisional troops from Algiers to Bone, three hundred miles nonstop save for meals, and within a couple of hours were on the hundred-mile journey to Souk-el-Arba with ammunition for the defence of the airfield. They would be back at Bone in fourteen hours to move troops forward—eventually having covered six hundred miles with only what rest they could snatch while their vehicles were being loaded and unloaded.)

With the Division's headquarters and divisional troops already at Souk-el-Arba, General Anderson, on November 17, ordered the Division—still only two brigades strong—to advance on Tunis as soon as it had completed its forward concentration along the arrow-head of the roads Tabarka—Souk-el-Arba—Ghardimaou. The French were to cover the concentrations and the right flank of the subsequent advance.

It was to be a two-pronged advance: 36 Brigade on the left, along the northern road that runs roughly parallel with the coast from Tabarka, through Djebel Abiod, to Mateur, whence roads run out to Bizerta and Tunis, and 11 Brigade on the right, twenty-five miles farther south, from Beja along the road that runs through Medjez-el-Bab, Tebourba, and Djedeida to Tunis. A small column (known as Hartforce), recruited from 11 Brigade Group and under command of Major V. Hart of the Northamptons, was operating on the north road. Blade Force, a composite group under the command of Colonel R. A. Hull, 17/21 Lancers, consisting of one regiment of British tanks (17/21 Lancers), one motorised company of the Rifle Brigade, "C" Battery H.A.C., some armoured cars of the Derbyshire Yeomanry, and 1 Parachute Battalion, were sent forward to deny to the enemy the high ground between these two widely-separated roads, to act as a mobile link between the two brigades, and to be ready to help either side over its inner flank or to join in any break-through towards Tunis. In the event the lie of the land forced them towards 11 Brigade. The 17/21 Lancers were equipped with Crusaders and Valentines, and it was with these lightly armed fighting vehicles—the Crusader mounted a six-pounder and the Valentine a two-pounder—that they took on the redoubtable German Mark IV.

CHAPTER II

THE TWO-PRONGED THRUST FOR TUNIS

THE mild weather that had smiled on the landings soon changed. As the Division pushed into the high hills the rains came, the cold at night became intense, and the troops felt the shortage of blankets and the lack of winter kit. They encountered the hard weather, the difficult country, and a determined enemy all at the same time.

It was at Djebel Abiod on November 17, that 36 Brigade, on the left of the advance, made firm contact with the enemy, and it was here that the Royal West Kents, supported by the London Territorial 138 Field Regiment, fought the Division's first major engagement.

The village of Djebel Abiod, small as it is, was of great strategic importance. It lies in a pass in the hills where the two roads fork—the road from Bone to Bizerta and that from Bone to Beja, on 11 Brigade's axis. Control of the junction meant that we had lateral freedom of manoeuvre and communication between our two widely separated brigades; its loss would mean that we had to travel backwards fifty miles for a similar junction.

"C" Squadron of 56 Recce had already reconnoitred the village and the river bed beyond it. At this early, uncertain stage of the campaign much heavy and nerve-racking work fell, necessarily, on the Recce Regiment; by this time most of its men had gone four days and nights with no sleep or with brief snatches in their vehicles, and had eaten irregularly, inadequately, and on the move. "C" Squadron was glad to meet no trouble in Djebel Abiod and to hand over to the three companies of the Royal West Kents and eight twenty-five pounders of 360 Battery, 138 Field Regiment.

The Royal West Kents slipped unopposed and unobserved

into the village just after dawn on November 17. They had dug in and sited their defences when, in the middle of the afternoon, a column of German Mark IV tanks trundled unconcernedly towards what they thought was an unoccupied village.

The Royal West Kents were overrun but stayed put—a fine performance for green troops. Two anti-tank two-pounders, forward and to the right of the battalion, opened fire at 200 yards and the two leading tanks were knocked out. For three hours the infantrymen and the gunners held—and finally drove off from the closest possible range—a superior force of 400 German parachute troops, supported by mortars, and thirty Mark III and Mark IV tanks.

The Germans left behind them eleven of their tanks, but our losses had been heavier in relation to our strength at the time: five out of our six two-pounders and three twenty-five pounders all being put out of action. A light section of 217 Field Ambulance, under Lt. Perry, dealt with the casualties as best it could, in the darkness of a cave in the hillside.

The platoon forward of the bridge, thinking—with good reason—that the town was lost and the rest of the battalion destroyed, made their way as soon as darkness fell through the enemy lines and did a circling march of twenty miles to the road back to Tabarka. If victory and defeat were a matter of nicely balancing material losses, we had lost our first battle; in fact we had won it, for we had taken and held the important road junction we had intended to take and hold, and we had driven a heavier force of Germans from the field.

It was at Djebel Abiod that the Division first learned what warfare in North Africa meant. It was cold, the side-roads were mud tracks, and the attacks came not across hot desert sands but from between rock-strewn hills, from behind dense scrub, and out of the dark cork forests. The men at Djebel Abiod had no reserves within forty-eight hours' travelling distance, and the Germans had complete mastery of the air. The Royal West Kents had been bombed from the time they reached Bougie and they went on being bombed. They were wet through, they had no change of clothes, and they were short of sleep; at the end of the Djebel Abiod fighting—and there was more to come—they had gone for twenty days without taking off their boots. Meanwhile, however, the first battle for Djebel Abiod was over; the rest of the brigade came up; the Royal West Kents were relieved by the Argylls; and the way seemed open for 36 Brigade's advance along the left, or northerly, of the two roads that led to Tunis.

In the rear, the concentration went on, and on the right 11 Brigade was ready to move along the southerly road.

It was hilly country here, too—yet scattered with fertile fields as far as Medjez-el-Bab, the little white town that straddles the River Medjerda and looks out over the plain that stretches to Tunis. The river here is broad and muddy, with steep cliff-like banks, and three battalions of German parachute troops on the far bank covered the crossing with heavy machine-guns.

The Northamptons and the Lancashire Fusiliers—both of which battalions had already been in action on the road from Beja—reached that part of Medjez which lies west of the river on November 24. But what mattered was to seize the bridge, and it was intended to make a night attack. The Lancashire Fusiliers advanced, with the Northamptons on the right. The Northamptons crossed the river at Sloughia, moved across broken country to avoid the enemy's tanks, and then along the road to Medjez from the Grenadier Hill side. The plan was to converge on Medjez from both sides. But enemy posts on the flanks slowed down the Lancashire Fusiliers' approach to the river; the Fusiliers' C.O., Lt.-Col. Manly, was killed by a burst of machine-gun fire from one of the posts as he went forward to reconnoitre, and Major Kelly took over. The battalion raced over the open ground to the river, but it was already full daylight as the three companies waded breast-high through the turbid yellow Medjerda river, the men holding their rifles high above their heads.

Two companies climbed the sheer, twenty-foot bank on the far side and came under machine-gun fire before they could find cover in the scanty groves and cactus plantations. One company was held in the muddy river bed, one of its platoons being wiped out almost to a man. On the near side another company was pinned down by the accurate German field-gun fire. The Northamptons attacked over the hills from the right flank but were driven off by tanks, which then turned towards the Fusiliers.

There was nothing for it but to withdraw, and as we did so we saw the bridge, for which we had been fighting, blown up.

The withdrawal was made possible by the covering fire of 132 Field Regiment—the territorial unit from South Wales which normally supported this brigade. Captain Barker-Benfield, a forward-observation officer, got across the river with his wireless set tied to his back, and engaged the machine-gun posts whilst the Fusiliers withdrew in good order. He was awarded an M.C. for his coolness and courage.

Next day, November 26, the Brigade attacked again, with the East Surreys leading, and found Medjez abandoned. (Medjez-el-Bab means "gateway"—this was the gateway to Tunis). It was one of the minor mysteries of the war: a key-point in the campaign given up without a struggle by first-class German troops—who had had by no means the worst of it in the fighting so far. Presumably, the Germans still did not know how weak we were on the ground, how precariously supplied and supported. However it was, we took Medjez and held it to the end. Not only that. Within two hours of the German withdrawal Lt. Gibson and his section of 237 Field Company R.E., were putting up a hundred-foot span bridge to replace the one the Germans had demolished. It was the first Bailey bridge the Division's engineers had put up in action and it remained in use for the rest of the campaign.

The week that had elapsed since the Royal West Kents' battle at Djebel Abiod—to go back to 36 Brigade on the northerly road—was one of stalemate in that village and of confused fighting around it. The Royal West Kents continued to hold the hamlet they had defended so stubbornly, but German air superiority made it difficult to support and supply them during daylight. The Focke-Wulfs and Messerschmitts kept out of our Spitfires' range until they had to go back to refuel— the German airfields were so much nearer the front than ours— and then swept low over the roads, machine-gunning everything within sight. The German ground troops were active, too, and the Argylls in particular lost heavily in supporting the Royal

West Kents' flank and in night raids and patrols. On one such raid the subaltern in command—Lt. Mackay—was killed, and Sgt. Mackinnon carried a desperately wounded Cpl. Reid nearly two miles to safety.

In the darkness of the night of November 20, the Argylls relieved the Royal West Kents in Djebel Abiod and pushed three companies forward. Twenty-four hours later the Djebel Abiod garrison was reinforced by two companies of the Buffs, the remainder of 138 Field Regiment and a battery of the six-pounders of 64 Anti-Tank Regiment (Glasgow Yeomanry).

Five days of rain and of the inevitable compo rations, of German shelling and dive-bombing, of night patrols and of one Italian counter-attack, and on November 26, at dawn, the day that 11 Brigade entered Medjez, 36 Brigade advanced under what, for those early days, was a heavy barrage.

The Royal West Kents made a flank attack from the west on to Tamera, which they captured, whilst the Buffs advanced along the road. The enemy fell back, and next morning the Argylls passed through the other two battalions along the muddy road, and took Sedjenane without serious opposition.

It looked as though the Tunisian gamble might come off—as though we might reach Bizerta and Tunis before the Germans realised how lamentably small our force was and how ill-equipped. The brigade was ordered to push on at dawn next day, the Argylls leading, and to seize the cross-roads ten miles east of Mateur before dark. It meant an advance of twenty-six miles with only the daylight hours to do it in, through mud that clogged the tracks of the carriers, immobilised motor-bicycles, and weighted the men's boots with viscous grey clods. But hopes were high, and the Argylls covered fifteen miles by mid-day.

It was then that the enemy stood to fight, and it may be that a better combination of reconnaissance and intelligence work would have warned us. The Argylls were caught in a pass between thousand-foot hills. Heavy machine gun and mortar fire broke out from the bare, rocky, Bald Hill (Djebel Afred) on the right and from the scrub-covered Green Hill (Djebel-el-Azzag) on the left. (Lt.-Col. Mackellar gave them their names, and they stuck.) The Highlanders found little cover in the open fields between the hills and lost heavily; one company, deployed in the open, was overrun; the carriers, mortars and and trucks were immobilised if not destroyed; one of their platoons, fighting their way doggedly up one hill, was threatened from the other. It was well after dark before orders came through from Brigade to withdraw and concentrate short of the pass. Of the company that had been overrun only eight men got back; the battalion had lost one officer killed, four wounded, and five missing, five men killed, twenty-two wounded, and one hundred and thirteen missing. It was learned later that fifteen of those missing had been killed. After the withdrawal the medical officer, Capt. Hugh Macfie, Capt. Campbell Preston and Capt. Erskine, with stretcher-bearers, drove into no-man's-land in a gun-portee calling out, "Anyone there?" into the darkness. They saved and collected eight wounded. Lt. Dawson won an M.C. for his leadership of the platoon that had fought its way up to the top of Green Hill.

But the order now was to hand over forward positions to the Buffs, whilst Brigade headquarters planned a full-scale attack. This attack went in on November 30; the Royal West Kents on Bald Hill and No. 6 Commando on Green Hill fought stubbornly all night and all day. The Royal West Kents reached the summit of Bald Hill, but were too few to hold it, and at nightfall they withdrew. The Royal West Kents had lost no fewer than thirteen officers and a hundred and thirty men. For the next three days 36 Brigade held its positions short of the pass, whilst the winter rains filled the slit trenches and soaked the men's clothes.

This was check to the northerly prong of the advance. Meanwhile, after the capture of Medjez on November 26, 11 Brigade had pressed on along the southerly road, and in the early hours of November 27, a battalion-group under Lt.-Col. Wilberforce of the East Surreys entered the little town of Tebourba, fifteen miles further north, already bombed and shattered into ruins.

It seemed for a time—for a matter of hours, as it turned out—that our long-shot gamble to reach Tunis and Bizerta without enough men, supplies, or air cover might come off. We were out of the hill-country now, and the rains had not yet come to this southern sector of the front. Between Tebourba, set amid scorched fields, rocky outcrops, and large olive-groves, and the city of Tunis lay a mere fifteen miles of open country. But on November 27 came the first warning that our hopes were too high. At mid-morning seventeen German tanks approached through the olive groves surrounding the town and engaged our infantry and guns at the closest range all that day until dusk. The East Surreys had not had time to dig in and withdrew through the guns; the twenty-five pounders of 322/132 Field Battery knocked out fourteen of the seventeen tanks, but the German crews that escaped from them fought on from the cactus clumps, and enemy aircraft repeatedly dive-bombed the town itself, barely a mile to the rear. At the end of the action seven out of 322 Battery's eight guns were out of action—the one remaining gun had been manned for the greater part of the day by Sgt. Eustace alone. The knocked-out tanks were in a ring around the battery, one of them only three yards from the muzzle of the gun that had destroyed it. Sgt. Eustace won a D.C.M. that day, Lt. Owen Jones, a gun-position officer of the same battery, an M.C., and Gunner Deans, who had, from an unarmoured truck, kept up communications though under fire throughout, an M.M.

However, the town was held, and the Northamptons pushed on towards Djedeida, the one sizable place between Tebourba and Tunis. On its outskirts was the airfield that had to be seized to enable the R.A.F. to close up and give air cover for the last few miles to Tunis. There still seemed to be a chance of seizing Tunis. Blade Force, the composite armoured force that had been operating in the hills between the Division's two brigades, each on its respective road, was out of the hills and on to the Tunis plain, west of Djedeida. Its tanks were in action in spite of the rains that had already come to the hill-country and in spite of the heavy going; indeed, on the night of November 25-26, before the East Surreys had even left Medjez, the Derbyshire Yeomanry, strengthened by the addition of American light tanks ("Honeys") had carried out a dashing raid against the Djedeida airfield and destroyed thirty-seven Stukas on the ground.

Now, too, heartening news was received that 1 Guards Brigade, the Division's third brigade, consisting of 3 Grenadiers,

THE TWO-PRONGED THRUST FOR TUNIS

2 Coldstream and 2 Hampshires, with 17 Field Regiment R.A. and its other attached troops, had begun landing at Algiers, five hundred and fifty miles away, on November 22, and that its units would presumably be coming forward, as they disembarked, to reinforce the tired and depleted 11 and 36 Brigades.

It was becoming clear, at the same time, that the Germans, fully reinforced and with their air strength steadily increasing, were ready to stand and fight along the entire front. The Northamptons, pushing along to Djedeida, came in for a new weight of dive-bombing; they were short of light anti-aircraft weapons and they had outrun our own fighter cover. (Our fighters were still operating from Bone—their advanced landing ground at Souk-el-Arba was thick in mud.)

At midday on November 29 the Northamptons, supported by American Grant tanks and by 496 Battery, 132 Field Regiment, attacked the outskirts of Djedeida. The advance went across open ground, and it was easy for the enemy guns, from the hillocks overlooking the plain, to knock out four of the Grants. The second advance, at daylight on November 30, saw the leading company of the Northamptons practically wiped out as they crossed the open, swept by machine-gun fire. As the Northamptons, with the tanks and guns, repulsed for the second time, fell back into the knolls east of Tebourba the German tanks and infantry were at their heels and assembling to counter-attack the town. This strong enemy reaction ruined the plans that had been made for an armoured attack on Tunis. It had been intended that Blade Force and Combat Command B of U.S. 1 Armoured Division should drive for the city, whilst 1 Parachute Battalion was to drop at Depienne and attack from the south. The parachutists made their drop, but the armoured attack—because of the enemy stand at Tebourba —had to be cancelled; the parachutists attacked Oudna airport, only eleven miles outside the city, and there destroyed half-a-dozen planes on the ground, but were forced back into the hills by tanks and armoured cars. Their survivors eventually rejoined the Division after an eighty-mile march through the mountains, hiding by day and moving by night.

Meanwhile, for the four days from November 27 to 30, the

East Surreys and their supporting gunners had been holding Tebourba against tanks, infantrymen of the Parachute Division, and dive-bombers, which they had the doubtful pleasure of actually watching take off from Djedeida. Major T. A. Buchanan of the East Surreys won the M.C. and R.S.M. A. H. Adams of the same regiment the D.C.M. in the stubborn defensive fighting here.

By the evening of November 30 it was necessary to relieve the Northamptons, falling back on Tebourba after their failure to progress at Djedeida. The East Surreys were, by now, thoroughly tired too, and in need of relief, had relief been possible; the Lancashire Fusiliers, the third battalion in the brigade, were already detached with Blade Force; the only infantry reserve in the battle area was 2 Hampshires, which had landed a week before as part of 1 Guards Brigade, and had been sent on ahead of the Grenadiers and the Coldstream, to come temporarily under command of 11 Brigade.

On the night of Sunday, November 29, the Hampshires, relieving the Northamptons as the forward unit in the sector, took up positions on the Djebel-el-Hamara ridge and in a copse half-way between Djedeida and Tebourba. Beside the copse were the Medjerda river and the road and the railway between the towns. Two twenty-five pounder troops of 496 Battery, 132 Field Regiment, were with them, one six-pounder troop of 72 Anti-Tank Regiment, and one battery of 4 Medium Regiment's 5.5s.

It was a bad position to be in, overlooked from high ground to the right, the front and the rear. But the enemy was quiet throughout November 30—except always for his dive-bombers —and the Hampshires' C.O., Lt.-Col. James Lee, made the best dispositions he could in the circumstances, and the men dug in. Fighting patrols that night made little or no contact, and the German attack did not come in until the early afternoon of December 1, when infantry, with mortar and machine-gun support, attacked the forward companies. They were held by rifle, machine-gun, and artillery fire.

Meanwhile, Blade Force was being pressed towards Tebourba by a force of thirty enemy tanks which appeared, on the morning of December 1, in the Chouigui Plain, three miles

5 Northamptons on patrol

Point 667, near Medjez-el-Bab

View towards Chaouach from 5 Northamptons' positions

237 Field Company R.E. clearing mines

west of the town, and which was supported by incessant attacks from the air.

Before noon this enemy force (which was fortunately without infantry) was within five hundred yards of 11 Brigade's H.Q., whose troops, covered by a few guns of 321 Field Battery and 457 Light Battery, held a pivotal position four miles south-west of Tebourba, where the head of the valley leading to Medjez was confined between the hills and the Medjerda river.

The few headquarters troops (and particularly the field and light guns firing over open sights in their anti-tank role) drove off the attack with the loss to the enemy of six tanks, but the enemy thrust had shown that communications between our forward troops at Tebourba and our Divisional H.Q. behind Medjez were now precarious to a degree.

Beyond Tebourba itself, the Germans tried, that same evening, to get men and machine-guns into farm buildings on the Hampshires' left flank, and Lt. Griffith led a platoon in a counter-attack which suffered heavily as it advanced down an exposed forward slope. The platoon reached the farm but was ordered to withdraw, as being too weak to hold it. After dark, Lt. Wright, second-in-command of the company, though himself wounded, took a stretcher-bearer party out and brought back the badly wounded Lt. Griffith, eight other wounded men and seven who had been reported missing.

At dawn next day machine-guns opened up along the whole front and the enemy advanced, this time with tanks. The gunners and the Hampshires' anti-tank gunners engaged them hotly, but one tank destroyed a whole platoon, firing at it at a range of a dozen yards, whilst another destroyed the battalion headquarters' signals carrier, killing the signals officer and five men.

By midday "X" Company was overrun, not before two enemy tanks had been destroyed by its two-pounders and the gunners' six-pounders, and after it had made repeated attacks, led by the company commander, Capt. Thomas, on the enemy infantry. Now only Capt. Pearce-Serocold, second-in-command, one sergeant, and five men remained. At about the same time the battalion's second-in-command, Major Chamberlain, was killed whilst tending the wounded.

DECEMBER 2-3, 1942

At another point of the perimeter a bayonet charge under Lt. Freemantle drove off an infantry attack, at a cost to us of six wounded (Freemantle among them) and to the Germans of fifty killed and wounded and six prisoners. Meanwhile it looked as though "Y" Company, out of wireless communication, had been overrun, but two runners—the company clerk and the transport N.C.O.—braved a dash across the bullet-swept open (after they had seen a previous runner seriously wounded) to report to battalion H.Q. The company was out of water and ammunition, had suffered heavy losses, but was holding on. Capt. Wingfield took a carrier through to it.

The liaison officer with brigade made two journeys to report and to bring back brigade's orders: the battalion was to fall back for two miles and stand with its right on the river, its left on Point 186, a high feature which the East Surreys were holding.

The East Surreys and their supporting troops had been fighting against odds for six days, in the olive-groves of Tebourba, towards El Bathan and on Point 186, in a battle only a little less grim than the Hampshires' bitter struggle on the ridges east of Tebourba. Now they were worn out and desperately thin on the ground. On December 3 they lost the dominating Point 186, thus enabling the Germans—quick as ever to exploit a success—to by-pass and outflank the Hampshires, establishing themselves on the crest and pounding "Z" Company of the Hampshires from that vantage point with heavy machine-gun and mortar fire. Time and again "Z" Company sent detachments against the summit; time and again they were driven off. Finally, in the company's last gallant assault, Major Le Patourel with four volunteers charged, and fell. One badly wounded man was the sole survivor to be rescued. The enemy consolidated his position, and a company of East Surreys, supported by all the available guns, failed in a last counter-attack.

By now—the evening of December 3—the Hampshires were down to ten officers and two hundred men. They formed square round Battalion Headquarters and Capt. Tatham and Capt. Waldron led one bayonet charge after another. Col. Lee had hoped until now that at dark he could break out, seize

Point 186 and hold it till further orders. But the Hampshires were short of water and ammunition, and their anti-tank guns had been destroyed. So had the twenty-five pounders. (The gunners of 496 Battery had already been told they could withdraw, but Capt. Shaw and his men had elected to stay and share the Hampshires' glory as infantrymen.) To have broken out for Point 186 would have meant death for all of them, or capture.

So the C.O. ordered all ranks to arm themselves as well as they could from the dead and to fix bayonets. "Walk towards them slowly and when you get close enough charge and give it 'em," was Col. Lee's order. Charging, firing their Brens from the hip, the remnants of the battalion cut their way through Tebourba, led by the C.O. himself and his adjutant, Capt. Barber—both already wounded.

Meanwhile, after dark on December 3, the C.O. of the East Surreys, unable to get through to Brigade H.Q., decided on withdrawal for the remains of his hard-pressed group. The enemy was across the road to Tebourba, so it was necessary to make their way as best they could along ill-defined tracks through the olive-groves. At one place here ill luck led a number of carriers and some twenty guns of all types into a bottleneck—an impassable slippery track beside a deep water tank—only twenty yards from the main route. Officers and men struggled in the dark, under fire, and in deep and clinging mud, to free the vehicles, but it was no good: they had to be abandoned. It was a serious blow, on top of what had been lost in action, to the fast-dwindling force. Most of the men, though, got through and many managed to make their way between the enemy and the fast-flowing river, to re-form at the head of the valley leading to Medjez.

So when the remnants of the Hampshires reached Tebourba, the shattered, empty town had been evacuated and the road beyond it was cut. But it was here that the Brigade's order to withdraw reached the gallant battalion. The men marched through the town in column of threes, the colonel leading and calling the step, and when it was realised that the road to Medjez-el-Bab was under fire, the colonel told the men they could surrender if they wished. They refused, and he ordered

DECEMBER 3, 1942

them to break up into twos and threes, take to the hills, and work their way back to Brigade as best they could.

That was on December 3; on December 6 four officers and 120 men had reached the collecting point, five miles from Medjez-el-Bab. Reporting on December 31, the adjutant wrote laconically that "from that date until the time of writing, no other officer or other rank has reported, except wounded on discharge from hospital." Lt.-Col. Lee—subsequently awarded the D.S.O.—was among the missing, and so was Major Le Patourel, a company commander recommended for the V.C.

Le Patourel's Victoria Cross was gazetted in the following March. It was believed at first to be a posthumous award, but his friends and those who had read with admiration and pride the account of the Tebourba battle were heartened to learn that he was a prisoner of war at Naples, and recovering from his wounds. The citation of this, the Division's first V.C., ran:

"On the afternoon of December 3, 1942, the enemy had occupied an important high feature on the left of the company commanded by this officer. Counter-attacks by a company of another battalion and detachments of Major Le Patourel's company had been unable to regain the position. This officer then personally led four volunteers under very heavy fire to the top in a last attempt to dislodge several enemy machine-guns. The party was heavily engaged by machine-gun fire and Major Le Patourel rallied his men several times and engaged the enemy, silencing several machine-gun posts.

"Finally, when the remainder of his party were all killed or wounded, he went forward alone with a pistol and some grenades to attack enemy machine-guns at close quarters and from this action did not return. From reports received from wounded men, this officer died of wounds.

"Major Le Patourel's most gallant conduct and self-sacrifice, his brilliant leadership and tenacious devotion to duty in the face of a determined enemy was beyond praise."

The day after the Hampshires' withdrawal two war correspondents talked with the survivors. Evelyn Montague, of the

Manchester Guardian, himself to fall a victim later to his own courage, cabled to his paper and to *The Times* that his "lame account may serve to hint now at the unshakeable valour with which they (the Hampshires) faced strange new terrors and agonies." Lt.-Col. Heber-Percy of the Grenadiers assembled his officers in the back of a lorry and by the light of a hurricane-lamp repeated to them the news of the Hampshires he had just received. "For most of us", wrote one of them, "it was our first realisation of what war means. People with whom we had laughed and talked a few days before were dead. Germans, angry and successful Germans, were waiting for *us* to follow behind the Hampshires. We must have looked a bit glum when we clambered out of the lorry, but for the moment we did not tell the men the reason why."

* * * * *

Meanwhile, during the night of December 3, in all kinds of scratch parties, the retiring infantry was making its way to the next feasible defence position—the point, four miles west of Tebourba, where the river valley narrowed and where Brigade headquarters had been. Our rush to reach Tunis before the enemy had made himself strong enough to halt us—our two-pronged thrust for Tunis—had failed.

CHAPTER III

A PLAN THAT FAILED

IN spite of the terrible losses they had suffered, both of men and equipment, and in spite of their having had to withdraw, the Hampshires and the gunners had done great service to the Division and to the Allied forces in Tunisia. To the Division because, newcomers though the Hampshires were, the other regiments felt that Tebourba was a crowning glory in which they all shared. It did not put into the shade Djebel Abiod, Medjez, the battles at Green Hill and Bald Hill, all the nameless little actions in which the men of 11 and 36 Brigades had already tested themselves and found themselves to be soldiers: it made them part of a distinguished litany of honours.

That was the moral value of Tebourba. Its tactical value was this, to quote *The Times*, "that it gave us breathing space in which to adjust our minds and military dispositions to the fact that the gamble had failed and that the two brigades of the 78 Division were out on a rather precarious limb. The breathing space was not wasted; by the time the inevitable German counter-attack came we were more or less ready for it, and though we lost valuable positions we did not lose Medjez, by far the most valuable of them all".

The adjustment to our military dispositions lay chiefly in the Argylls being switched from 36 Brigade in the north to 11 in the south—the first of the moves that were to make this battalion the hardest-worked and furthest-travelled in the Division—and the bringing up of the Grenadiers and the Coldstream (recently arrived at Beja) to the Medjez area. The Division was now, at last, three brigades strong, though two of the brigades had been necessarily overworked for a month and were depleted, and the new brigade, the Guards', was already a battalion short.

V Corps had taken over command of the British and

A PLAN THAT FAILED

French troops in the sector, and General Evelegh, commanding the Division, was wholly responsible now for the safety of his small force—with no available reserves at his back and maintained five hundred miles from his base (Algiers) by a railway in a hopeless state of disrepair, which took a week to bring men and stores to the forward areas.

While we held the narrow front south-west of Tebourba it was realised that we must also hold the high ground east of the river if we were to use as our axis of supply the long, exposed defile that stretched back, for eighteen miles, to Medjez. An American armoured group was moved there, but they were not strong enough to dominate it in the face of an enemy found to be of considerable strength.

A further withdrawal was decided upon, to be completed in two stages, first to "Longstop Gap", ten miles further south (itself untenable without our holding the hills across the river on its right flank), and later to the heights of Oued Zarga, twenty miles west of Medjez.

Longstop was a large, isolated hill, north of the Tebourba-Medjez road, which completely commanded the northern and western approaches to Medjez. On the map it was "Djebel Ahmera", but the Division had already named it Longstop, because an anti-tank position in depth had been created there, as a longstop against an armoured break-through. It was a name, and a feature, with which the Argylls and others were to become better acquainted.

The initiative was now in the hands of the enemy. Secure at last in Tebourba, he attacked towards Medjez on December 6, and the Argylls, who had taken over from the Northamptons in the olive groves at the bottleneck south of Tebourba, fell back on the night of December 6 to Longstop and the hills north-east of Medjez.

At about the same time the weather broke. 36 Brigade, in the north, had already experienced the cold drenching rain of North Africa. Now it was the turn of 11 Brigade and the Americans, in the south. It rained for three days and three nights; there was no cover for the men and the slit trenches filled with liquid mud. By December 10, when the weather lifted, all vehicles were bogged down, and that night one

American battalion, withdrawing from east of the river, lost most of its equipment in a morass.

Divisional headquarters was still in a group of farms just north of Oued Zarga, unavoidably isolated from the brigades it had to control, in an endeavour to be accessible to them all.

Meanwhile the original Divisional order to withdraw from low-lying Medjez to the Oued Zarga heights had been reversed by higher authority. It was a decision based—as often happens in operations in which allies are engaged—on non-military considerations, yet it was to stand us in good stead.

So two French battalions remained holding the Medjez bridgehead, with American tanks (Combat Command B) on the south-east and 11 Brigade on the north-west. A two-pronged German tank and infantry attack on Medjez on December 10, simultaneously from Tebourba and Massicault, was thrown back by French artillery and a counter-attack by American tanks, and the Guards Brigade—less the remnants of the gallant Hampshires—moved into the town. That night, in heavy rain and through thick mud, the Americans, 11 Brigade and Divisional headquarters withdrew to the main Oued Zarga position, leaving the Guards Brigade and supporting arms to hold the advanced point at Medjez, the Grenadiers occupying a steep hill just south of the town—Grenadier Hill—and the Coldstream the railway station.

The Germans made one more serious attempt, with tanks, to take Medjez but were driven off, and the Guards settled down to ten days of consolidation and patrolling.

Meanwhile, on December 13, General Anderson had ordered General Allfrey, commanding V Corps, to prepare for another all-out drive on Tunis. General Allfrey hatched a plan which entailed, first of all, the capture of Longstop, followed by an advance of the Guards and 11 Brigade, with an American combat team, north-east to Tebourba, while 6 Armoured Division moved direct on to the high ground at Massicault. From Massicault and Tebourba 78 Division and 6 Armoured Division would drive straight for Tunis. An American combat command was to be in reserve.

This concentrated attack would take up four-fifths of the existing First Army's strength; the rest was committed in

A PLAN THAT FAILED

36 Brigade's attempt to get behind the Germans at Jefna and drive on to Mateur, whilst the French and a commando held the enemy in the high ground between the two main roads.

The success of the plan depended on the weather. Unless there was fine weather for at least a week the ground in the Medjerda valley would never harden enough to carry tanks, and the efforts of the infantry would be wasted. The sun baked the surface of the ground, but underneath was three or four feet of oozy clay; even a light shower was enough to soften the outer crust and let the tanks through into the clinging mud. Rain held off for six days, and it was decided to begin to put the plan into effect.

A quarter-of-an-hour's barrage by sixteen field guns and a few mediums of 138 Field Regiment Group—a very tiny barrage compared with those that the Division was to see later—opened the attack on Longstop, which went in at 2230 on December 22.

The Grenadiers held the tiny village on the right bank of the Medjerda river, both as a right-flank guard to the Coldstream, attacking Longstop, and as a jumping-off place for the exploitation of the first phase. An American battalion of the 18th Combat Team was to be ready to take over Longstop as soon as it had been seized by the Coldstream.

The Coldstream attacked in bright moonlight, and in two hours they had taken their first objectives. One company had seized the col which connected Longstop with the main range of hills to the left, another under Major the Hon. A. P. S. Chichester, who was mortally wounded, cleared the top. A third company had suffered heavy losses in a battle for the railway halt to the east of Longstop, and as we seemed secure in possession of the hill, Lt.-Col. Stewart-Brown, commanding the battalion, decided not to commit his reserve company to an attempt to regain this railway halt.

None the less, the hill had been more strongly held than we had expected; prisoners told us that it was held by one of the two battalions of the 69 Panzer Grenadier Regiment, of the 10 Panzer Division. Our own reconnaissance and intelligence had estimated the German strength at only one company with half-a-dozen machine guns.

What is more, it was not clearly appreciated—though it should have been realised from the map—that Longstop was not the single feature we thought, but that jutting out to the north-east, separated from Longstop itself by a deep gulley, was the distinct and dominating Djebel el Rhar.

For the time being, however, both the existence and the tactical importance of Djebel el Rhar were hidden from us, and the Coldstream continued to hold the hill, even though it was impossible to mop up all German resistance, and though some of their many counter-attacks were locally successful.

At half-past three in the morning of December 23 heavy rain came down, just as the American battalion was moving in to take over. It turned out that the Americans had expected to take over a defensive position, completely free of the enemy, and were not ready to take over under battle conditions. In the early morning, however, they said they were ready, and the Coldstream were back in their concentration area, fifteen miles away, by 10.30 that same morning.

Meanwhile the German counter-attacks continued, and so did the rain. The Commander of the Guards Brigade moved five tanks up at dawn to help the Americans, but the ground was too soft for them.

Throughout the morning the Americans were appealing for support and, as the Grenadiers were fully employed, the Coldstream had to be brought back, only twenty-four hours after their first assault. In the meanwhile it had already been decided to cancel the major operation—the all-out drive for Tunis—because of the weather, but the Guards Brigade was ordered to carry on with the battle for Longstop.

What had happened there was that the Americans had lost the summit of Longstop and were in difficulties and the Coldstream, who had fought all night, marched fifteen miles back from the battlefield in the rain and had been attacked from the air on the way, were summoned from their breakfast at Medjez to retake the hill.

All through the day of December 23 the rain fell in torrents, and the Coldstream sent one company after another to support the Americans on the slopes. (A pocket of excellent American heavy machine-gunners was still sticking it out in the middle of Longstop.) On December 24 the Coldstream reached the summit and swept it from west to east, only to see in the fading light of Christmas Eve what nobody had seen or appreciated before—the sinister bulk of Djebel el Rhar looming up to the north. The leading company assaulted it in vain and all that night the companies on the crest of Longstop were subjected to an accurate and heavy mortar-fire that made the task of digging-in on almost solid rock extremely difficult for very weary men. Tired, though, as they were, not an officer or man but distinguished himself, and the comment of the battalion's medical officer, Lt. Grey-Turner, that Roddy Hill (the second-in-command) "was magnificent, standing boldly on the ridge and rallying the troops" could have been applied to many an officer, W.O. and N.C.O. that day.

So heavy had the rains been that wheeled vehicles could not get within 5,000 yards of the forward companies, tracked vehicles not nearer than 3,000. Ammunition had to make the last stretch by hand, and casualties were manhandled down the hill the same way. On the summit the knee-high rosemary and coarse heather were sopping wet—painfully slow to get through. As night wore on, under heavy mortar-fire, it was clear that in spite of the handful of reinforcements—a draft from England (hurried into battle as soon as they had dropped their heavy packs) and a company of French native troops—more troops still and more guns would be needed if Longstop was to be held and Djebel el Rhar taken.

As Christmas Day of 1942 dawned German armoured cars and infantry could be seen moving to the attack. The French were shot up and had to withdraw; the artillery and mortar fire on the Americans and the Coldstream intensified; the work of the carrying parties became impossible. Casualties were mounting, ammunition dwindling. It was clear that Longstop could not be held. The Coldstream withdrew through the Grenadiers, who had moved up to give them cover, supported by 138 Field Regiment, whose C.O., Lt.-Col. Clive Usher gained the D.S.O. for his personal action on Longstop.

The C.O. and the Adjutant of the Coldstream were both wounded. (The C.O. was awarded a D.S.O. and the battalion won three M.C.s and a dozen D.C.M.s). The battalion had lost nearly two hundred killed and wounded, the Americans possibly a hundred. The American heavy machine-gunners, incidentally, and their medical teams, earned high praise from the Coldstream's survivors.

The lessons these actions had brought were that, for future co-operation in the field, differences of terminology and organisation between the British and the Americans would have to be ironed out at brigade and battalion level; that gunner O.P.s must remain in position during hours of darkness: that units should not be expected—for the sake of those relieving them— to take a position and hand it over the same night, and that mules were needed as carriers in this mountainous country where rain could so suddenly and so completely make tracks impassable to wheeled and tracked transport. Most important of all, it had given us a new view of Longstop and Djebel el Rhar: the troops that were to seize it at Easter would be better briefed than the Guards and the Americans had been.

Now, however, on Christmas afternoon, the Corps and Divisional Commanders, up at Brigade Headquarters, decided against a further assault. On Boxing Day, the Grenadiers took over Medjez station—where the following day they were to fling back a German attack—the Argylls held Grenadier Hill, and the Coldstream, who had lost ninety killed and missing and eighty-seven wounded, were in reserve.

The Northamptons had been detailed, according to V Corps' plan, to work through the hills to seize the pass west of Tebourba, and they set off with their wireless equipment carried by four mules over rough country. The mule carrying the set itself went over a precipice, so the order cancelling V Corps' major operation never reached the battalion, which pushed through very difficult country in dense fog right up to the Djebel Lanserine before the commander, realising what had happened, halted his battalion and brought it back after some minor clashes.

This exploit was accomplished with only limited mule transport hastily acquired from the Arabs, with improvised pack saddling and no trained muleteers. It taught us the valuable lesson that the British soldier nearly always loses an argument with a mule—especially an Arab-speaking mule; in future operations in North Africa (though not, unfortunately, in Sicily) the Division was supported by a properly trained pack-transport unit under Lt.-Col. J. Hume Dudgeon.

* * * * *

It was on Christmas Eve, at a conference between General Eisenhower, General Anderson, and General Allfrey, that it was decided to abandon any hope of another major attack on Tunis until the rainy season had ended. (Eisenhower accordingly withdrew all the American trooops except 18 Combat Team from V Corps area so as to put in, instead, an American attack in the south against Sfax.) This was the end of the First Army's hopes of capturing Tunis by storm—a sad decision, in the words of General Anderson's despatch, but inevitable owing to the weather—and it was clear that when the time came for a new attack in the spring, it would have to be on a heavier scale against greatly increased opposition. So there was to be a stern winter race to decide which side could build up its forces the faster for the next campaigning season.

Whether we could do it was doubtful, but the doubt in no way depressed the spirit and morale of the Division and the spring offensive was awaited with supreme confidence that given equal terms we had proved ourselves equal or superior as fighting men to the Germans. In the meantime extensive patrolling was to be the order of the day and night. Patrols were often out for forty-eight hours or more in the many wide and desolate areas where no troops of either side were permanently established. The Division thereby dominated these areas and denied them to the enemy. The experience thus gained raised the standard of resourcefulness and cunning to a level that was to stand the Division in good stead in the fighting that lay ahead.

CHAPTER IV

THE NINE ATTACKS OF VON ARNIM AND THE TEN-DAY BATTLE OF THE TEN PEAKS

AT home there was anxiety and deep disappointment. Excited, only a couple of months back, by the news of the North African landings—and by the fact that they coincided with the Eighth Army's success at El Alamein—Britain's newspaper readers had been led to believe, partly by their own wish to believe, and partly by the optimistic accounts of the initial success in North Africa, that the First Army would race through to Tunis unchecked.

The requirements of military security prevented the correspondents on the spot revealing that First Army was less than a corps in strength—less than a division, even, until mid-December —and that the Germans were in command of the air. And if the same correspondents had been unduly optimistic in the first couple of months of the campaign, so had the intelligence officers who had briefed them, and so were the earliest communiqués. There had, indeed, been grounds for optimism at first. What was impossible to explain completely to the public was why those grounds no longer obtained.

Now, with the news first of Tebourba and then of Longstop, the public at home realised fully for the first time that First Army was unlikely to reach Tunis until Eighth Army arrived to lend a hand. "This was a humiliating situation," as Capt. Nigel Nicolson of the Grenadiers has written, "which the world's press did not hesitate to point out. The First Army, compared to the Eighth, had sunk in the esteem of a public who naturally tended to measure fighting ability in terms of the miles gained and of prisoners captured. When the word 'mud' was mentioned, derisive fingers were pointed at Rostov, where the Russians were making contemporary gains of great importance in similar conditions. Shortage of supplies? Surely the Eighth Army's difficulties . . . were at least equally severe? Mountains? But since when had any British Army been halted by mere mountains? Shortage of troops? Security regulations forbade the explanation that an army can sometimes be smaller than a corps. The truth was that First Army, alone of all the armies with which they were disparagingly compared, faced all these difficulties simultaneously, and therefore they alone were halted."

There was more to it even than this. The Americans, so far, were only sketchily represented in the battle area: they were occupying and policing Morocco and Algeria, holding the ring, as it were, for our invasion of Tunisia. From the beginning to the end of the Tunisian campaign the Americans never provided more than a quarter of the troops engaged. So the brunt had fallen on the Division and on Blade force, only now growing up into 6 Armoured Division. The French were lamentably ill-equipped, though their spirit was high, and far too short of arms, vehicles and signal equipment and too unpractised in staff-work to be used for offensive action. What they were capable of doing, they did well—covering the mountainous right boundary (the "Eastern Dorsale") of the battleground.

Our own lines of communication were stretched to snapping point: most of the fighting was done at a distance of 500 to 550 miles from Algiers. Even Bone, when it became fit to use after its bombing, was more than a hundred miles as the crow flies. And everything had to be carried from the ports—there was no coal, no petrol, and precious little food to be got locally—over the one ramshackle railway or the two roads, now dusty, now deep in mud, and daily swept by the Luftwaffe's fighters. As A.B. Austin, the *Daily Herald* correspondent, put it, it was like fighting in the Highlands and being supplied from Plymouth.

In fact Austin was putting the position too favourably. It was like fighting in the Highlands and being supplied *through* Plymouth but *from* the continent of Europe. For Algiers, 500 miles away, was only an entry port. Unlike any other army in the field First Army had no firm base nearer than the

JANUARY, 1943

United Kingdom—requirements, if not already in transit, took three months to arrive.

It was along the two roads from the entry ports that the men of the R.A.S.C. drove incredible journeys by night; these roads that the Royal Engineers (who eventually had their own ten Tunisian quarries producing 2,000 tons of stone a day) metalled and bridged, often under fire, and on which the men of the Pioneers worked till their hands bled.

What nobody had realised—General Anderson admits it in his despatch—is that North Africa is a European, not an African, country. It rained from December till April. There was mist as well as rain and always there was mud, "thick, sticky and bottomless", as it is described in Alan Moorehead's *African Trilogy:* "the dead were buried in mud and the living were in it up to their knees. They were wet to the skin all day and all night. They had mud in their hair, and mud in their food. When the mud dried it set like iron and had to be beaten off the boots with a hammer or a rifle-butt. Before the astonished eyes of the commander, tanks went down to their turrets in mud. A spell of a few fine days made no difference—the mud was there just the same, and if you sent out a squadron of tanks you never knew whether or not they would be caught in another downpour and so abandoned to the enemy."

The mud was a factor not only to the foot soldier and the tank commander: it added to our difficulties in the air. Our few forward airfields were far enough away from our fighting troops as it was—Souk el Arba some fifty miles and Bone a hundred miles back and more: often the fighters were so bogged down on them that they could not take off. The German fighters were on sandy airfields near the coast—and a mere score or so of miles, most of the time, from the battle. This enemy air superiority had a serious effect on operations, and administration; 250 casualties in one week on the ten kilometres of road between Medjez and Oued Zarga is a measure of the effect—and this in spite of restrictions on the daytime use of transport.

We were already short of transport, and this inability to use what we had by day in the forward areas made matters worse.

(Opposite) A patrol of 2 Lancashire Fusiliers near Chaouach

Gen. Sir Harold Alexander and Maj. Gen. Evelegh at an O.P. near Heidous

Mule Harbour near Bettiour

But we dared not take risks, when it was a matter of three months before wrecked vehicles could be replaced.

* * * * *

We were attacking, the Germans defending: the mud hampered us, not them. And how well they defended! And how well the lie of the land helped them! Except for the narrow coastal plain, and the plain around Tunis, this was a country of defiles, djebels and wadis, hills, rocks and narrow gulleys, every narrow track or road dominated by some feature from which a well manned machine-gun post could hold up a battalion.

And the posts were certainly well-manned. The German troops in North Africa were highly trained, skilful, courageous, and at their best in defensive, delaying fighting. They sited their posts admirably and their half-inch machine-gun was heavier, more accurate, and had a longer range than anything we possessed at first: indeed, their defence of Tunis was built on the heavy machine-gun together with—to a lesser degree—the heavy mortar.

Where we had the advantage—an advantage that was to be increased as time went on—was in artillery, chiefly twenty-five pounders. The front, according to the Army Commander, seemed sometimes to be held largely by artillery fire alone. Except that "front" is hardly the word: we covered the chief defiles through the mountains with never more than a brigade and often less; there were inadequately patrolled gaps of a score of miles between units; there were huge unpoliced areas as big as England behind and on every side, peopled by French farmers, some of doubtful friendliness, and by Arabs some of whom spied now for one side now for another, and who stripped the dead of their clothes.

We were not only superior in artillery. Our service rifle was better than the Germans' and the men who had criticised the slow rate of fire and the small capacity of the Bren came to bless its accuracy and reliability. The bayonet proved itself at Tebourba. Above all, the Division—except when there were brief local breakdowns of supply—was well clothed and well fed. The compo ration made its first appearance in

Tunisia, a one-man load holding enough for fourteen men for one day—forty-two tinned meals, together with sweets, cigarettes and toilet paper. It could be eaten cold, or heated, and it was a first-class, and even a palatable diet. Moreover, battledress is probably as good a kit as any army has yet devised for European or near-European conditions, and the men, thanks to the food and clothes, kept very fit. There was a certain amount of mild dysentery, especially at first, but malaria was kept in check—largely owing to the ubiquitous, the ineluctable Mepacrine.

Above all, morale was high. The Division had met the Germans face to face and felt that given the supplies and the support it needed, it would be fully their match. And the Germans, in spite of their quick build-up of forces, their superiority in armour and in aircraft, never succeeded in pushing us out of our point of access to the Tunisian plain—Medjez.

For the time being, however, all that was asked of the Division, as we awaited better weather and heavier forces, was that it should contain the enemy, seize ground that we should need later by limited attacks with full artillery support, and to be ready to advance—even without armour—if the enemy moved south against the French.

The sappers of the Division, and the field companies with the brigades, who had been busy mine-lifting and bridge-building, were now more occupied with mine-laying and the placing of demolition charges. Sgt. Laird, of 237 Field Company, who won an M.M. for his coolness in placing a charge under a bridge on the Tebourba–Medjez railway whilst being machine-gunned, was only one of many sappers whose cunning was matched by their courage. And some field-company sections, besides providing fighting patrols, were known to lay as many as a thousand road-mines in a single night. All this in addition to bridge-building and road work: Dryshod Drive, Auchinleck Avenue and Heartbreak Highway were routes by which bullets and biscuits got to the men who needed them.

January 3 saw the first of the new "limited" attacks made by 36 Brigade on Green Hill and Bald Hill—the dominating positions, ten miles short of Mateur, that they had come to know so well only two months before. This time the Argylls, who had suffered heavily there, were not with the brigade—they were now, after a spell in 11 Brigade, filling the Hampshires' place with the Guards. The plan was for the Buffs, with a parachute company, to take Green Hill, while a commando was to take Bald Hill; the Royal West Kents were in reserve.

The Buffs went into the attack—under a thirty-gun barrage from 132 Field Regiment and 456 Light Battery—in a night of rain, and at dawn they were still on the lower slopes, being heavily and accurately machine-gunned. They held on through the day while the parachutists took the summit—only to be driven off again. Meanwhile the fight for Bald Hill had taken a similar course: the commando took it, lost it, and took it again.

We had to withdraw, and by January 5 we were back at our original position. A memorandum by the Division's C.R.A., Brigadier Wedderburn-Maxwell, pointed out that the operation had failed, as had the Longstop attack at Christmas, largely because our forces were inadequate. He asked C.O.s for their ideas on how best to cope with the German method of defence—excellently sited heavy machine-guns and mortars and the bulk of their infantry held back to counter-attack on D+1.

On our right both the enemy and 6 Armoured Division were active: on January 18 newly-landed German mountain troops, supported by the new Mark VI "Tiger" tanks—the first we had seen—swung down the Bou Arada valley, to drive a wedge between us and the French, threaten our right flank, and widen the coastal corridor between Von Arnim's army, facing us, and that of Rommel, now falling back before Montgomery's Eighth Army. The Germans were feeling their strength; they were still being steadily reinforced from Sicily, and now also from Rommel's retreating forces.

The attack against 6 Armoured Division was stopped after heavy fighting, in which the lorried infantry, the Irish Brigade—who were to become part of 78 Division in the spring—especially distinguished themselves. But the French were overrun; they lost their few anti-tank guns and their field pieces;

seven infantry battalions were cut off in the mountains; and the Germans were at Robaa and Ousseltia, far to the south of our old stamping ground, on January 20.

The position had to be strengthened, or the Germans could divide First Army and the approaching Eighth—perhaps even swing round behind First Army. So it came about that 36 Brigade, only a couple of weeks after their reverse in the hills of northern Tunisia, found themselves under French command in the mountains of the interior.

These reinforcements, together with American troops and armour, helped General Juin to stabilise his front along a line covering Robaa and running southward to the west of Ousseltia.

Again there was a lull of sorts. And made all the pleasanter for our feeling more at our ease now in the mud and mountains of North Africa, for bread at last after the three dreary months of dry biscuits, and for more regular mail from home. But there was no lull in Tunisia without its patrol work, and no lull that ever lasted long. On January 31 the enemy renewed his attack on the new and stiffened line in the south. Thirty-six Brigade took the brunt of it at Robaa, where the Buffs stood their ground and knocked out five tanks—two of them "Tigers"—with their anti-tank guns whilst the unfortunate French garrison at Faid was destroyed before the American tanks could reach them.

The first days of February were a trying period for the Allied forces as a whole, and their commanders. The French were overstrained; First Army was still undermanned and underequipped; and the approach of Rommel's army westward from Tripoli was beginning to be felt before its Eighth Army pursuers could link up with First Army.

Everything now centred on the mountain area south and south-east of Tunis, through the passes of which the railway runs to Sousse and in which French, American and British troops were more closely linked than they had been in the earliest days of the campaign.

Far away to the east the Eighth Army had taken Tripoli on January 23. Its long desert campaign was over; now its function was to act as one arm of a pincer on to the German stronghold in Tunisia.

Axis strategy, on the other hand, was to prevent the pincers from closing, to fuse Rommel's army and Von Arnim's and to hold on to the Tunisian tip as long as possible so as to deny us the Mediterranean passage and the jumping-off point for "the soft underbelly of Europe".

By mid-February the Eighth Army's forward troops were up against the Mareth Line. This meant a halt to its advance: its main forces and supplies had to be moved up, and the Mareth Line reconnoitred.

Rommel used this breathing space to turn west and try to prevent First Army's American troops in the hills of Tunisia breaking through into the Sfax plain and driving a wedge between him and Von Arnim. He no doubt calculated that if, better still, he could take Tebessa, the road and railway junction which was the communication centre and supply base for the whole of First Army, that army might have to withdraw along the whole of the Tunisian front and Von Arnim could enlarge and strengthen his western perimeter.

Rommel's attack, in mid-February, did not concern the Division directly, and it can be summarised briefly as follows:

The enemy, after heavy fighting in which the Americans were chiefly engaged, took Sbeitla, the last inhabited place before the Kasserine Pass. This pass gave access to Gafsa (a communication centre to the south) and westward to Tebessa itself, and the allies fell back to a line covering it.

The French were on the left, the Americans covered the pass itself, and the Guards' Brigade reinforced an American division at Sbiba, on the right. (The Guards Brigade had left the Division permanently to join 6 Armoured on February 2, and had since seen heavy fighting at Djebel Mansour.) The Guards held firm against attacks by tanks and infantry, but on February 20 the Germans broke through the American line at the Kasserine Pass and sent their Panzer divisions west towards Tebessa and north towards Thala. The Americans checked the threat to Tebessa and a British composite force, "Nickforce", found largely from 6 Armoured Division and commanded by Brigadier Nicholson, that division's deputy commander, but including also American gunners and the Hampshires, halted the German advance short of Thala. So by the time the Guards Brigade had been sent across from Sbiba to Thala the enemy had already begun to withdraw; British and American troops pressed on his heels slowly through the Kasserine Pass.

It seemed, no doubt, to Rommel—commanding in the south —that, although he had had to withdraw, he had done so much damage to the American II Corps that it could no longer intervene between his army and Von Arnim, commanding in the north. Now it was Von Arnim's turn to try to force us to withdraw from our jumping-off points for Tunis and Bizerta.

Von Arnim's nine attacks, between Ousseltia and the north coast (at Cap Serrat) fell on V Corps, and two of his objectives were, obviously, Medjez and Beja. The newly arrived 46 Division was now holding the sector from the coast in the north through the hilly country facing Mateur, down on the right to a notable valley, named Hunt's Gap after the C.O. of 49 L.A.A. Regiment, who had just reconnoitred it. This gap covered the northern approach to Beja from Sidi Nsir and Mateur and, as had been foreseen, it was the line of one of the strongest German tank attacks. Although the isolated battalion at Sidi Nsir was lost, the main attack—although it penetrated to within a few miles of Beja—was just held. In the end it was resolutely repulsed by 46 Division at Hunt's Gap, but it was an anxious time. Meanwhile, 78 Division took the brunt of the attack south of Medjez.

This is the place, perhaps, to explain that for a time it becomes difficult to follow the fortunes of the Division as a whole. As an intelligence summary in the Division's war diaries plaintively puts it, "the chain of command had become somewhat tangled". The Guards, as already mentioned, had left the Division for good to become the 6 Armoured Division's lorried infantry brigade: the Irish Brigade were not to become part of the Division until March, when the Division at last took the shape it retained throughout Sicily and Italy to the end of the war. Meanwhile 36 Brigade fought under French command for a while, the much-travelled Argylls were at one time with the Guards, at another with the French, at another with 11 Brigade instead of their own 36, at still another under

46 Division. In return, 78 Division, throughout this period of confused command and confused fighting, had under command 138 Brigade, consisting of the K.O.Y.L.I., the Lincolns, and the York and Lancaster, from 46 Division.

At this particular time from February 26 to March 3, the period of the nine attacks of Von Arnim, 78 Division consisted of 11 Brigade and 138 Brigade. The Parachute Brigade, the Guards' Brigade, and 36 Brigade were at this time all being used as army troops to stop the gaps and to counter-attack whenever required on our extended front. The Argylls were used as an independent battalion in army reserve—an arduous honour, with the moves coming so thick and fast that their C.O. had not time to get one plan down on paper before another had to be formulated.

All was a measure of the fact that First Army had not enough troops to hold an enemy who was constantly probing and pressing in one sector after another.

The attack on 78 Division's front came in at 3 a.m. on the morning of February 26, when the patrols of 11 Brigade found themselves engaged all along the line. The enemy infiltrated into the French hill positions on our left and penetrated between the French and the Northamptons. By seven o'clock or thereabouts he was within 2,000 yards of 11 Brigade H.Q., and heading for our gun areas.

Guarding the approach to the valley from Bou Arada to Testour, where was Divisional H.Q., was 1 Commando, under Lt.-Col. Mills-Roberts. It held "The Green Patch" against two infantry attacks, but was then overrun by tanks. The commando had only arrived during the previous night.

Five Survey Regiment R.A. cut their way out after being surrounded, and the Lancashire Fusiliers joined with 56 Recce in pushing the enemy slowly back along the road. The Survey Regiment were not the only gunners to find themselves in an infantry battle: the 4 Medium and 49 Light Anti-Aircraft Regiments took prisoners, also without infantry help.

One company of the East Surreys, holding an outlying hill known as Fort MacGregor, was overwhelmed. Major Brooke-Fox, its commander, was killed and almost all his men killed, wounded or captured.

The rain hampered the enemy more than it did us—this time he was the attacker—and 56 Recce Regiment briskly engaged at Tally Ho corner, had manna showered on it from heaven when the Germans, unable to supply their forward troops by road, dropped supplies by parachute. The men of the Recce regiment watched anxiously as the parachutes descended on them: could they be landmines? Anxiety changed to triumph and delight—there was Danish butter and Swiss chocolate in the containers. But there was little else for rejoicing: the enemy came on in force and the Recce regiment had to give way. Tally Ho Corner was lost—for a time.

By the middle of the first day of the battle a company of each of the Lancashire Fusiliers and the East Surreys, with 56 Recce, all that we had in reserve, were counter-attacking, and the enemy was withdrawing, but still holding Tally Ho Corner.

On the second day a full counter-attack, under a heavy bombardment and in pouring rain, was launched by the East Surreys to recapture Fort MacGregor. This was completely successful, and among those who distinguished themselves were Sgt. John Davies, who won an immediate M.M. for his leadership of the carriers, and Pte. R. Moore, whose D.C.M. was the reward for carrying messages and tending wounded under fire. While being sniped he repaired his faulty Bren, stalked and killed the sniper, and brought back his papers as proof of the kill.

Elsewhere, counter-attacks were maintained, and concerted action by the Recce regiment and the Northamptons succeeded in clearing Tally Ho Corner.

Throughout these first two days the K.O.Y.L.I. of 138 Brigade were fighting hard at Banana Ridge, overlooking the Medjerda river from the south, and the French and Northamptons were kept busy.

There was not a unit in the Division that did not find itself hotly engaged. Pressure on the enemy from our right flank—from a scratch force known as "Y" Division, which included Guards, the Irish Brigade, 1 Parachute Brigade, Frenchmen, commandos, tanks and guns—helped the Division to force the enemy back, but for five days the fighting was close and harassing. The Recce regiment particularly distinguished itself, continually taking on tanks and sticking out its neck as Recce regiments must.

At Bou Arada, as part of "Y" Division, our own 17 Field Regiment saw its first engagement of the campaign, an engagement that took place, as it had with 132 and 138, against tanks over open sights—not without loss to the regiment but with even greater loss to the German armour.

Over on the Division's left the Argylls, under 46 Division for the time being, took heavy losses in an attempt to relieve the 2/4 Hampshires, holding the isolated group of rocks known as the Pinnacles, near Hunt's Gap. They were mortar-bombed in a rocky ravine: Capt. Anderson, who had exposed himself recklessly, won a D.S.O.; Sgt. MacInnes, Cpl. Moody, and Pte. Dignal won M.M.s. The Argylls did their job and for a fortnight held the position they had seized—for most of the time isolated, and unsupported by other infantry on the flanks.

By March 3 the situation was in hand, but the enemy pressure went on against 46 Division in the north, where he again reached the outskirts of Djebel Abiod, which we had taken so long ago. Further south, French withdrawals in the Medjez area left the Germans occupying all the high ground overlooking the Oued Zarga–Medjez road, including the important hill villages of Toukabeur and Chaouach. We still held Medjez, but it was on low-lying ground, supported only by our holding the village of Naceur, 3,000 yards away and itself overlooked. Thus, Medjez was a dangerous salient, but to help in its protection we were able to deploy three or four seventeen-pounder anti-tank guns for the first time. On the right we had fully restored the position—again in command of Tally Ho Corner and the protective ring of hills that formed our defence line eastward from it.

Spring came to Tunisia—or to those patches of it, between the crags and rocks, where spring could come. There were marigolds in clefts on the hills, great-headed marguerites in the valleys, and red poppies thick amidst corn. There were longer periods of sunshine between the rainstorms, and the roads began first to dry and then to become dusty. Strategically, the time had come to strike back, and the season of the year now made it possible.

On March 18 General Anderson gave the orders to V Corps: no more withdrawals; in the north the enemy to be driven back to the line Sedjenane–Cap Serrat; in the south the Beja–Medjez road and the high ground overlooking it to be cleared—all as a preliminary to a major assault on Tunis and Bizerta.

In the northern sector, 46 Division—and it is to be hoped that somewhere their achievements, too, will be recorded—reached all their objectives in the attack launched between March 28 and 31. 36 Brigade had fought under their command and were now switched back to their own division.

Now, for the first time in its history, 78 Division was assembled in the field as one complete formation under its G.O.C. It consisted of the old faithfuls—11 and 36 Brigades—with the newly joined but well-seasoned Irish Brigade. Under command it had its former units, 17, 132, and 138 Field Regiments, 49 L.A.A., 64 Anti-Tank, and 4 Medium Regiment R.A., with an array of other gunners, and the tanks of 142 R.A.C. and the North Irish Horse—their Churchills in action for the first time. Fifty-six Recce and all the other divisional units were at hand.

The Division's turn came before dawn on April 7, when it opened its attack northward to clear the Beja–Medjez road. The mountain country that had to be swept has been described by General Anderson himself: "a vast tract of country, every hill in which is large enough to swallow up a brigade of infantry, where consolidation on the rocky slopes is very difficult, in which tanks can only operate in small numbers, where movement of guns and vehicles is very restricted, and where the Division had to rely on pack mules for its supplies and to carry wireless telegraphy sets, tools, and mortars. The general impression is one of wide spaciousness—a kind of Dartmoor, or Central Sutherlandshire, but with deeper valleys and steeper hills."

So this was essentially an infantry battle, though the attacks went in under admirably planned artillery concentration, and with the best possible support from the R.A.F. bombers and from the Churchills of Brigadier Maxwell's 25 Army Tank Brigade. For the first time a complete model had been made, at Divisional H.Q., of the ground to be fought over, and on it commanders and staff were coached for the coming battle. Everyone knew, this time, who would be on his either hand.

* * * * *

There was a cold night wind blowing as the barrage opened from a twelve-mile arc of guns manned by something like 15,000 gunners. A. B. Austin, the *Daily Herald* correspondent, on the ridge above Oued Zarga in the darkness, heard the growling and barking of the guns, and saw a white flicker like summer lightning run up and down the valleys and ridges, throwing the high ground into sudden relief and filling the hollows with light. It was, he wrote, as if the hill waves really were pitching and rolling.

The red and white Very lights went up and the infantry attacked. General Evelegh's plan was to attack with all three brigades at once, and then to stretch the enemy to the full.

Eleven Brigade was on the right, having assembled south of Djebel Touila. The Northamptons and the East Surreys had taken their first objectives before first light; the Lancashire Fusiliers were in reserve.

In the centre the Buffs and the Argylls also seized the small hills that had been allotted to them, whilst the Royal West Kents awaited their turn. On the left the Irish Brigade was fighting its way up the grim slopes of the Mahdi.

By the first light of dawn the Churchills were moving out of Oued Zarga's eucalyptus groves, over ground that had been too sloppy for tanks a short month before, but was now hard and dusty. Soon they were climbing the hills to get at the German machine-gun and mortar posts, some of them coming in from behind and driving the machine-gunners out of their nests on to the advancing infantry—for the Germans had not counted on the tanks taking to the hills.

As soon as the first hill positions had been taken the arc of guns broke up, the 25-pounders and the mediums jolting up the dusty hill tracks to be ready to open up the afternoon's barrage.

Mortars and machine-guns could not stop them; the enemy's tanks were down south on the Kairouan plain and he had not thought it necessary to site anti-tank guns in the hills. So out came the Focke-Wulf fighters, attacking gallantly at close range. But the targets were too difficult to spot and too scattered. The Luftwaffe did little harm, and its activity dwindled again to next to nothing.

A detailed history of the next ten days would be a chronicle of the hills and valleys that the Division took, one after another —a maze of Arab names as confusing on the page, to a reader, as the maps to the fighting troops themselves. It came to be known as the Battle of the Peaks, but the features that mattered in this barren and desolate waste of hills were those known as the Mahdi, Hills 512 and 667, Djebel el Ang, and Tanngoucha and the Berber villages of Toukabeur, Chaouach and Heidous. All had to be cleared and held for Medjez to be freed of pressure and the threat of counter-attack so that we could build up there for the final offensive.

On the night of April 7/8 units which were to continue the attack next day had to transfer much of their equipment from M.T. to Pack Transport. Lt.-Col. Hume Dudgeon's 4 Pack Transport Group of mules and muleteers (the formation of which has already been mentioned) took over the transport of much of the attackers' equipment that night. The transfer of signal equipment went through without a hitch, thanks to the two company commanders, Capt. Adderley and Capt. Johnson, and in the subsequent fighting Sgt. Sifi, an Arab N.C.O., won the M.M.

The advance northward from the road was on a ten-mile front and was intended to cover a depth of ten miles, in the forbidding mountain ranges. By the afternoon of the second day the East Surreys were in Toukabeur ("Touk is took" was the signal), with the Northamptons and the Lancashire Fusiliers on the high ground on either side, and Lancashire Fusilier patrols feeling towards Chaouach.

That was on the right of the line. In the centre, by the same time, the Buffs had reached the summit of Hill 667 and the Argylls were throwing back a German counter-attack and consolidating, as were the Royal West Kents, on the slopes of the hills by Chaouach.

The Irish Brigade, on the left, were "tidying up" the slopes of the Mahdi. The 16 Durham Light Infantry, briefly attached to the brigade since the day before the attack began, were on the southern slopes, while the Royal Irish Fusiliers were on the north. The 2 Hampshires—the reformed Tebourba battalion —fighting in place of the London Irish, who were resting, had taken one of the smaller hills, and were soon to be relieved by the Royal West Kents. The Inniskillings were in reserve. (Throughout this battle there was a certain amount of fluidity between the three brigades, according to the progress made, and there were loans from other divisions: the Royal West Kents fought under 36 Brigade and under the Irish Brigade; the 6 Black Watch from 4 Division relieved the Royal Irish Fusiliers on the Mahdi for a time; the tanks of the North Irish Horse were used as support for each of the brigades in turn.)

On the morning of April 9 the East Surreys, with the Lancashire Fusiliers and tanks of 142 R.A.C., occupied Chaouach, and April 14-15 saw the same brigade (11)—with the Royal West Kents from 36—engaged in the heaviest fighting of the battle, for the hills Tanngoucha and Djebel el Ang, the two 3,000-foot ridges that overlooked Longstop and Medjez. Meanwhile the Argylls were holding the slopes of Hill 667.

Eventually, the following day, it fell to the Royal Irish Fusiliers to take Djebel el Ang, but the Inniskillings were driven off the top of Tanngoucha, and the Buffs, in the centre, had to withdraw from the outskirts of Heidous.

By April 16 we held the high ground north and south of Heidous. Djebel el Ang was already ours, one of the two ridges eight miles from Medjez. The other, Tanngoucha, was still occupied by the enemy. Medjez itself was free at last from any real threat from the hills, and the object of the ten-day battle had been achieved. We could build up there, in security, the stores and forces needed for the final thrust.

All this had been achieved by units which, in General Anderson's words, had been in contact with the enemy without a break since November 1942. They had taken 1,080 German prisoners in a series of extremely fierce hand-to-hand fights, including much night work over cruelly difficult ground. "I consider", General Anderson wrote in his despatch, "that 78 Divison deserves the highest praise for as tough and prolonged a bit of fighting as has ever been undertaken by the British soldier".

CHAPTER V

INTO THE STRAIGHT

NOT only was Medjez free to become a building-up area for a full-out assault: First Army at last had a total superiority of men and material (an advantage minimised to some extent by its division into three components of different nationality), and Eighth Army was near enough now to draw off enemy forces towards Enfidaville. Divisions were now packed into sectors we had once had to hold with battalions; three corps—one American and two British—held the sixty-mile front that the Division, two brigades strong, had occupied in November.

General Anderson's orders were to go all out for Tunis and (with the Americans) Bizerta, beginning on April 22. Apart from the coast road to Bizerta, there were three routes through which he could break into the plain of Tunis. The Division was chosen for the shortest, the most direct, and the one most suitable for tanks—the road through Medjez and Massicault. But it was the most heavily guarded, and it was so narrow at Medjez, where the river Medjerda ran between Banana Ridge and the high ground of the most recent battle, that General Anderson knew there would be very heavy fighting before he could break through.

One further advantage we now enjoyed: at last we had superiority in the air. The landing-fields that had been too muddy for take-offs were now dry, and in any case we had ten times as many—and seven times as many aircraft—as we had had in November. For the first time since they had landed the men of the Division did not look up when they heard aircraft—they were almost certain to be Bostons and Spitfires.

So much the better, but the German infantryman, with his machine-guns and his mortars, had still to be beaten on the ground, and the fighting began, necessarily, with an attack on

Longstop and simultaneous attacks on Heidous and Tanngoucha to protect its left flank. Not only did Longstop's dark sullen hump dominate the Medjez–Massicault–Tunis road: unless it were taken its guns could reach the French and the armoured division when they broke through from the south, or the Americans from the north, if they swung around against Tunis.

36 Brigade (commanded by Brigadier Howlett), the Buffs, the Royal West Kents and the Argylls, with the East Surreys from 11 Brigade under command, and the North Irish Horse in support, were given the task of taking Longstop—a task on which the Guards and the Americans had battered themselves in vain at Christmas.

This new battle for Longstop started on Good Friday eve, on the night of Thursday, April 22. Four hundred guns, served by gunners, stripped to the waist, who had already given the Irish Brigade a good send-off in its attack on Heidous and Tanngoucha, pounded the positions on the hill, while the Royal West Kents and the Buffs moved forward to the attack.

By dawn on Good Friday (it was St. George's Day, too), the Buffs were on the slopes, and the Royal West Kents, checked in the night by minefields and by heavy machine-gun fire, were going into the curtain of fire again.

The plan now was for the Argylls, followed by the East Surreys, to go through in an assault on the western summit, whilst Churchills of the North Irish Horse worked round to the right to give covering fire.

At 11.30, under a repetition of the original long artillery supporting programme, the Argylls' new C.O., Lt.-Col. Macnab, moved his men into the attack. It was a warm, spring day; flowers were blooming on the slopes. The Argylls advanced to the foot of the hill through a cornfield, and soon the machine-guns, mortars and field guns opened up on them.

Once on the slopes, because of the fire and the thickness of the scrub, the Argylls lost formation, and they advanced more as a body of men than as a battalion in companies. The fire was heavy now, and it was here that Colonel Macnab was killed. Major Anderson, D.S.O., leading, and now in command, soon found that he had only four officers and thirty men with him, exhausted by the heat and the climb—they had been fighting hard for the past fortnight, too—and likelihood of more. All communications were gone, and Major Malcolm made his way back with messages for Brigade.

The citation which accompanied the award of the V.C. to Major Anderson, in June, tells as well as anything can the story of the Argylls on Longstop:

"Over a period of five hours Major Anderson led the attack through intense enemy machine-gun and mortar fire. As leading company commander he led the assault on the battalion's first objective, in daylight, over a long expanse of open sloping hillside and most of the time without the effective cover of smoke. Enemy infantry opposition was most determined, and very heavy casualties were sustained, including all other rifle company commanders, before even the first objective was reached.

"On the first objective and still under continual enemy fire, Major Anderson reorganised the battalion and rallied men whose commanders, in most cases, had either been killed or wounded. The Commanding Officer having been killed he took over command of the battalion and led the assault on the second objective. During this assault he received a leg wound, but in spite of this he carried on and finally captured 'Longstop' Hill with a total force of only four officers and less than forty other ranks. Fire had been so intense during this stage of the attack that the remainder of the battalion were pinned down and unable to advance until Major Anderson had successfully occupied the hill.

"During the assault he personally led attacks on at least three enemy machine-gun positions and in every case was the first man into the enemy pits; he also led a successful attack on an enemy position of four mortars, defended by over thirty of the enemy.

"Major Anderson's force on the hill captured about 200 prisoners and killed many more during the attack. It is largely due to this officer's bravery and daring that 'Longstop' Hill was captured, and it was the inspiration of his

Mule train on the path to Tanngoucha

Tanngoucha

Maj. Gen. Evelegh and Brig. Wedderburn-Maxwell preparing the attack on Longstop, April 22, 1943

8 Argylls advancing to attack Longstop, April 23, 1943

Looking towards Tunis

Entering Tunis

example which encouraged leaderless men to continue the advance."

With their C.O. the Argylls had lost their I.O., Capt. Barry Erskine, and Lt. McLeish, the Adjutant, and the whole of the battalion headquarters' staff. Of the company officers, Lt. Fraser was killed and six others wounded. Twenty-five N.C.O.s and men were killed, sixty-six wounded, and sixteen missing.

By Good Friday evening the Argylls and the East Surreys, both sadly depleted, were in possession of Longstop, newly joined by the Royal West Kents, who had come up in support. The whole force was commanded now by Lt.-Col. Wilberforce of the East Surreys, who won a D.S.O. in this Longstop fighting.

But, on Longstop, it still remained to take Djebel el Rhar, the distinct feature on the north-east separated from Longstop itself by a deep gulley, the existence of which had been unknown to the Guards when they first attacked Longstop at Christmas, and which had proved the key point to the battle. The remnants of the three battalions on Longstop were suffering heavily from fire across the gully.

That night, the night of Good Friday, the Royal West Kents, who had fought stubbornly on the approaches to Longstop twenty-fours hours before, made an attack on Djebel el Rhar that was checked by heavy mortar-fire. Next day and the next the Royal West Kents, the East Surreys, and tanks of the North Irish Horse were kept pinned down. Clearly a new plan was needed, and a heavier scale of attack. Brigadier Howlett, commanding 36 Brigade, went forward in a tank on the morning of Monday, April 26, to conduct a battle in which the tanks of the North Irish Horse, supported by the Buffs and by much artillery, made the main assault, whilst one squadron of tanks and a fighting patrol of Argylls made a diversion on the right. Night patrols by the Royal West Kents had given us the information we needed.

As the tanks advanced they attacked an 88-mm. gun in position and one machine-gun post after another. The Buffs pressed on with them. The gunners' F.O.O. was killed, and

(Opposite) Gen. Sir Kenneth Anderson presenting decorations after the capture of Tunis.

sappers of 256 Field Company went ahead with the tanks and the infantry, lifting mines and blasting enemy posts with "beehives". "A" Squadron of 56 Recce, with Major Russell's company of the East Surreys and with tanks, worked round to the north of the hill and prevented the enemy from Djebel el Rhar, and those who had joined him from Longstop, from escaping.

The Buffs took more than 300 prisoners, at a cost to themselves of forty casualties. The Brigadier reported that it was "impossible to speak too highly of their steady advance under shell-fire" and of the support of the North Irish Horse. Lt.-Col. Dawnay (10 Hussars), who commanded, received the D.S.O. for this action.

On the left of the weary but victorious 36 Brigade was Brigadier Nelson Russell's Irish Brigade, fighting now in a last battle to clear the ten peaks, where 11 Brigade, under Brigadier Cass, had fought so hard only a fortnight before.

The Irish Brigade had taken over from 11 Brigade in the hills on April 16, with orders to take Tanngoucha, the Kefs, and the village of Heidous—all still in enemy hands. Eleven Brigade itself, its companies' strengths down to an average of fifteen to twenty, all ranks, had been holding grimly on to the rocky feature of Bettiour. From now on it concentrated on holding the Djebel Ang, then covering the Irish Brigade's left flank whilst it cleared the last hills.

This operation began with the Inniskillings' attacking Tanngoucha, the capture of which, it was thought, would cause the fall of Heidous and the Kefs. There was a long approach march, and the noise of a counter-attack on Bettiour in their immediate rear. But the attack went in, and the Inniskillings took half the hill. But the mules bringing up the tools, beehives, and ammunition were machine-gunned, and the battalion had to withdraw just before dawn.

It was decided now that a battalion attack on Tanngoucha was too much at the mercy of the machine-gun and mortar-posts at Heidous and on the Kefs. So a brigade attack was planned, and the following night (April 22) the Inniskillings again advanced against Tanngoucha whilst the London Irish attacked Heidous and the Royal Irish Fusiliers the Kefs and the fortress that the Germans had made of Hill 622.

The Inniskillings got half way up the Tanngoucha and dug themselves in; the London Irish were thrown back from Heidous; the Fusiliers took the Kefs but not Hill 622. The brigade hung on—there could be no help from 36 Brigade, in the middle of its bloody Longstop battle, nor from 11 Brigade, desperately weak after its ten-day battle among these same crags and gullies.

At midday on April 25, a fresh assault by the Fusiliers was launched against Tanngoucha and three Churchill tanks of the North Irish Horse helped to turn the tide. It was not tank country. As the Brigade commander said, it was scarcely mule country. But the troop commander thought he might get one of his three tanks near enough to the enemy to matter, and he and the Fusiliers attacked from the left to threaten the defenders of Tanngoucha, the Inniskillings to exploit any signs of worry.

All three tanks got through. And it took seventy-two mules to carry up the petrol and ammunition the three tanks needed. They lumbered up Butler's Hill and Hill 622, blazing at everything, with the Fusiliers advancing alongside. The Inniskillings charged up the Tanngoucha cheering, and the defenders surrendered. That night the London Irish entered Heidous. The left flank of the Longstop front was cleared, and it was the following morning—April 26—that the Longstop battle was finally won.

Had we been able to take Tanngoucha on April 14, in the course of the first battle for the Ten Peaks, the fight for Longstop might not have been so hard; for the men on Longstop were machine-gunned and mortared from it. Had the Irish Brigade not taken it when they did, on April 25, the final capture of Djebel el Rhar might have been still more difficult.

In taking Tanngoucha and completing the capture of the Ten Peaks, the Fusiliers had lost six company commanders in four days, the Inniskillings at the finish could just muster three rifle companies each about thirty strong, and the London Irish had suffered similarly at Heidous. Every man in the Brigade who could fight—clerks, anti-tank gunners, cobblers—had served in a rifle company during the battle. The medical services and stretcher-bearers were more than usually splendid. The corn was standing so high and, in other places, the undergrowth was so thick, that the A.D.M.S., Colonel Cheyne, had to organise special search parties from the R.A.M.C. and the Pioneers to follow up each attack and search for the wounded.

This was virtually the end of the Division's fighting in North Africa. And a fitting end, for it set the seal on Major General Evelegh's planning, on that of his subordinate commanders and on his soldiers' fighting quality. Except for the artillery and for the Royal West Kents, who secured the start-line for the final attack, the Division did not take part in the final attack on Tunis. That was for fresher troops. The Division had been fighting in the crags and ravines north of the all-important Tunis road for twenty-nine days without rest—some of its men for forty. Far to the north, the French went through the Sedjenane river-gap to Bizerta, the Americans along the Sedjenane road, between Green Hill and Bald Hill, other Americans through Sidi Nsir and Mateur. Other French forces swung up to Tunis from the south through Pont du Fahs. And through the Medjez gap, the quickest way to Tunis, came the major British attack of the campaign, made possible by joining forces of the First and Eighth Armies into one composite IX Corps. With Banana Ridge on their right and the Ten Peaks and Longstop on their left, astride the road that the Division had opened for them, 4 British Division and 4 Indian Division attacked, under a great barrage, on May 5. And through the gap they made, the armour broke out.

So, on May 7, 1943, Eighth and First Armies went into Tunis together—the 7 Armoured Division's 11 Hussars and the 6 Armoured's Derbyshire Yeomanry—and very proper it all was: Tunis had been taken, the enemy destroyed, as a result of the co-operation of the two armies. But when the tired infantry of 78 Division entered the town on May 8 (given pride of place by the Army Commander), six months to the day from their landing at Algiers, the French were still hysterical with gratitude. "Though the French may not have known it," observed *The Times*, a fortnight later, "they were thanking the right men."

For six months they had been laying the foundations of this victory. For six months, short of men and equipment, they had borne the main burden of the Tunisian campaign. For most of the time they had been virtually the whole of First Army, which until the last weeks was an army in name only; for most of the time they had been short of air cover, short of rest, unappreciated at home.

The millworkers from Lancashire and the Midlands, the clerks and city folk from Kent and Surrey, the men from the bogs and the shipyards in the Irish Brigade had become as agile and as tireless in the mountains as the Highlanders they had fought with. What was more, and what was to matter to them in the battles still to come, they had learned to fight a European campaign—the first we had fought since Dunkirk. Whilst the units of Eighth Army had been manoeuvred over the trackless spaces of the desert like so many ships at sea, 78 Division had fought in mountains and in valleys, over mined roads and through olive groves. They had blown up bridges and put up new ones, they had forded rivers and battled in railway sidings. In Sicily and in Italy it was they who were the experienced troops, after their six months of battle; it was the men of Eighth Army, seasoned as they were after their three years, and proud as they were of their superb record, who still had lessons to learn.

Meanwhile, as von Arnim's beaten army was herded into the cages on Cap Bon peninsula—twenty-two generals and a quarter of a million men—and as General Alexander cabled to Mr. Churchill, "We are masters of the North African shore," the men of 78 Division took their rest and found it good.

BOOK II

SICILY

CHAPTER I

INTRODUCTION

A TENTATIVE plan was already in being for the invasion of Sicily, hatched by the Joint Planning Staff in London in 1942. In January 1943, at the Casablanca conference, it was decided to put the plan into effect as soon as possible after Africa had been cleared, so that the Mediterranean should be opened and a jumping-off place secured for the invasion of Italy; detailed planning began at Algiers in February.

General Montgomery's advice was that both Germans and Italians would fight hard for Sicily, and as this, in any case, was our first big amphibious operation against a defended coast-line he produced a plan of his own on which he was surer of success. So the first London plan was altered: instead of the Americans landing in the north-west around Palermo while the British landed in the south-east between Gela and Syracuse, as had originally been intended, both landed side by side in the south-east, to avoid what was feared would be a dangerous dispersion of the allied forces and the possibility of the invasion's being defeated in detail.

The first landings were made in the early morning of July 10, 1943, after preliminary airborne landings by British and American troops. Lt.-Gen. Patton's U.S. Seventh Army landed in the Gulf of Gela, General Montgomery's British Eighth Army south of Syracuse. The two armies (Fifteenth Army Group) were under the over-all command of General Alexander, responsible to General Eisenhower as Supreme Allied Commander.

The Division had been transferred, whilst in North Africa, from First to Eighth Army, and at the time of the landings was Eighth Army's reserve, waiting in the hot and sandy country around Sousse and Sfax to be ferried across when needed. Meanwhile, Eighth Army, the larger of the two allied armies in

INTRODUCTION

Sicily, consisted of two corps, XIII and XXX; four British, one Canadian, and one airborne division, and one infantry brigade.

By July 20, Eighth Army was being firmly held short of the Catania plain with its network of canals and its Gerbini airfields. The Germans, reinforcing from Italy, were intent on denying us the airfields as long as possible and on delaying our clearing of the island and, especially, the Messina peninsula, whence they would escape at last, and whence our invasion of Italy would probably come.

Patton's army was occupied in reducing the west of the island, seizing the northern ports—Palermo especially—and guarding Eighth Army's flank. It was clear that Eighth Army had tough fighting ahead of it if it was to regain its momentum and drive forward on either side of the vast bulk of Mount Etna, 11,000 feet high, which filled and dominated the base of the isosceles triangle which was the Messina peninsula. On July 20 General Montgomery ordered forward his one reserve division, 78 Division, from North Africa.

There was a lull on Eighth Army's front in the last week of July, whilst the men rested after their hard slogging in the damp heat of the Sicilian summer and until the fresh troops arrived—all the more eagerly awaited because this was the division that knew more about mountain fighting, thanks to Tunisia, than any other division in the army. And it was mountain fighting that lay ahead.

CHAPTER II

FORTNIGHT OF FIGHTING

THE Division's landing was spread over the period from July 25 to July 30, two or three weeks after the invasion had begun, and was made over the beaches from Syracuse to Cape Passero, in the south-east corner of the island. For most it was a peaceful crossing by landing-craft and a well-organised landfall in the sunlit Sicilian afternoons. Only 138 Field Regiment, the last to land, lying off Avola on the night of July 29-30, were subjected to a disturbing—but ineffective—bombing attack.

It was over rough roads among the olive groves and vineyards, on steep mountain tracks, and through steamy, dusty heat that the Division moved forty miles to its concentration area at Palagonia, overlooking from the south the Catania Plain. Every man's throat was parched by the heat and the slight sulphur fumes of Etna, so many miles away. And the dust was the worst trial of all—a heavy white dust that clung to the skin, whitened hair and moustaches, and yet was fine enough to penetrate the handkerchiefs that officers and men wore over their mouths while driving.

In the squalid, picturesque, smelly little villages the Sicilians waved amicably and produced their rough wine, while the dark-eyed children gathered around any halted vehicle to plead for "cioccolati," "caramelli," and "biscotti." It was a foretaste of the sights, sounds, and smells, of the charm and the squalor, of Italian generosity and Italian beggarliness, that the Division was to come to know so well.

The Division was under XXX Corps, along with the Canadians and the Highland Division. The Germans were still resisting strongly in the Catania Plain, and General Alexander's plan was to push the left flank of Eighth Army northward, west of the plain, towards Etna, whilst the U.S. Seventh Army continued its advance eastward along the northern coast road. By reaching the southern slopes of Etna that great mass would be interposed between the two halves of the German forces and the enemy would have to withdraw from the Catania Plain and uncover the port of Catania itself. The task allotted to the Division was to carry out this advance of twenty miles to Etna, moving by means of the high ground west of the Catania Plain and so outflanking the Germans who still opposed the rest of Eighth Army.

There were four days of forward concentration, of reconnaissance and of mapwork, from July 25 to July 29. The Division's sappers toiled in the heat, and under shellfire, to make a track that would carry the Division forward from Castel di Judica to Catenanuova—there was no proper road—and the gunners worked over what was to be a major fire-plan for Centuripe. What impressed everybody was the scale of the mountainous country that had to be covered.

A Canadian brigade, temporarily under command of 78 Division, forced the crossing of the Dittaino river, on the night of July 29-30 and moved into the little town of Catenanuova in the early morning, followed by 11 Brigade, which saw its first fighting of the new campaign in a brisk battle to enlarge the bridgehead over the river. The Luftwaffe was in action, and on the ground was the reinforced and re-formed Hermann Goering Panzer Division, part of which we had met and destroyed in Africa. The East Surreys and the Lancashire Fusiliers suffered small losses in the hills overlooking the town, being harassed mostly by mines and machine-gun fire, but the Northamptons took the worst of the air attack, which destroyed their attached field-ambulance unit. This day and the next the enemy air force was active in the rear of the battle; Divisional headquarters was attacked, the two brigade headquarters and the convoys on the roads.

But Catenanuova was taken, which meant that a bridgehead over the Dittaino had been secured, the enemy was falling back behind his usual rearguard of machine-gun posts, minefields, blown bridges and snipers' eyries; 36 and 38 Brigades were ready to go on, over the mountain tracks towards Adrano and the lower slopes of Etna.

It was in the fighting for Catenanuova that L/Cpl. D. Chidwick of the East Surreys won an immediate M.M. for bringing in, from a patrol, a wounded German officer under fire. The officer—he was from the Hermann Goering Division—had valuable information: in his attaché-case were orders giving the whole German plan for the future operation in Sicily. The case was sent to Divisional headquarters, and General Montgomery arrived while the intelligence officer was translating the orders, and the translation was passed to him and to General Evelegh, paragraph by paragraph.

It became clear as the campaign progressed that the German withdrawal was being carried out strictly according to this plan: General Evelegh recalled later, in the fighting at Centuripe, that the orders had insisted that this was the pivot on which the German front was hinged, and that it was to be held at all costs. And one stern paragraph stuck in his mind, years later: no German soldier was to be embarked in the final evacuation of Sicily unless he was in possession of his arms.

* * * * *

Between Catenanuova and Etna the earth heaves itself into a tumult of ridges and hills, each seeming higher and steeper than the last, separated from each other by rocky gorges. Crowning this great outcrop of rock, and barring the road to Adrano and the foot of Etna, was the fortress town of Centuripe, on its razor-backed ridge—known soon and for ever to every man in the Division as "Cherry Ripe."

It was like Tunisia all over again, save that here was high summer, and the slightest exertion meant an outbreak of sweating in the clammy heat. Above all, it was dusty. Mingled with the dust of the parched Mediterranean landscape was the fine volcanic dust from Etna, the cone of which could be seen at night, a dull red glow in the darkness.

Mules and packhorses were needed, and the staffs and battalions were searching and scrounging for animals and equipment. Tunisian experience had taught them how necessary they were, but Army Headquarters had not given the Division even the lower deck of one L.S.T. to bring them from North Africa; shipping was too scarce, they said, even for one company of mules and muleteers. Some Italian army mules were captured, but it was largely a matter of requisitioning from the local population, and pressing civilian drivers into service. The drivers decamped whenever they could, and we found to our cost—especially at Centuripe—how unused civilian mules were to army accoutrements. Lt.-Col. Browne (the Division's A.Q.) had one nervous moment when, having taken 140 mules from one village, he was told by the mayor that they had shot the German officers who had once tried to take them. The brigadier recalls that he withdrew cautiously—but not without the mules.

* * * * *

The vast Centuripe feature, occupying a width of five miles or so between the Dittaino and Simeto river valleys was the main outpost of the Adrano position and it was defended—with what General Alexander later described in his despatch as "fanatical vigour"—by the best German troops in Sicily, the Hermann Goering Division and the 3 Parachute Regiment. It was approached by a narrow corkscrew road that ran for a couple of miles along the flank of one of the precipitous ridges jutting out from the main mountain mass. Every yard of this road was commanded from the steep slopes above; the steep slopes below were death traps to men, mules and vehicles. It had been mined, breached and blown and its hairpin bends were made for ambush. The town itself had been built on the steep edge of the final slopes of the outcrop, slopes which ran up at angles sharper than forty-five degrees. Immediately round the town the slopes were terraced for cultivation, in six-foot steps; farther away they were dizzy angles of coarse, slippery grass or loose crumbling stone. "The strongest mountain position I have seen", cabled a correspondent who had seen the worst that Tunisia could show.

The original plan was to go for it in the darkness of the night of August 1, moving across the hideously difficult country west of the road from Catenanuova to Centuripe. Eleven Brigade was to hold a covering position north of Catenanuova, so that 36 Brigade could move during the night along the mountain tracks to secure an outlying feature on the Centuripe plateau, across which it would attack at first light. The Irish Brigade was in reserve.

The move to the covering position went so well that General Evelegh decided on a bold move. He knew from the captured orders how hard the Germans would fight for Centuripe, and how likely it was that they were reinforcing their troops there as busily as they could. Every day's delay meant a bigger garrison there, so, with time in hand because of the success of the night march, and knowing that the Division was well enough trained for anything that was asked of it, he ordered the main attack to go in at midnight, twenty-four hours ahead of schedule.

Luckily, the fire plan was ready, but the snap decision meant that the complete divisional artillery, with extra ammunition, and two brigades with all their mules and supporting arms, had to be deployed on the single one-way road that ran north of Monte Scalpello to Catenanuova.

As the road was under shellfire, the units could not move until darkness fell, and there was no time even for reconnaissance until the middle of the afternoon. The Division deployed in pitch darkness over boulder-strewn country, the only mishaps being the inability of certain observation-post parties (their equipment carried on newly-acquired and ill-trained mules that lay down and refused to budge as soon as they were saddled), to reach their battalions in time. Apart from that series of hitches this move saw the Division probably at its best as a smooth-working and well-practised team.

In spite of this successful deployment, German parachute troops hiding in the caves between Catenanuova and Centuripe nearly wrecked the plan at the beginning, and did, in fact, prevent its full realisation. The East Surreys (11 Brigade) had secured their objective but failed to flush the parachute troops from the caves in the rear of their forward positions. The Germans came out as dark fell, attacking the Buffs (36 Brigade) moving up to their start line.

So it happened that by dawn on August 1 the Buffs were still disorganised, and were not established on the high plateau close to Centuripe before daylight, as had been planned. On the left of what was to have been a two-battalion front the Royal West

Kents had made a creditable advance over more than a mile of precipitous going, but were already meeting opposition. Because of the failure to flush the caves this was going to be a hard and a bloody battle. To add to the difficulties the operation was still hampered by the behaviour of the pack-mules, awkward and stubborn under the unaccustomed military saddling.

Brigadier Howlett, commanding 36 Brigade, ordered the Argylls, who had been the brigade's reserve battalion, to assault Centuripe head-on, straight up the menacing hill, while the Buffs re-formed and the Royal West Kents carried on their advance. On the right of the road the Northamptons of 11 Brigade were securing some intermediate high ground, harassed by the snipers of the slowly withdrawing enemy.

It was desperately hot, and the men were both overloaded and hungry. The main advance was over the jumble of rocks and ravines to the left of the road. It was impossible country for vehicles and the improvised gear for the mules was unsatisfactory, so that the carrying sections fell far behind. The rifle companies, therefore, had only the arms they could carry—no supporting weapons. The gunners' observation officers could bring up only their new portable radios, so that communication with the supporting artillery was uncertain. In any case this stretch of country was so full of dead ground that it could not properly be viewed.

From 9.30 on the morning of August 1 until dusk the Argylls and the Royal West Kents were under heavy machine-gun fire from the peaks, pinnacles and ridges of the broken country as they felt along the bluffs and mule-tracks towards Centuripe itself. The Royal West Kents were harassed by fire from the high ground to the left of the town; the Argylls—nearer the road—came under fire from the nearest houses and from the cemetery. Among the wounded was Major Moodie, commanding "R" company, who died the following day.

General Evelegh, reconnoitring along the road in his jeep (and ordering 56 Recce to disperse its vehicles), decided that afternoon that 36 Brigade must capture the town that night if it were humanly possible: the longer the delay the more reinforcements the enemy could bring up and the bloodier the final battle. He switched the East Surreys from 11 Brigade to 36, and Brigadier Howlett gave them the job of advancing along the mule-track and taking the cemetery whilst the Royal West Kents took the heights commanding the western, and the Argylls those commanding the southern, approaches to the town. The Buffs were in support and Brigadier Russell's Irish Brigade was moving up to exploit success or to redeem a failure.

It was a grim battle in the warm dark. The East Surreys approached the cemetery along a stepped, cobbled track. This cemetery, a maze of vast baroque tombs, is perched on a high hill separated from the town itself by a deep ravine. From this natural bastion the Germans put up flares and machine-gunned the East Surreys on the exposed track and the Argylls on the bluffs south of the town. To the west the Royal West Kents were playing a deadly game of hide-and-seek with German snipers whose accurate rifles were fitted with telescopic sights.

At daybreak the East Surreys had to make a frontal attack on the ridge to their right; under rifle-fire from the crest, they climbed a series of rocky ledges, each six feet high, handling their tommy guns and their bayonets as best they could. They cleared the ridge and all that day—August 2—they and the Germans in the cemetery, 400 yards away across the gorge, kept up a running fire at each other. One platoon reached the cemetery only to be driven from a nightmare battlefield where every grave and tomb was a strongpoint.

By that afternoon the Royal West Kents and the Argylls had been on the move for forty-eight hours, fighting every inch of the way not only against a tough and determined enemy but also a malignant landscape. The East Surreys—without food, for no transport had been able to reach them—were pinned to their exposed ridge. General Evelegh considered that although 36 Brigade had failed to capture the town it had dented the defence by its steady pressure and that it had taken the points necessary for the final thrust. It was clear afterwards that the Germans had not expected the attack to take place when it did, and did not believe that it could get so far.

The whole of the Division's artillery therefore slapped down a concentration on to Centuripe; the Royal Irish Fusiliers moved up near the hairpin road towards the cemetery, through the East Surreys; the London Irish attacked from the west; and the Inniskillings over the highest and roughest approach of all towards the town itself. Their C.O., Lt.-Col. Grazebrook, won an immediate D.S.O., as did Lt.-Col. Butler of the Royal Irish Fusiliers.

By dusk on August 2 the Inniskillings had a foothold in the southern edge of Centuripe, after being closely engaged all day, and by first light on August 3 the Royal Irish Fusiliers, after four hours of bloody fighting in the narrow, twisting cobbled streets, were through the town and pushing out patrols towards the north.

It had been an infantry battle, worthy of the great mountain fighters of Tunisia, and the other arms were quick to acknowledge the fact. The gunners had given splendid support, handling their guns over a cruel country into unbelievable positions, but a gunner officer's diary reads, "this is an infantry story". And 56 Recce, hot on the heels of the Argylls at the end of the battle, found itself in Centuripe before it knew it: "Thank God", said the squadron commander, and "we congratulated the infantry from the depths of our hearts" noted one of his subalterns in his diary. General de Guingand, Montgomery's chief of staff, had watched the attack from the hilltop to the south: "it appeared too much," he records in his book, "to ask any troops to undertake, yet . . . this fine division climbed the heights. . . . It was an imposing sight and will for ever spell valour in the records of the 78th." The Army Commander himself was quoted in General Evelegh's order of the day: "a wonderful feat of arms and he doubted if any other division in his army could have carried out this operation successfully." High praise, as General Evelegh added, from General Montgomery himself on the Division's first battle in the redoubtable Eighth Army. General Alexander's comment in his despatch was that "the storming of Centuripe was a particularly fine feat and its effects were widespread, for from that time the front once more became fluid. In face of the threat to Adrano the enemy position covering Catania became untenable." Mr. Churchill was able to announce the taking of Centuripe in a statement to the House of Commons, only a few hours after it had fallen, and the leader-writer of *The Times* referred to it that night with "it looks as if . . . the admirable 78 Division which fought with such courage and skill throughout the long Tunisian mountain campaign, may have Adrano for its objective." Yet nothing that the great ones said gives a clearer picture of how tough the fighting for Centuripe was, how dizzy and how deadly its slopes, than the comment an officer of the Division made to Reuter's correspondent on the day the town was taken. "Worse than Longstop", summed it all up.

It was a good guess of *The Times* leader-writer's. Adrano was the next objective, the largest town on the road that circles the vast bulk of Etna. But first there were the Salso and Simeto rivers to cross, and the Irish Brigade, pushing through Centuripe on the morning of August 3, descended the steeply terraced and thickly wooded hillsides and, in spite of demolitions, were at the banks of the Salso by midday. It needed fit troops and keen commanders to follow up so quickly after thirty-six hours of gruelling mountain fighting, and their speed paid dividends: the exposed approach to the river was free from enemy interference all that morning.

The bridge across the river had been blown, leaving a crater in the road that needed twelve hours' work on it. By the time the bulldozers were up the road was under shell and mortar fire from the bluffs across the river. That day the Irishmen and the sappers reconnoitred the river banks; that night the sappers bulldozed the crater, the infantry sent out fighting patrols, and the Division's artillery, ahead of the other arms, moved up the steep tracks of the Centuripe ridge to occupy what positions it could, however awkward, that would give them the range of Adrano. On the heights of Centuripe itself was 138 Field Regiment, whose ammunition could only be brought up by jeep and by manhandling with ropes, while 132 Field Regiment's position had been made feasible only by the extensive use of bulldozers. On the afternoon of August 4, under a heavy barrage from our own artillery and that of 51 Division, together with Army's mediums, the Royal Irish Fusiliers and the London Irish waded the Salso river, and climbed the bluffs on the far side. They were across in broad daylight; the Inniskillings followed through to take over the bridgehead, whilst the Royal Irish Fusiliers, who had had a good deal of opposition from machine-gun posts and snipers, pushed on to the next river, the Simeto. By early morning of August 5 the Royal Irish Fusiliers already had a rifle company across this obstacle; the London Irish were close behind them, with the supporting weapons moving into position; and the Inniskillings held a firm, wide bridgehead across the Salso and between the rivers. The sappers, working at night, and still under shellfire, had bridged the hundred-foot gap across the Salso in twelve hours and their patrols were looking to see what engineering problems the Simeto presented. Across their Salso bridge the cars of 56 Recce were nipping along to scout the flanks of the advance.

Technically, the Simeto was a harder nut than the Salso. The banks were steep and rocky, and the further bank was strongly held. There was three feet of fast-flowing water in the river and the sappers reckoned that they needed twenty-four hours to bridge it. But the brigade was well under way; it had reconnoitred the river approaches whilst the enemy was still taken aback by the speed of the advance.

It was again an afternoon attack, and again it went in under full-scale divisional artillery support—with four medium batteries and two platoons of heavy mortars for good measure.

Across the river the face of the bank was a honeycomb of caves, each a machine-gun post or a sniper's nest, each having to be cleared in turn. There were scattered houses along the road on the far side, too, and each of these had to be cleared. At dusk on August 5 the last two of these—the "Casinc" and the "Palace", two strongly-built stone villas—were being engaged by the Fusiliers' anti-tank guns at 800 yards' range and a Piat of the London Irish at a mere 100, respectively, and by nightfall yet another bridgehead was secure. Again the Inniskillings had followed through, and again a bridge was being put up at night by the divisional sappers in record time.

Twenty-four hours later 11 and 36 Brigades were crossing what an Irish infantryman described as "a sapper miracle", and the Irishmen were resting on the banks of the Simeto and bathing in waters that they felt were their very own. (It was malarial country they were in, had they known it: the local peasants were accustomed to flee these mosquito-ridden valleys in the summer for the hills. The Division suffered several thousand cases of malaria after the Sicilian campaign.) They had come twenty-five miles between August 1 and August 5, helped to take Centuripe, and forded and fought for two rivers. Among their heavy losses was one of the brigade's characters— Major Peter Fitzgerald, of the London Irish, who had already won an immediate M.C. for his gallantry at the Salso crossing.

On the Division's left the Americans were moving due east and fighting their bloodiest battle of the brief campaign at Troina; on the right XIII Corps had taken the important port of Catania, opened up for them by the capture of Centuripe. For the Division, Adrano was still ahead.

The first to reach the outskirts of the town were the scout cars of 56 Recce, not before the leading car of "A" Squadron had come to grief on a bank of mines and "C" Squadron had lost its two leading cars, only a hundred yards short of the town, to shellfire. These were not "C" Squadron's only losses: another of its patrols lost one car on mines, whilst two others were halted by machine-gun fire and surrounded by enemy infantry. The regiment's losses were high in this skirmish on the outskirts of Adrano, and two subalterns, Mitchell and Weeks, distinguished themselves by rescuing wounded men under fire. The cars withdrew under orders, so that a heavier attack could be made.

This time, though, the credit for actually taking a town fell not so much to the infantry as to the gunners and to the bombers operating from the Gerbini airfields. The concentration put down on Adrano on the night of August 6-7 seemed, said an observer at Tactical Headquarters, to lift the town out of the ground, and when the East Surreys moved in on the morning of August 7, through the battered, cratered streets and among the smoking ruins, the enemy had gone. The taking of Adrano, unopposed, had become, as the divisional commander said later, "an excellent training exercise". But we learnt that, in spite of the bombardment, rear parties had been in the town at nightfall, and it is likely that they would not have withdrawn had the final attack not been so well staged; had the planning been casual they would have fought it out.

The fall of Adrano gave us the key to the enemy's only

remaining lateral road south of Etna. But although this had been a much-coveted objective, and although the whole complexion of the campaign altered after its fall, there was no time yet for rest, and the enemy continued to delay as well as to evade our advances.

Now was the time, though, for General Evelegh's previously-arranged plan to be put into operation—for 11 Brigade to turn north and, supported by the whole Divisional artillery and other arms, advance round Etna's western flank on to Bronte. The ground restricted the advance to a one-brigade front but the plan allowed for 11 Brigade to be relieved, as it tired, by a fresher brigade passing through and keeping up the pace.

The Division had now reached the lowest slopes of Etna's lava fields, and difficult country it was, consisting of miles of hard, rough, rocky surface, broken up by deeply terraced vineyards and stone walls. Through this inhospitable landscape one narrow, single-way tarmac road led to Bronte, hedged in by two solid stone walls, unbroken by any gate.

The Lancashire Fusiliers led the way along this road supported by detachments of 56 Recce Regiment, the sappers of 256 Field Company and by tanks of 50 R.T.R. In spite of the rough going and of craters often covered from enemy gun-positions and hedged by mines the brigade made good headway and the evening of August 7 found the East Surreys five miles beyond Adrano, slithering and scrambling over the glassy rocks and the lava beds just south of Bronte.

But Bronte proved a harder town to take than Adrano. The German defence followed the pattern that had become so familiar: sappers and machine-gunners held on till the last minute and then fell back on to new vantage points; mines and booby-traps alternated with blown bridges and culverts. The whole advance was as much a sapper's as an infantryman's operation. This had been true of Tunisia; it was truer still of Sicily, as it was to be of Italy.

It was here and now that the Division made its first acquaintance with the German multiple mortar, the nebelwerfer. As the men got to know it better they learned how inaccurate it was, but at first its hideous whine was unnerving, and it did enough damage to make the whine seem a ghoulish threat.

The main cause of what delay there was at Bronte, apart from the German defence, was that supplies and supporting arms could be moved, backward and forward, only on the one narrow and congested road already mentioned. Cross-country movement for guns and vehicles was impossible and the four field regiments, 17, 132, 138 and 57, and detachments of 64 Anti-Tank Regiment, broke gaps in the stone walls and deployed from the road as best they could, in country that was virtually one vast slag-heap—except for the few and equally impassable terraced vineyards and olive groves. At times guns could come into action nowhere but on the road itself: it was remarkable in these circumstances that the artillery support was always so prompt and efficient and that positions were always found or made, somehow, so that the fire of the whole divisional artillery was available all through the advance.

In these conditions there had to be the strictest control of traffic into the narrow Adrano–Bronte road—a problem made all the more difficult by the forward move of the Division's rear echelons from south of Centuripe across the Salso and Simeto bridges. It was lucky for us—considering the inevitable delay at the river crossings—that we had air supremacy and that the Divisional "Q" staff coped so well with the re-routing of the axis of supply from the Centuripe to the Catania-Adrano road.

Forward, the nebelwerfers pounded away at the East Surreys as they hung on, short of Bronte town, overlooked from the high ground, through the night of August 7 and through the next morning. On the afternoon of August 8, however, the East Surreys and the Lancashire Fusiliers attacked and captured the heights on either side of the town and the Northamptons advanced along the road and into the town itself. At dusk 36 Brigade moved forward from Adrano in troop-carrying vehicles in readiness to pass through 11 Brigade and take over the lead at dawn in the advance towards Randazzo.

The nine miles or so from Bronte to Randazzo saw the most stubborn and most skilful German delaying action in the Division's experience of Sicily, save only for Centuripe itself—an action made all the easier for the Germans because they were now fighting on a very narrow front and because of the delays imposed by our own bombing and shelling of Bronte and its exits, which created a mass of craters and wreckage. The country was so difficult that there was no way to outflank the enemy, and the roads so mauled that we could use neither armour nor impetus to keep him moving.

The intermittent enemy shelling of the Bronte area throughout August 9 was particularly uncomfortable for 17 Field Regiment, normally with the Irish Brigade but now, with the other three field regiments, supporting whichever brigade happened to be leading the leapfrog advance. The regiment had been obliged to occupy a position two miles south of Bronte which was hemmed in by walled terraces and olive groves and under observation from enemy-held hills. A concentration put down on them after dark took especially heavy toll of 10 Battery, among whose casualties were Major Carey, the battery commander, killed, and Capt. Gibson, also killed, who had arrived from England only two days before.

Throughout August 9 the Buffs and the Royal West Kents were engaged in a long struggle with German infantry on the slopes of Monte Rivoglia, to the right of the road to Randazzo, whilst accurate German shelling harassed the supporting artillery—a long engagement in which Bdr. G. H. Evans, of 17 Field Regiment, won an immediate M.M. The Buffs established a foothold on the southern slopes during August 9 and, in the evening, the Royal West Kents pressed home a fine attack in spite of heavy and accurate gun and mortar fire. By the morning of August 10, 36 Brigade was firmly on Rivoglia, while on the left of the road the Lancashire Fusiliers and "B" Squadron, 56 Recce, were clearing the high, rugged lava slopes. That afternoon the Buffs advanced, in daylight, round the east flank of Rivoglia to try to secure the next isolated hill, Monte Macherone, and before nightfall they had a patrol on it.

It was steady slogging along the road, with our guns and aircraft pounding one position after another as the infantry battalions leap-frogged along. For four days the enemy had been using his guns, mortars and machine-guns against our infantry to good effect in rugged defensive country where it was virtually impossible to spot him in spite of ground and air observation-posts and flash-spotters. Our artillery had four particularly difficult days in trying to dominate this fire directed against our leading troops.

Boldly sited German self-propelled guns knocked out three of 56 Recce's scout cars short of Macherone on August 11 at just about the same time that patrols of the Lancashire Fusiliers, and then "B" Squadron of the Recce Regiment, made contact with the U.S. 9 Division on our left. Now the Germans were sealed off in the Messina peninsula—sealed off by the Americans and by 78 Division on the west, and by XIII Corps pushing northward from Catania on the east side of Etna.

But it was still the enemy's policy to hold us up as long as he could, so that as many of his troops could get away as possible and the defence of Italy be as well-organised as he could make it. So the last phase of the Division's campaign was no cakewalk. Monte Macherone and the heights by the little town of Maletto still barred the way to Randazzo and the far, or north, side of Etna, and it was given to the Irish Brigade to take Maletto once 36 had Macherone. In readiness for this General Evelegh ordered the commander of the Irish Brigade and his battalion commanders forward for reconnaissance, and arranged to move the brigade forward in transport to Bronte in the evening of August 10.

The pale dawn of August 11 found the small patrol of the Buffs—the regiment had taken heavy punishment in the last couple of days—still on Macherone, and by dark 36 Brigade had the feature secure and was able to protect the beginning of the Irish Brigade's night attack on the heights and village of Maletto. After a pounding by our light bombers and under a barrage by the divisional artillery and four medium batteries the Royal Irish Fusiliers on the left stormed the high ground and were firmly on their objective by dawn. (Capt. D. J. Anderson, of 17 Field Regiment, won an M.C. for the work he did with the Royal Irish Fusiliers in forty-eight hours of battle—work that ranged from observing under fire to manhandling ammunition across a minefield.) But that same morning found the London Irish still in difficulties on the high ground to the right, finding it impossible to handle their mules in the dark over the stone walls and terraces that barred their way, and being shelled and machine-gunned from the isolated hill,

La Nave, to the east. To counter this, the Inniskillings made a forced march in the heat of the afternoon across the grain of the fissured lava slopes, to take La Nave, with heavy artillery support. On the Division's left the American advance was weakening the enemy's resistance. By noon the London Irish were secure on the heights of Maletto and a few hours later the Royal Irish Fusiliers swung downhill into Maletto village, where they took thirty prisoners. By nightfall it was all ours—the high ground and the village of Maletto, and La Nave.

Relieving the Irish, the Argylls moved into Maletto in the darkness of the night August 12-13, and the Royal Irish Fusiliers pounded off down the road to chivy the enemy into and beyond Randazzo. There was a running fight in the darkness, there was some American shelling from the left that came uncomfortably close, there were mines and more mines. But there was little actual resistance now, and at 9.30 on August 13 the Royal Irish Fusiliers and the Americans made contact short of Randazzo itself.

The concerted Anglo-American pressure had decided the Germans to clear out of Randazzo, and when the American infantry and the Division's sappers settled a friendly Anglo-American rivalry by entering it together that morning there was no enemy—only a vast witness to the weight of the British air and artillery bombardment and to the skill of the German demolition experts. It was a town—it had once held a population of more than ten thousand—with not a house intact. "You could not tell what kind of town Randazzo had been", reported one correspondent. Every street was blocked by craters and by the rubble of houses that had been simply spilled into it. The Division had seen no devastation quite like it, though they were to see a lot more like it in Italy.

For the Division—greeting among the ruins their old American comrades-in-arms of Medjez, the 18 Combat Team, now sunburnt veterans—for the Division the Sicilian campaign was over. It had been a fortnight's war under a fierce sun in a cruelly difficult country, against the hand-picked rearguard of a stubborn and determined enemy. (For most of the time the Germans had been steadily evacuating Sicily through Messina;

the Sicilian campaign, from the German point of view, was a well-planned and successful disengaging operation.)

All that the Division had learnt in the Tunisian mountains was put to the test at Centuripe and on the slopes of Etna and, in addition, it had had to learn new lessons about movement along narrow, walled-in roads with no margin of manoeuvre on either side.

Above all, this had been not only an infantryman's but a gunner's, a driver's, and a sapper's fortnight. The closeness of the country, the thick crop of mines, the infinite number of craters and blown bridges had given the sappers more work than they had had even in Tunisia, and they had done it quickly and efficiently, usually under fire. So had the R.A.S.C., along fiendishly difficult roads and cinder tracks. The D.C.M. awarded to Driver Pye, of 217 Field Ambulance, for "continual devotion to duty" was a token of what the fighting troops owed to the R.A.M.C. He had made fourteen runs with his ambulance in one day, up and down a road continually under shell and mortar-fire, refusing relief until all the wounded had been brought to safety. The gunners, unable to deploy as they had been able to do in Africa, had made perhaps the greatest impression of all on the Germans. An intelligence summary recorded that "perhaps the most unanimous view in the German army is of our artillery, which is admired and feared at the same time. The close advance of our infantry behind a creeping barrage is something the Germans are quite unable to grasp. German senior N.C.O.s have stated repeatedly that even without heavy casualties a platoon or section is mostly unable to fight after a barrage of the intensity experienced in Sicily."

Our other advantages were that we soon established air superiority, and that there had been no German tanks: only one of our anti-tank batteries had been used beyond Adrano, and the L.A.A. regiment saw little action after the first three days.

These, though, were the exceptions. For the divisional artillery and the other supporting arms already mentioned it had been a fortnight of continuous fighting and movement over extremely difficult country. Most of the infantrymen had been able to snatch a little rest, because of the way in which fresh units had leap-frogged those that had been in action, but many a gunner and sapper—and this was even more true of commanders and staffs—was able now to look forward to his first full night's sleep since the invasion of Sicily. The Division had been severely tested, not only operationally but administratively, and it had earned tributes from the commanders of higher formations that were obviously more than mere phrases. General Montgomery, who had congratulated General Evelegh on the taking of Centuripe as "a wonderful feat of arms" now wrote to tell him that he thought the Division had added to its North African reputation, and General Leese, commanding XXX Corps (and soon to succeed Montgomery as Eighth Army commander) also sent his congratulations on the Division's "magnificent fighting".

After Randazzo, on August 13, the Division passed into reserve; the Americans entered Messina three days later, and the allied guns massed to bombard the mainland of Italy and to prepare the way for the next campaign. While the infantrymen of the Division took their ease in the olive groves, or visited Taormina or Catania, its artillery—17, 132, 138 and 57 Field Regiments, covered by 49 L.A.A.—moved up from August 24 onwards to the north coast of the island, west of Messina. There was a week of preparation there, on the heights above the straits, of concealed gun-positions, entailing a good deal of manoeuvring among the walled lanes and terraced vineyards and a hazardous ammunition-dumping programme that lasted four nights—on each of which drivers covered sixty miles over one-way mountain roads between dusk and dawn.

As a result, at 4.30 in the morning of September 3, the Divisional artillery joined with the guns of three other divisions and of the Navy in putting up a barrage for the landing, north and south of Reggio, by 5 Division and the Canadians of XIII Corps. The Division itself was transferred back from XXX to V Corps, under which it had served in North Africa. Its turn was to come.

BOOK III

ITALY

CHAPTER I

INTRODUCTION

As in the case of Sicily the invasion of Italy was a twofold operation, and as in the case of Sicily the Division landed after the first foothold had been secured.

Mussolini had fallen on July 25, 1943, and Marshal Badoglio, charged by the King of Italy with the formation of a new government, was in secret negotiation with the Allies. One British and one Canadian division of General Montgomery's Eighth Army (5 Division and 1 Canadian Division) landed at Reggio, in the tip of the toe of Italy, on September 3, 1943, against little or no opposition, and on September 9 the newly formed Fifth Army, a mixed British and American force under the American General Mark Clark, landed at Salerno, near Naples, and established a precarious beach-head against heavy German resistance.

The Salerno landing coincided with the announcement of the Italian armistice. From now on the Italians were no longer our enemies—they were soon, in fact, to become co-belligerents —but the Germans had had time to organise their defences and the geography of Italy remained an ally of the Germans, whatever may have been the mood of its people. The Allied armies were faced with a campaign which would have to be fought up a long narrow peninsula, against the grain of a country all the rivers of which flowed east and west, forming a series of obstacles to a northward advance. A mountainous country, too, in which the machine-gun posts and single guncrews of a well-trained, well-disciplined enemy could hold up bodies of men greatly superior in numbers. Such plain as there was between the mountains and the sea was in most places very narrow, with only one major road to take the heavy traffic of a mechanised army, and with little room for manoeuvre.

It was soon clear that the Germans had no intention of holding the heel and toe of Italy. By September 16 Eighth Army had marched 180 miles in thirteen days, across this difficult country, and had made contact with the Fifth Army—to its intense relief—in the Salerno beach-head. (The first contact was made by a jeep-load consisting of three correspondents and a conducting officer all of whom wore the Division's battle-axe flash—they had been with the Division since the North African landings, and had now landed in Italy ahead of their old comrades.) This meant a threat from the right that obliged Kesselring, the German commander in Italy, to abandon his hopes of pushing the army at Salerno into the sea; the allies now held all Italy south of a line joining Salerno on the west with Bari on the east; it remained to be seen how far and how fast they could push northwards from it. It was at this stage that the Division landed to take its place again in Eighth Army.

CHAPTER II

FROM THE TOE TO TERMOLI

THE Division landed in Italy over the period from September 19 to September 29. A small advance force landed at Reggio on September 19, the rest sailing in groups from Syracuse and Messina—the men direct to Taranto, the naval base inside the arch of Italy's foot, most of the guns and vehicles to Reggio, then by road to Crotone and by sea again to Taranto.

The Division was soon to be committed to taking over the right-hand sector of Eighth Army's front, and meanwhile, its forward party reached Bari, on the east coast, on September 22. The bulk of the German army in Italy was still contesting the Allies' advance from the Salerno beach-head; the sector in front of the Divison was only lightly held by their parachute troops, so that a light mobile force under Lt.-Col. Chavasse (commanding 56 Recce. Regiment) operating under the Division, was able to push fast and far ahead while the remainder of the Division was held up near Bari, awaiting the stores needed to establish a new base on this side of Italy.

The mobile force was soon expanded into "A" Force, when it consisted of a squadron each from 56 Recce, the Royals, and 3 County of London Yeomanry (the Sharpshooters); a company of the Kensingtons; 17 Field and 64 Anti-Tank Regiments, R.A.; 237 Field Company and 2 Parachute Squadron R.E.; patrols of S.A.S. and the Airborne Recce Regiment; and 217 Field Ambulance. It now came under Brigadier John Currie's 4 Armoured Brigade (which was under command 78 Division) and it was in this expanded form that it reached Foggia, the town that had grown in recent years to market the produce of Mussolini's small-holding settlement scheme for the Foggia plain, and which controlled the same plain's vast network of airfields.

It was clear that the enemy had not the armour with which to give battle in the plain, and cars of 56 Recce, racing ahead of "A" Force, had little difficulty in reaching Foggia by September 27 and in adding to the damage already done by our air forces—to aircraft on the ground, to armoured cars and self-propelled guns, and to the retreating German infantry.

But it was felt that this rate of advance was too good to last; that resistance would not remain a matter of mines, demolitions, harassing patrols, and a few well-placed anti-tank and machine guns; and that the enemy would turn and fight in the high ground. Sure enough, and soon enough, the first hint of increased resistance was met at Serracapriola.

But Serracapriola was not to be taken until the Division's infantry caught up with "A" Force, and meanwhile the Division —its commander and staff chafing under the administrative delays—had been assembling in the olive and almond groves near Bari, undergoing company training and hardening its feet by marching, occasionally buying the cheap watches, the thin beer and the raw wine of the large but gimcrack town, surely the only ugly town of its size in Italy.

Many escaped prisoners of war had by now rejoined our lines. Two of them were Sgt. MacCrimmon and Cpl. Lamont, who had been captured at Green Hill a year before; by a happy coincidence the first British troops they met after their escape on September 3, and their long and hazardous journey south, were their own platoon of the Argylls.

On September 29, 11 Brigade marched 25 miles north from Bari to Trani, and the following day the Northamptons were placed under command of 4 Armoured Brigade and moved forward to San Severo. On October 1 the Northamptons, supported by 56 Recce and tanks of 3 County of London Yeomanry, were ordered to attack and capture the little hill village of Serracapriola, on the one main road that was all there was to take Eighth Army's northward advance.

The tanks moved forward first, and made steady progress against little or no opposition. Loud explosions were heard, and there was a heavy pall of smoke over the little town. Although it had been expected that the enemy would stand here, and although he had gone through the motions of doing so, it was clear that he was withdrawing without any serious fighting, and that he was destroying what he could before doing so. Five hours after zero hour the Northamptons were being mobbed and embraced by the people of Serracapriola.

Next day the advance was continued northward towards Termoli, twenty-five miles away. The going was slow: enemy aircraft caused casualties as they harried the advancing column, there were continual diversions to avoid the craters, and in the first four miles three bridges had been demolished that had to be repaired before the advance could be continued. But by the morning of October 3 we were through the villages of Portocannone and San Martino and moving slowly on beyond the high ground on which they stood.

Our forward troops were already at the Biferno river (about five miles south-east of Termoli), where the bridge was blown, and here they were joined by 11 Brigade. It was obvious that the Germans meant to hold as long as possible the high ground, north of the river, dominating his lateral supply road—the road that runs across Italy from Termoli through Campobasso to the Volturno river at Capua, north of Naples. Obvious, because he was holding the Volturno against Fifth Army (which had entered Naples on October 1) and because it was vain to do that unless he also held Termoli against the Eighth.

Nevertheless, there seemed a good chance—thanks to the speed of the Division's advance—of taking Termoli before the enemy could assemble enough troops for serious resistance. Although there was some doubt at Corps as to the whereabouts of 16 Panzer Division, Eighth Army's Intelligence was confident that (apart from the parachute division falling back before us) Termoli was held only by a few garrison troops; it would be a month, said the weather experts, before the weather would break; and there were landing craft available by means of which a right hook by sea could be swung into the town.

True, the Division was still short of its second-line transport (much of it still in Sicily) and Army could provide none to make up for it. The Divisional artillery had to dump 25-pounder ammunition forward and then lend many of its vehicles to 11 Brigade to help it lift its battalions. But speed and surprise were the elements aimed at, and it was decided to land two commandos of the Special Service Brigade in Termoli by landing craft, for 11 Brigade to join them as quickly as possible by land, across the Biferno, and for the other two brigades to follow by sea when Termoli had been secured. As the commander of the Irish Brigade noted, "as far as my Brigade was concerned it was to be a pleasant peacetime cruise, with fighting unlikely for a fortnight or so. And Termoli was known to be a nice little town." Adding ruefully, "Note: this did not go according to plan."

But it all began smoothly enough. The two commandos, 3 and 40, with the Special Service Brigade's reconnaissance squadron, all under command of Lt.-Col. Durnford-Slater, embarked at Bari and landed successfully. By eight o'clock on the morning of October 3 they had easily overcome the weak garrison, and 36 Brigade was able to land unopposed that night and to begin to push towards the north.

11 Brigade had already made contact, and the leading battalion, the Lancashire Fusiliers, had already crossed the Biferno into the town by wading and in small boats. Eight of 64 Anti-Tank Regiment's guns were got across by raft, and by dusk a folding boat bridge was in use, across which, in driving rain, 56 Recce Regiment (less two squadrons) passed to join the commandos and the Fusiliers. Short of the river, covering the infantry, was the Divisional artillery, with 17 Field Regiment in close support. One field regiment only, 138, was across the river.

But that rain had not entered into our calculations. As had so often happened in North Africa, we had been misled by inaccurate weather information, and the rain, not officially due until the end of the month, began on October 3 and fell continuously for eighteen hours. In much less time than that the four diversions immediately south of the Biferno were virtually impassable to anything but tracked and four-wheel drive vehicles. What vehicles we had were stuck at them at every angle. Drivers were feverishly loading straw at nearby farms to dump on to the slippery river banks to make them wheel-worthy, whilst others hacked down bushes and the branches of trees. The traffic jams were easy meat for the occasional air attacks that the enemy was able to put in, relatively unhampered by our own slight air support—for Foggia was not yet in service as a base.

The coming of the rains was bad luck for us, and the Germans had a corresponding stroke of good luck that made it possible for them to react more sharply than we had expected. Sixteen Panzer Division had already set off eastwards from the Volturno, along the lateral road that both sides wanted so desperately, for rest and refitting. They had left before our landing at Termoli, but now their tanks and lorries were racing across with orders to retake the town and to destroy the British forces west of the Biferno. They were to be committed to the battle as they reached it.

This fact was still hidden from us, and on the morning of October 4 the Argylls, the Royal West Kents, and 56 Recce began to probe outwards from the area we held around Termoli. There was no doubt that there were plenty of Germans in the wooded heights and gulleys about the town; the Argylls were held by tank and mortar fire, the Royal West Kents had to put in a bayonet attack against a farm and a wood, at a cost of forty casualties, and the Lancashire Fusiliers and the Special Service Brigade, holding the little port itself, were suffering from well-directed artillery and mortar fire, controlled by an enemy observation post still in Termoli's church tower. On the coast road 56 Recce had found itself in action against German Mark IV tanks, and there was far more infantry about than we had expected. The capture of an unsuspecting motor-cyclist gave us the answer: we were up against not only the parachute battalion we already knew about but an armoured division to boot.

We had a small bridge across the Biferno, capable of taking nine-ton loads; the Division's Bailey-bridging had been taken by Army for railway repairs, and we had not the equipment for a bridge that would take tanks, or even the gunners' anti-tank guns. True, infantry vehicles and anti-tank guns were across the river with 11 Brigade (less the East Surreys) but, thanks to the unexpected and heavy rain, the ground was sodden and the carriers could not get the guns across country to the Buffs and the Royal West Kents.

The Irish Brigade, on its way by sea from Barletta, was

divorced from its transport, and all but one of the field regiments were still south of the river, and with only 200 rounds of ammunition a gun. Because of the impossibility of getting tanks across, and the difficulty in getting anti-tank guns to the forward troops, the infantry was caught, as a senior officer has recorded, "with one leg off the ground." It was no fault of the Division or of its staff—which had been misinformed both as to the weather and as to the German dispositions—but everything now was to depend on the morale of virtually immobile and far too lightly supported infantrymen, face-to-face with tanks.

This new phase of the battle began with confused fighting in the night. The Argylls came under heavy fire as they tried to get on to the heights three miles west of the town, whilst behind them, only 500 yards away from the Lancashire Fusiliers, then handing over to the Buffs, were enemy infantry digging in.

October 5 dawned in a drizzle to find the Argylls out in the open, holding tanks and infantry with precious few anti-tank guns and no tank support at all. The sappers were slogging away under shellfire to make a ford across which the C.L.Y's tanks could come to the rescue. The guns of 17 Field Regiment were putting down a curtain of fire on to the advancing Germans, only a hundred yards ahead of the Argylls.

Six of the C.L.Y's Shermans got across the ford before it became a morass again: they went to the support of the Argylls with great dash, but lost four of their number before they and the infantry had to fall back to the shelter of a brickworks, a couple of miles outside the town to the west.

It was there, at the brickworks, that Brigadier Howlett, commanding 36 Brigade, and Lt.-Col. Scott Elliott, commanding the Argylls, met to discuss a situation that had become grave indeed, and it was only a short time after the brigadier had left that German tanks turned the Argylls' right flank, and the colonel, with two volunteers from the Recce Regiment, was manning an anti-tank gun. The brickworks was being heavily shelled—by both sides—and the battalion's survivors began to move back, in good order, through the Lancashire Fusiliers' positions. But not before Major Anderson, the Longstop V.C., had been hit and killed—one of the five officers killed, seven wounded, and 150 casualties among the other ranks.

Gunner officers who had gone forward with the battalions as forward observation officers found themselves fighting as infantrymen (it was here that Capt. J. Gilbertson, of 132 Field Regiment, earned and was awarded an M.C.) and there was one period at least when the R.A.M.C.'s dressing stations were cut off—Lt.-Col. Crerar, M.C., won a D.S.O. and Sgt. S.F. Burrit, of 217 Field Ambulance, an M.M. for their fortitude in this Termoli fighting. It was later in the same battle that Capt. J. O. D. Williams and four other ranks were killed and nine other ranks wounded when the section of 11 Field Ambulance working with the Lancashire Fusiliers was hit by shellfire.

While the Argylls were withdrawing, the Royal West Kents and the Buffs, over on the left, were also falling back, under pressure from the German tanks. The ground was too wet by now to move forward even the few anti-tank guns we had on this side of the river, and six Mark IV tanks overran the Royal West Kents (who retreated in confusion towards the Larino road), and then turned towards the Buffs. The Buffs too were disorganised, and their left flank was open. But Brigadier Howlett put new heart into the men, and ordered them to hold where they were. The Royal West Kents were down to eighty men as they took up positions holding the left flank.

That afternoon—the afternoon of October 5—the position was critical. Army had returned the Division its Bailey-bridging and at last there was a heavy tank-bearing bridge being built and thirty tanks of the C.L.Y. and the Canadian Tank Regiment waiting on the wrong side of the Biferno river for it to be finished. Would it be finished in time? Would it be ready for our own tanks to cross before the enemy tanks finished off the desperately depleted infantry on the far side?

It was finished at twenty to three in the afternoon of October 5, built in twenty-four hours by 214 Field Company, in pouring rain and under shellfire that had cost them twelve casualties. General Evelegh was across the river, at Brigade Headquarters, to see the first of the C.L.Y.'s reinforcement of Shermans attack the German tanks on the plateau overlooking our positions. By dusk that evening the situation was partially restored, but our Termoli bridgehead was still ringed by the tanks and infantry of an eager and skilful 16 Panzer Division, and we were still under heavy shellfire. Five of the first nine Shermans had been knocked out, and there were at least twenty-five German tanks still in action. We needed more tanks and more men before we could break that hostile ring. More ammunition too. Had the Division failed at Termoli it would have been primarily because of the absence of a tank-bearing bridge at the beginning, but partly, too, because of the impossibility of maintaining gun ammunition in the forward area; every gunner O.P. which called for fire on a good target was distressed by the quantitatively poor response. There were seven river crossings between Serracapriola and Campomarino, at each of which the bridge was blown and at each of which the diversion climbed down and up a steep and slippery slope—almost impassable for the lorries of the R.A.S.C. and the divisional artillery regiments, which had rear-wheel drive only.

Those first few Shermans, though, had prevented the enemy from coming in to make the kill he expected, and at dusk that night came the real turning-point of the battle. Two squadrons of the Canadian Tank Regiment clattered over the Bailey bridge, and seven landing-craft put into the battered harbour bearing the Irish Brigade, surprised that the fighting was not all over, but disembarking at the rate of 300 men every hour and a half, all fresh for battle after a smooth and uneventful voyage.

That night the brigade and the tank-regiment commanders met to hear General Evelegh's plan—a conference that took place against a background of heavy artillery fire, whilst on the flanks of the Termoli position the Recce Regiment and the Lancashire Fusiliers were holding enemy counter-attacks with the aid of concentrations from our own guns. When the enemy put in an attack that included five tanks the Fusiliers had to withdraw, but the enemy was halted by a heavy and accurate concentration.

The time had come now to put the Divisional commander's new plan into action. The tanks were across, and the Irish Brigade was assembled. The attack began early in the morning of October 6, with C.L.Y. and Canadian tanks, followed by the Buffs, making slow progress on the left against well-placed anti-tank guns. Other Canadian tanks, supported by the Irish Brigade, first against shellfire and machine-guns, but then against a withdrawing enemy, took the brickworks and began to make headway up the coastal road towards Pescara. This eased the situation for the Buffs, who—helped by "B" Squadron of the Canadian Tank Regiment—made contact with the Inniskillings and then pushed quickly forward with the C.L.Y. as the Germans began to fall back in disorder.

By nightfall the battle of Termoli was over, and the enemy was withdrawing from every point of the perimeter, leaving our hold on Termoli secure and the road to Pescara open.

It had been touch and go, and if the enemy had not been obliged to commit his 16 Panzer Division piecemeal it might easily have gone differently. But 78 Division, caught by an armoured division on the far side of a river across which—deprived of its Bailey-bridging until it was almost too late—it could not get its own supporting tanks and unable, because of the state of the ground, to get its anti-tank guns forward, its units necessarily committed to battle with dangerous haste—sometimes straight from the landing-craft—had held that enemy armour for three days and three nights of the bitterest and most confused fighting. All arms and all ranks shared in the glory, and all arms and all ranks shared, too, in the feeling that 78 Division had begun its Italian campaign as promisingly as it had begun in Africa and in Sicily.

It remains to add that the few units of the Division that did not take part in the Termoli action joined in an equally gallant engagement of their own. The East Surreys had been given an independent mission: along with 322 Battery of 132 Field Regiment and two platoons of the Kensingtons, they had been ordered on the day of the landing at Termoli to advance and capture Larino—fifteen miles to the south-west of Termoli, on the important lateral road.

By nightfall they were in contact with the enemy at the entrance to the town, and at daybreak two companies, under Major Andrews and Major Hill, carried out a dashing assault on the first ridge in front of it. They cleared the enemy from the ridge, but soon came under heavy fire and were obliged to dig in. For four days the East Surreys held on to their positions

OCTOBER 8, 1943

under continuous artillery, mortar, and machine-gun fire—with the nearest friendly troops fifteen miles away and in desperate difficulties of their own. It was not until the afternoon of October 8 that the town eventually fell, and on that day they were rejoined by Sgt. Bunting, who had been missing, believed killed, since the patrol he was leading at the beginning of the battle had been engaged by enemy armoured cars. He had been living, hidden by Italians, in the cellars and granaries of a nearby enemy-held village for four days. The East Surreys had suffered many casualties, and two of their stretcher-bearers, L/Cpl. Kemp and Private Ramsay, received immediate M.M.s for tending them under fire.

CHAPTER III

RIVERS TO CROSS

FROM Termoli onwards it was a matter—to use a phrase of General Alexander's—of "slogging up Italy". It was rough going. There was one decent road, parallel with the coast, to take virtually the whole of the advancing Eighth Army; there was one river after another to cross—invariably with its bridges blown; the second-rate little railway was shattered. There was snow already on the peaks of the Apennines, for the Italian winter had come—a colder, harder winter than anybody expected. The men began to joke bitterly about "sunny Italy" as Moore's men, in their hideous retreat over the snow-clad mountains to Corunna, a century-and-a-half before, had jested about "sunny Spain". How was it possible that twentieth-century Englishmen should have been so ignorant beforehand about the climate of another European country? The only explanation seems to be that peacetime visitors to Italy knew only the big cities and the favoured resorts; that few people penetrated to this eastern side of Central and Southern Italy where both the summer mosquitoes and the winter cold were so much more savage than in Rome, or Capri, or the Italian Riviera; and that Italy was sufficiently near and familiar country for us to have taken it too much for granted in our planning.

Now, though, it was obvious that the local inhabitants were used to hard winters. Before the end of October they were wearing fur caps and great black woollen cloaks. There was snow on the hills by then, grey skies, bitter winds, and drenching rain. The Eighth Army officers from the desert divisions began to appear in Syrian sheepskin coats and flying boots. Seventy-eight Division was soon hung with mufflers, greatcoats, and leather jerkins, and the R.A.S.C. brought up, just in time (thanks to the efforts of Lt.-Col. Kenny, the A.D.O.S.), new battledress, woollen underclothes, greatcoats and gum-boots. There was even a rum ration for some of the luckier night patrols. Before the end of October radiators were being drained at night.

This period immediately after the Termoli battle, as the winter closed in, was one of regrouping, reorganisation, and gradual development of our gains. In the Army's regrouping the Division passed under the command of V Corps, and pushed slowly forward up the coastal plain. One squalid little town after another fell to the advancing infantry: Guglionesi to the Buffs, Montecilfone—after some gallant fighting by 56 Recce's "A" Squadron—to the Royal West Kents, Petacciato to the London Irish and 46 R.T.R., Montenero to 56 Recce.

The first patrols to reach the next river, the Trigno, found the road bridge intact but as the leading troops of the Royal Irish Fusiliers arrived, in the early hours of October 23, they heard a roar and saw, in the first light, a 200 foot gap in the bridge. The enemy had blown it up as the main body was seen approaching.

The Trigno is wide but shallow, and the Royal Irish Fusiliers waded across only ankle deep. There were mines about, but apart from some spasmodic shelling there was little active interference with our establishment of the proposed bridgehead. The rest of the Irish Brigade moved up to our own side of the Trigno, astride the main road, and 11 Brigade on its right, near the coast, also came up to the river. The Lancashire Fusiliers established a second bridgehead by wading it, and by October 27 we had three companies each of the Royal Irish Fusiliers and the London Irish across and two companies of the Lancashire Fusiliers. The rest of the Irish and of 11 Brigade were in close support, with 56 Recce, the Kensingtons, and 36 Brigade strung out, farther back, between Termoli and Montenero. So far only the Lancashire Fusiliers had met opposition: they had been scrapping hard with German offensive patrols and with the enemy's forward defences as they felt towards the little town of San Salvo and its railway station, a couple of miles away from the town, on the coast. Later they had pulled back again to consolidate their bridgehead area.

On our side the ground dropped sharply to the river except

at its mouth and at one point near the road. At both places the Royal Engineers built fords which were firm enough except for their approaches, inevitably susceptible to rain.

On the far side there was a wooded undulating plain, suitable for the concealment of men and vehicles. Behind it was a narrow sluggish stream and a low escarpment, and behind that again the highest points between the Trigno and the Sangro —the ridge of San Salvo and Vineyard Hill, by the town of Cupello. Our opponents were the Panzer division with which we had swopped heavy blows at Termoli; here they were more favoured than we were by the lie of the land. They were reorganised and in good heart too—our bridgehead troops had found that out—and there was no getting through them or pushing them aside without a major divisional attack.

This fact received melancholy proof when the Irish Brigade was ordered to take San Salvo in a night attack on October 27-28. The London Irish went in on the right, and the Royal Irish Fusiliers on the left, over rain-sodden ground, protected by a heavy barrage. It was not only that the German artillery and mortar fire was particularly heavy: it was particularly lucky, too. The Fusiliers lost their commanding officer, Lt.-Col. Beauchamp Butler, their two leading company commanders, Proctor (who had won an M.C. at Termoli) and Dunn—all killed—as well as all the leading platoon commanders, killed or wounded, just as they were about to assault the ridge. So too with the London Irish, who lost Major Kevin O'Connor and two company commanders. The men dug in and were withdrawn at daylight. For a week it was left to the bridgehead troops to probe the enemy's defences—it was lucky that the enemy, though alert and quick to react to patrols, was not in an aggressive mood—until, on November 3, it was possible to attack again, and in greater strength.

An unusual feature this time was support from the Navy— the attack opened in the early hours with a bombardment of Vasto and Cupello by two destroyers and a flotilla of M.T.B.s. This was designed chiefly to lead the enemy to expect a seaborne landing, and he was further confused, and prevented from firing into the flank of the attack, by 49 L.A.A. Regiment and the Kensingtons, the one unit firing tracer ammunition from its six Bofors guns on fixed lines, the other making warlike noises with its mortars and machine-guns—both on the left and both successfully creating the illusion that the attack was being mounted there.

The destroyers were not the only craft in support. In order to reduce traffic at the fords and on the bridge (when it was built), ammunition for the gunners and the tanks was conveyed by DUKWs, which were loaded at Termoli and sailed under the cover of darkness to a point north of the mouth of the Trigno. Of thirty DUKWs in use, only one was lost—and that because the skipper omitted to close his sea-cocks!

Meanwhile the advance of the tanks and infantry, controlled by 36 Brigade, and consisting of the Buffs, the Inniskillings, and 46 R.T.R., was going on towards San Salvo against heavy machine-gun fire. General Evelegh had ruled that the attack was not to begin until all anti-tank guns, carriers, and tanks were across the Trigno, and zero hour was put back for twenty-four hours because of a collapse of the approaches to the bridge. Fortunately, it was not until the Inskillings entered San Salvo that the first enemy tanks were seen, and by that time 50 R.T.R. was crossing to support 46.

A tank battle did, in fact, develop in the olive groves on the outskirts of the town. The Shermans, slowed down and restricted in movement by the soft ground and with their visibility hampered by the olive trees, were at a disadvantage against the lower-built German Mk. IVs, but they knocked out six, and two self-propelled guns, before they were obliged to withdraw. But the rest of the German tanks were able, then, to press the Buffs back into San Salvo. The Buffs' C.O., Lt.-Col. A. D. McKechnie, D.S.O., was badly wounded, and handed over to Major Monk; Major Fewson was among the killed.

Over on the right, 11 Brigade had made little progress during November 3: the enemy stood firm at San Salvo railway station, and our infantry was harassed for a short time, too, by one of the Italian campaign's rare manifestations of enemy air activity. Twelve fighter-bombers attacked the forward infantry and caused casualties.

All the same, the attack passed into its second phase during the night, but the Royal West Kents and the Argylls were checked, in turn, by enemy tanks as they sought to push along the road beyond San Salvo to Vasto. Curiously enough, however, the shelling of the crossings slackened. It looked as though the enemy was pulling back his tanks, covering the withdrawal of his guns and main forces. So supplies and reinforcements crossed the river, and as resistance also slackened on the right the East Surreys were able to occupy the railway station and the Lancashire Fusiliers were freed to make a difficult night march south of the river from right flank to centre and to cross over in support of the main attack.

It was during the East Surreys' fighting in the town that two of their stretcher-bearers—Privates Poll and Merritt—earned Military Medals for their gallantry in tending wounded under fire.

The main attack was resumed at dawn. We were now at the foot of Vineyard Hill, which had dominated the battle. The Royal West Kents and 50 R.T.R. took it by assault and that afternoon the Argylls were on the lesser hills beside and beyond it. Through them came the Northamptons, pressing on over difficult ground against heavy machine-gun and mortar fire. They lost their anti-tank platoon to an ambush, but by dusk they were at the cross-roads just short of the little port of Vasto, and on the morning of November 5 the Lancashire Fusiliers were in Cupello and 56 Recce and the Royal West Kents in Vasto, clear of the enemy.

There were prepared defence positions both in Vasto and Cupello and it was pretty obvious that, orderly as the enemy's withdrawal had been, it had been made earlier and more quickly than he had intended. The weight of our artillery fire and the steady advance of the infantry had forced him to withdraw to positions on the high ground beyond the Sangro that he had meant to fall back on later, and hold through the worse weather that was to come. This in spite of the fact that the weather was already bad enough to have delayed our crossings of the Trigno for a week and thus give him time to improve his positions along that river by digging and mine-laying.

We gave the enemy no rest, harrying his slow withdrawal, and there were brushes between his rearguard and 4 Armoured Brigade, which was under command and led the pursuit for a time. A patrol of East Surreys cleared a German rearguard from two houses and destroyed its armoured car, in a night attack in which Lt. Woodhouse won an M.C. and L/Cpl. L. Wood an immediate M.M.

By November 9 there was no enemy on our side of the Sangro river, and our forward troops, the Lancashire Fusiliers and the East Surreys, were looking from the heights northward across the Sangro valley.

What they saw was very like the view they had had across the Trigno—a wide river bed of many channels, with a steep bank on our side, a plain on the other about a mile in width, and an escarpment, 150 feet high or so, beyond that. Behind the escarpment there was higher ground still. As with the Trigno the approaches to the river were muddy and treacherous, and the bridges were blown. The river bed itself was about four hundred feet across, little wider than that of the Trigno. The enemy—65 Infantry Division and our old friends of 16 Panzer Division—held the line of the escarpment and the high ground beyond. Prisoners told us that this was the winter line and that the orders were that there was to be no withdrawal from it.

These first prisoners had fallen to the battle patrols of the Buffs and the Royal West Kents which, with those of the other battalions, so completely covered and dominated the plain across the river from November 10 to 15 as to confine the enemy to his escarpment and to give us a free hand in our reconnaissance of the river line.

The Royal West Kents established a system of patrolling by specialists. All activities were controlled by one officer, who was allotted a proportion of men from each company who were used for nothing else. They put in raiding parties, smaller parties to draw fire and otherwise reconnoitre the German strength and dispositions, and protective patrols for the sappers' and tanks' own reconnaissances. One of the raiding parties, led by Major Forman, was more than sixty strong: it killed or wounded some ten Germans, captured three machine-guns, a mortar and a number of rifles. Another, a reconnaissance patrol, consisted of only two N.C.O.s—Sgt. Knight and L/Cpl. Lingham, who had already won the M.M. They were a day

Entering Centuripe

Centuripe

Looking North across the Sangro

The Sangro Escarpment

and a half behind the German lines, and gathered very valuable information, but the river had swollen under the rains whilst they were across, and in swimming back Lingham was swept away and drowned.

It was the rain and its effect on the river, which broadened from a stream of a hundred feet wide to fill the 400 foot channel, and rose from a foot-deep trickle to a fast-flowing river five feet deep, that interrupted our patrolling for a couple of days after November 15. We could not get across and we lost, for a time, our ascendancy over the mile-wide plain on the far side. The enemy, alert to this situation, hastened to strengthen his outposts and lay fresh mines, so that when we got across again tracks that had already been swept once by the sappers had to be swept again, and much other work re-done.

After discussing various plans, Corps decided that 8 Indian Division should secure the high ground in the area of Mozzagrogna by daylight on D day and that 78 Division should then pass through, with 4 Armoured Brigade under command, sweeping right-handed along the ridge to the sea before swinging north again up the coastal road. A conference at General Montgomery's headquarters at Vasto, where General Montgomery himself, General Allfrey (V Corps), General Freyberg, v.c. (2 New Zealand Division) and General Evelegh all spoke, enabled all the subordinate commanders to issue operation orders of more than usual clarity.

In pursuance of the plan hammered out at Vasto, General Evelegh ordered 36 Brigade to secure a bridgehead across the river, and one company from each battalion waded across knee-deep through pouring rain and under shellfire, on the night of November 19-20. The Buffs lost Major Milton, M.C., and thirty-seven other ranks; the Royal West Kents suffered several casualties on a mine-field—one that had been sown during the couple of rainy days that had lost us our control over the plain; and the Argylls were heavily counter-attacked from three sides in the misty morning of November 20. One platoon fought its way forward and was never seen again; the others, as they withdrew across the river, saw all their officers wounded and then ran on to a minefield. They returned that night and re-established their position.

It was clear that the enemy had regained control of the river plain and that the bridgehead could not be held by three companies. The more so as the renewed rains meant a postponement of the Indian Division's attack and a longer holding period in the bridgehead than we had bargained for.

So 11 Brigade was committed to the assistance of 36, of which the Royal West Kents were to reinforce to battalion strength. Along with these fresh troops went the 2nd 60th from 4 Armoured Brigade.

The river was deeper than ever, waist-high on the shorter men, and running seven knots. No vehicles could get across, no Vickers guns or anti-tank guns. The infantrymen carried one day's rations apiece and what small-arms ammunition they could manage.

The heaviest fighting fell to the lot of the 60th and the Lancashire Fusiliers. The riflemen were pinned down to the river bank all day, whilst the Fusiliers, after losing six men killed on a minefield, and nine wounded, had to take a farmhouse against machine-gun fire. They lost, all told, ten men killed and twenty-three wounded, killing at least twenty-five Germans and taking thirty-eight prisoners. The commanding officer, Lt.-Col. Mackenzie, was among the wounded (the two gunner observation officers with him were killed) and so was Major Charles Walke, commanding "A" company who, armed with a tommy gun, had led four men in a charge against a machine-gun post, killing three and capturing sixteen Germans.

The bridgehead was firm enough now so long as there was no counter-attack by tanks, for the rains continued, the going was heavier than ever, the river faster and deeper, and it was still touch-and-go when, how, and in what numbers we could get our own tanks and anti-tank guns across.

Meanwhile the infantrymen on the far side were running short of food and ammunition. They were shelled all the time and their only line of supply and reinforcement from the river was narrow, mined, flooded, and open to shellfire. They went from Sunday night to Wednesday without a brew-up and they lived, waking or sleeping, in wet clothes in holes in the ground.

The Corps and Divisional engineers worked steadily in the rain and under shellfire, and it was here that Lt.-Col. Blake,

D.S.O., O.B.E., the Division's C.R.E. since its formation, was killed when his scout car overturned during a reconnaissance of a seashore route to the Sangro. Five bridges were built and four were weakened by shellfire and destroyed by flooding. The one bridge left undamaged had been built by 78 Division's sappers on what was regarded as an unsuitable site by Corps, who omitted it from their main bridge plan. We got tanks across by fording—their weight prevented their being washed away—first, half a squadron of 50 R.T.R. which had to return because they could not get beyond the mud on the far bank, then nine tanks of 3 County of London Yeomanry, then 50 R.T.R. again. On the night of November 22-23 the first two anti-tank guns crossed the river.

These first tanks were not engaged, but their presence had its effect. The enemy withdrew to his main defensive line—the summit of the ridge—where he was heavily bombed by the Tactical Air Force and pounded by a concentration of something like 400 guns.

All this time the Divisional engineers had been working with the utmost devotion, under the greatest difficulties and danger. They built the biggest of the five crossings on the Corps front, and one other. Their unprotected patrols had reconnoitred both banks of the river; they had piloted their vast, clumsy, bulldozers under shellfire to make half-mile long diversions to the river down steep inclines and had humped metal track, railway-sleepers, and brushwood along them; they had seen their Bailey bridge submerged, then swept away, and had built it again. All arms can be proud of the Sangro battle, but none prouder than the Sappers.

The continued rain led not only to a postponement but to a revision of the Corps plan for the assault. In fact, there were alternative plans, but what it boiled down to was that 8 Indian Division was to crack the line at Mozzagrogna and the Irish Brigade—the one brigade of the Division that had had no bridgehead fighting this time—was to exploit the crack along with 4 Armoured Brigade, clearing the high ground to the coast.

November 28 was a bright and beautiful day. Our medium and light bombers, fighters and fighter-bombers were busy over the ridge, and the German ME 109s and FW 190s came out in half-dozens at a time to harass our batteries. The Indian attack went in, up the narrow sunken lane that leads to Mozzagrogna. Their leading brigade (17) got to the village, but the way up was impassable to supporting arms, and the Gurkhas were driven back by flame-throwing tanks, making their first—and a terrifying—appearance in the Italian campaign.

That afternoon—the afternoon of November 28—General Allfrey, commanding 5 Corps, met General Evelegh at H.Q. 4 Armoured Brigade (Brigadier John Currie) and, with Brigadier Nelson Russell of the Irish Brigade, they discussed the new situation, caused by the Indians' failure to take Mozzagrogna and crack the line. General Allfrey gave General Evelegh his choice: the Indians could have another go, or the Division could secure its starting-line for itself. General Evelegh chose the latter course. The weather had been fine for a few days now, the going was better, and he decided to put in his tanks.

At 6.30 in the morning of November 29 the tanks of 44 R.T.R. along with the Inniskillings, made a frontal attack on the Colle, a high point on the dominating ridge. The tanks were held up for a time on minefields, lumbered over deep trenches and dug-outs, whilst the Inniskillings, with tommy-guns and grenades, cleared up the scattered houses and machine-gun nests. By three in the afternoon they had the Colle and by five they were in Santa Maria.

The main attack went in on the two following days. The Argylls came under command of the Irish Brigade and took over Santa Maria and the Colle. The Sharpshooters' tanks, with the London Irish on their backs, went up to the escarpment, the Irish Fusiliers assembled at its foot, where they were heavily shelled and suffered, among more than forty casualties, the loss—badly wounded—of Capt. Lang, the battalion's M.O. since North Africa.

On November 30 the Germans were taken by surprise by the Sharpshooters' tanks coming straight at them over country which they had thought to be too steep and broken for tanks, and which they had mined for good measure. The tanks kept close to a creeping barrage from the massed 400 guns, and the London Irish kept close to the tanks.

Soon after midday the Sangro line was broken by their taking of Fossacesia at the eastern end of the ridge and the opening of the coastal road to the north. At almost the same moment General Montgomery, just behind the battle front, was standing in his car in the winter sunshine, grinning at a group of correspondents and saying, "We've broken into and through the German winter line on the Adriatic axis." The victory was marred for many in the Division, though, and for 36 Brigade in particular, by the death on the previous day of Brigadier Howlett, killed whilst visiting forward posts. Brigadier Howlett—cheerful, friendly, hearteningly confident "Swifty" Howlett—had commanded the brigade since December 1942. He was succeeded by Brigadier J. L. Spencer. (Another change in command that took place during the battle was the appointment of Lt.-Col. Scott Elliott of the Argylls to the command of a brigade of 8 Indian Division; he was succeeded by Major Hamish Taylor, his second in command, who was promoted and confirmed in his command.)

At two that afternoon the barrage opened up again, the tanks and the Royal Irish Fusiliers moved forward on the last lap—Fossacesia to the sea—and by four it was all over. Brigadier Nelson Russell was reporting "Seven hundred prisoners and much booty" to Division before nightfall, and General Allfrey, the Corps Commander, was telling General Evelegh that the only thing an Irishman would call "booty" must be whiskey.

The final punch in the battle had been delivered by the Irish Brigade and 4 Armoured, but if ever there was an all-out divisional battle this was it. The sappers who had done such good work at the river crossings and in the minefields; the gunners who had pounded the Germans' four-mile front so that the first prisoners we took looked dazed and terrified; the infantrymen of 11 and 36 Brigades who had fought and endured in the bridgehead on little food and less warmth, and with no tank or anti-tank gun support—they all shared in the victory.

More, perhaps than anyone's it was the divisional commander's battle. The Corps plan had been flexible, and so had the Division's. General Evelegh had changed his plan first because of the weather; then because of the Indians' failure at Mozzagrogna. And the final assault was made all the easier for the tanks and the Irishmen by his copy-book feint. As the attack began on the west of the ridge he moved infantry into position on the river plain as though for an attack from the east, laid a smoke-screen in front of them, and withdrew them. The German artillery swung into action on the empty clouds of smoke—on to an empty plain. Meanwhile our own artillery, besides putting down a barrage, acted as the flank of our advance.

Seven days of fine drying weather, after days of rain, had made the tank attack possible. Now the weather broke again, and the Division pushed on towards Lanciano on the lateral road, and up the coastal road, under thunderstorms, sleet and icy winds.

The total of prisoners mounted to over a thousand; we lost ten officers and seventy-eight other ranks killed between our arrival at the Sangro and the end of the battle—485 casualties in all (less than a hundred in the attack on Santa Maria and Fossacesia—the rest in the bridgehead); the booty—Brigadier Russell had been wronged—included tanks, self-propelled guns, tanks mounted with 215 mm. mortars, and all sorts of arms. But the highest prize was to have broken the winter line. It was not, perhaps, so formidable in itself as we had expected, but the Division's pace from the Trigno to the Sangro had taken the enemy by surprise. We were six weeks earlier at the banks of the Sangro than he had expected; if we had not reached it till the end of December, the weather would have been an even tougher outer line of defence than it was. The supply services, therefore—notably the R.A.S.C. drivers—and the military policemen, sorting out tangled traffic on over-congested and muddy roads, also share the honours of the battle. So, too, do a group of Italian farmers who helped to build up the Division for the attack by driving a chain of bullock carts over a mile-long diversion about five miles short of the river. Umbrellas were their protection against both rain and enemy air attack, and an armed British sentry on each cart saw to it that it did its full day's work.

There was another week of scrappy fighting, as the Division pursued the enemy over the Feltrino and up to the River Moro. We were now facing the reconstituted 90 Light Division, worthy successors to the gallant Afrika Korps unit which had surrendered to General Freyberg in Tunisia; but it was the Canadians who were to clash with them seriously in the fierce fighting at Ortona. Now it was rest for the Division, who handed over the right of Eighth Army's line to the Canadians on December 7.

It was good-bye, too, to General Evelegh, whose departure from the Division was a sad blow, for he had been with it since its formation and had seen it through all its teething troubles. To knit a division into a fighting formation in a few months, and to have it ready for a major operation overseas, is no small undertaking. That it had been well done was clearly shown by the way the Division had fought, and General Evelegh can take the full credit for it. For in addition to producing it ready for battle he had ensured that it had the best possible launch. He would be the first to acknowledge that he was lucky to have first class material to train, and our country was lucky too, for had they not been of the highest class, they would certainly not have stood up to the task they were called upon to carry out soon after landing in North Africa.

Looking back on what his Division had done in the past year, General Evelegh was certainly entitled to be satisfied and very proud of their achievements. Throughout the period since the Division was formed, all ranks were clear that efficiency for battle was the only thing that mattered. There was no time for half measures, no room for anyone who was not prepared to put it all in. General Evelegh knew what he was aiming at, and was quite clear that he was going to get it. The troops under him trained with hardly a let up, and gave of their best in the fighting. Naturally they did not always like it, but they were all clear that, in return, they would be put into battle with the best possible chance of success with the means available. This feeling bred confidence, and success followed almost automatically. General Evelegh had a real tactical flair, and an uncanny knack of seeing the weakest point in the enemy defence and going for it. But for this the casualties in the Division, which were high enough in all conscience, would certainly have been higher. In putting the Division into any attack the fullest use was always made of the supporting arms.

His artillery supported him magnificently and his tanks often got over country which was considered impassable.

All ranks saw him leave therefore with regret and with the knowledge that he had put them into battle with courage and great skill.

He was succeeded by General Charles Keightley who was already well known to many in the Division as the Commander of 6 Armoured Division in North Africa.

CHAPTER IV

THE MOUNTAINS AND THE MONASTERY

THE Division had been in almost constant action since November 1942, and in contact since September 1943. Its losses had been heavy; the Argylls, for instance, had lost some 156 officers and about a thousand men since the landings in North Africa, and the Buffs was another unit that had only two or three men left of those who had embarked in the Clyde not much more than a year ago. Morale was still good, but the Division was thoroughly tired, and the intention now was that it should have a month of rest, reorganisation, and training.

* * * * *

Campobasso, which was to be the rest and training centre, was far back from the front in the mountainous centre of Southern Italy, had been a holiday resort as well as a market town in peacetime, and had already become an Eighth Army leave centre. The Canadians had made good use of its amenities, which included three cinemas, an E.N.S.A. theatre, and clubs for officers and N.C.O.s.

But not everybody in the Division had a month's rest. Eleven Brigade and 132 Field Regiment were sent into the line on December 9 to take over 5 Division's sector along the high ground overlooking the Sangro; on December 22 the Inniskillings moved forward to spend Christmas at Capracotta; and 49 L.A.A. regiment manned its Bofors guns for weeks on end in the bitterest weather without even the modest satisfaction of firing an occasional shot. For most of the men in the Division, though, this Christmas of 1943 was in sharp contrast with that of the previous year, spent in the bleak hills of Tunisia, with soggy biscuit as the main dish on most of the menus. This time the N.A.A.F.I. and the R.A.S.C. were given the chance to

JANUARY, 1944

excel themselves, and took it handsomely: Christmas dinner for most of the Division—even though some of the men got it a day late—included turkey, roast pork, plum pudding and mince pies; beer, whiskey and local wine to wash it down with; and cigarettes and chocolates to comfort many a distended belly and suddenly jaded palate.

* * * * *

Meanwhile, a plan was on foot which was soon to swing the Division into a new sector of the front. An allied landing was to be made at Anzio, south of Rome, with the object of cutting the enemy's communications with Rome and of threatening the rear of his XIV Corps, which was denying Fifth Army's advance up the west coast. A long period of planning, complicated and delayed by the demands of the planners of the Second Front for the Mediterranean's coastal and landing craft, culminated in a meeting between General Alexander and Mr. Churchill at Marrakesh on January 7, and as a result a British and an American division landed on the beaches at Anzio on January 22.

The immediate result of the new dispositions, as far as 78 Division was concerned, was that it took over from 5 Division—which was itself newly committed to the west-coast offensive intended to link up with the Anzio beach-head. The Division found itself, therefore, with thirty miles of front from Castel di Sangro to Casoli, overlooking the upper Sangro and in extremely mountainous country, broken by steeply precipitous valleys—a country in which nearly all the roads were already snowbound.

Thirty-six Brigade, holding the right-hand sector in the lowest ground, were in the foothills of the Apennines, close under the slopes of the great snow-capped peaks of Maiella, 9,200 feet high. Fifty-six Recce, in an unaccustomed infantry rôle, were in the central mountain sector, and the Irish Brigade had a loosely-defined twelve-mile front on the watershed of the Sangro and the Volturno. Their positions consisted of a number of independent company outposts—patrol bases rather than defence areas. The men were living in bivouac tents, in slit-trenches in the snow and in ruined houses, while the enemy, no better housed than we were, were much better placed tactically, for their positions were higher still than ours, with a complete and uninterrupted view of the whole of the Sangro valley.

It was a period of deep and dangerous patrolling, with great distances involved and with every man (the Germans, no doubt, as well as ours) only too well aware of the crunch of his boots on frozen snow, the depth to which his feet sank where the snow was dry and powdery, and the tendency of automatic weapons to freeze up in the intense cold. The vast no-man's-land gave the patrols of both sides so much elbow-room that it was as easy for an enemy patrol as for one of ours to reach the other side's forward posts—or even its Q.M.'s stores—for all the opposition it need have met. In the wintry conditions prevailing, both sides' activities were limited to the occupation of widely separated villages, to preventing infiltration, keeping contact, and finding suitable river-crossings.

The patrols operated in small numbers. One such patrol of the Argylls, consisting of ten men under Lt. Hugh Campbell Smith, was out in no-man's-land on a routine patrol when a party of Germans was seen approaching from high up on the hillside. Smith quickly spread out his men in an ambush and waited, until about two dozen Germans came in single file from above. The Highlanders held their fire until the last second, and achieved complete surprise. Eleven Germans were killed that night, for the loss of one of ours, and Cpl. Hefferland won a D.C.M. for the effect with which he continued to fire his Bren after being badly wounded.

An important factor during this period of patrolling was that the sympathies of the Italian civilians were with the British. Some of the farmers gave us useful and fairly accurate information about German troop movements, and others were even more active in their help. An enterprising and gallant band of partisans, known as Wigforce, was operating under the command of Major Lionel Wigram, a Royal Fusilier, with detachments from each battalion of 36 Brigade. They carried out many a daring and successful raid before Wigram was killed, on the night of February 2-3, leading forty British infantrymen and a hundred Italian guerrillas against the German-occupied village of Pizzoferrato.

JANUARY-FEBRUARY, 1944

Although there were no major engagements during these three winter months it was a difficult period for the men of the Division—a continual struggle for existence against the elements, with endless problems of supply and maintenance to be solved almost from hour to hour. The chief enemy was the cold. Winter is always hard in these highlands, but that winter— and the Italians were vehement in telling us so—was one of the bitterest in living memory. The first snow had fallen on Boxing Day, and within three days it was a foot deep in the narrow streets of the upland villages, and the roads leading down to the Adriatic coast were blocked. There were many cases of frostbite, and of 108 cases of exposure in the Division five men died. It was difficult to evacuate the sick, as so many of the regimental aid posts were snowbound. Major Joyce, of 11 Field Ambulance, himself an expert on skis, improvised skistretchers on which sick and wounded men were successfully handled down to hospital. Food and other supplies often had to be dropped to forward troops by parachute, and the Northamptons instituted a carrier-pigeon service in case they were cut off by snowdrifts. For three weeks 56 Recce were cut off in the snowbound mountain village of Capracotta, fed from the air. With them was a Polish commando that fought off most gallantly a German counter-attack, and other units in the Division were glad of the co-operation of a Belgian commando, notable especially for its skilled and dashing patrolling. Elsewhere the supply units worked wonders in handling their vehicles through snowdrifts and over frozen ruts to get food, mail, and ammunition to the forward companies, with the Provost companies and R.E.M.E. coming to their rescue when drifts and snow-filled craters proved too much. Even to keep the main roads open, bulldozers, flame-throwers, and whole battalions armed with spades had to be set to work—drifts of up to twenty feet would form in one night. In the rear snow ploughs and Italians by the hundred were kept hard at it.

The weather was still biting hard when orders were receieved, in early February, for yet another move. It had become clear to the higher command that little progress could be made up the narrow eastern coastal strip, between the Apennines and the Adriatic, and that seasoned troops could be better employed in adding weight to the proposed punch on the west than in dissipating their strength in mountain patrols. It was on the west—on the main Fifth Army front—that another attack was being prepared against Cassino; for the Anzio landings had had little loosening effect, the beach-head was contained, and operations were at a standstill. Nothing could be done until we had taken the position that closed the Liri valley and the road to Rome.

78 Division was relieved by the 3 Carpathian Division of the 2 Polish Corps, and began a long, painful, cross-country trek through rain, snow, and mountain blizzards. By February 19 they had all (except for 56 Recce) arrived at Capua, and pitched their bivouac-tents under the olive trees. It was here—or in the little town near by—that a Carthaginian army had once frittered away its victories in idleness and luxury: but no such future faced the Division in those cold February days of 1944.

As the Division moved to its new area near Mignano the men caught their first glimpse of the battlefield of Cassino—the town, the mountains, and the monastery that had already withstood so many attacks during the past weeks. Major Fred Majdalany, who commanded a company of the Lancashire Fusiliers during this phase of the campaign, has described it in *The Monastery*:

"From the crest above the village we could look down over the whole of the Cassino battlefield. Even at a distance, and to eyes not unused to destruction, the ruins of Cassino were awe-inspiring. This was indeed a stricken town. Not a single whole building remained, only fragments of walls and heaps of rubble. Those jagged fragments of buildings had a ghostly, slightly obscene quality that is hard to describe; it was like a forest of stalagmites. Cassino in destruction was different from all the other places.

"Away to the left ran the thin streak of the Rapido River, stretched like a steel cord across the entrance to the Liri Valley. The fortifications on its far bank linked up with the mountain range which began behind Cassino, and became higher as it went east till it culminated in the towering peak of Monte Cairo, over five thousand feet high, and the anchor of the Cassino defence system.

"Stark and clear now was the one that was the most important of them all, because it was the key to all the others—Monastery Hill. Having seen the country we could properly understand now the difficulties of this battle that had already been going on for nearly four months. The Monastery, converted into a fortress and securely planted on the crest of the precipitous rocky slopes of Monastery Hill, commanded a perfect view of every single approach to the Liri Valley, through which an army marching on Rome must pass. This amazing viewpoint—from which the German artillery was so accurately directed for so long—was protected on its eastern side by the mountains and to the west by the narrow but fast-flowing Rapido, and the steel and concrete defences behind it. It was obvious now why the Monastery had become the bogy of every operation."

* * * * *

An advance by the French and the Americans as long ago as December had placed them within striking distance of Cassino, and the French had done magnificently in the north of the Liri Valley, getting up behind Cassino and the monastery on to the Castellone and Belvedere mountains, sub-features of the mighty Monte Cairo, and themselves more than two thousand feet high.

The plan had been for the troops who had landed at Anzio on January 22, eighty miles from the Cassino front, to advance —not northwards towards Rome, but eastwards to cut the Frosinone road and the coastal roads behind the German army. At the same time a massed frontal attack was to be launched at Cassino by the main bulk of Fifth Army, so as to catch the Germans in a sort of vast nutcracker. But the splendid resistance of the German parachute division had set the operation back, and prevented the junction of General Clark's two forces. Kesselring had succeeded in sealing off the Anzio beach-head, and we had made no further progress at Cassino.

The American II Corps had made two determined attacks on the monastery, on February 4 and 10, and had suffered heavy casualties. The sector was then handed over to the New Zealanders, who attacked on February 15; the Indian Division supporting them was strongly counter-attacked, and the attack had to be called off. Two days later a new attack by the same formations also failed, the New Zealanders suffering particularly heavy losses.

It was at this point that 78 Division joined forces with these two divisions—2 New Zealand and 4 Indian—and with U.S. Combat Command "B" under the command of II New Zealand Corps of Fifth Army. The intention now was that the New Zealanders and the Indians should take the monastery and the town while 78 Division, as soon as the American armour debouched from Cassino on to the road to the north, was to cross the Rapido and drive on towards Rome.

But the weather remained unfavourable, and day after day the attack had to be postponed. The Division trained and exercised in a dreary landscape of pools and semi-liquid quagmires until it went into the line brigade by brigade. Eleven Brigade, which was intended to lead the river-crossing in assault-boats, learnt its new trade on the stretches of grey rainwater, while patrols were already active in covering the groups of R.E. who were working against utterly depressing and frustrating conditions in trying to prepare reasonably solid tracks down to the river. The Germans were patrolling strongly too, and clashed time and again with patrols of the East Surreys, manning the forward positions. With a gradual inevitability the Division got sucked into the battle before the great assault was even launched. Eleven Brigade took over a sector of the river line on February 23, and 36 Brigade moved up three days later.

The Irish Brigade, which found the time and the enthusiasm in this dreary waiting period to celebrate its Barossa Day on March 5, now found itself under a new commander. Brigadier Nelson Russell, who had led the brigade since the first North African days, was now obliged by ill-health to give up his command. In a farewell message he paid a moving tribute not only to his three infantry battalions but also to the remainder of his brigade group: to 17 Field Regiment, under Lt.-Col. Rollo Baker, to 254 Anti-Tank Battery and 280 Light A. A., to

Lt.-Col. Lytle and his 152 Field Ambulance, to the newest unit in the brigade, the Kensingtons, and—above all—to 214 Field Company, R. E., "never defeated by any task," and with "the Salso, Simeto, Trigno, and Sangro as proofs of their worth." To offset the brigade's ill luck in losing Nelson Russell there was an officer available who had commanded two of the brigade's battalions and was known to everybody. Colonel Pat Scott took over from Brigadier Russell and was confirmed in his appointment and promoted.

* * * * *

On March 15, which dawned bright and dry, the long awaited new attack on the monastery began with a tremendous onslaught from the air. At eight o'clock in the morning the first wave of bombers was seen, flying high above Cassino. They circled over the town, looking to the men below like lazy silver insects, and soon the ground itself seemed to shake with the fury of the bombardment. For over three hours the machines went over in waves—Fortresses and Liberators, in formations of eighteen and thirty-six. Over a thousand aircraft took part: some five hundred blasted Cassino with 1,100 tons of metal, while 300 fighter-bombers, with as many fighters as cover, attacked targets immediately nearby. There was no opposition from either enemy aircraft or flak.

No land forces in the war had yet seen such a massed attack on so small a target, and it seemed to those watching that at last we had found the key to success in attack without the inevitable casualties of an infantry assault. In any case, success or failure, this was a historic moment in the annals of war—the first instance of the close support of land forces by a mass attack of strategic bombers.

Surely no enemy could live through this? It was only as the battle wore on that these hopes were dashed—that it became clear that enough of the enemy, at any rate, could live through it, and that the problem was whether, and how soon, our own troops could advance through the barriers thrown up by the bombing.

At midday the artillery barrage opened, and the New Zealand infantry and sappers headed for Cassino town, while the Indians

Rest Camp at Portocannone

Winter; line of communication

made for the monastery. Eleven Brigade was on its toes waiting for orders to advance—orders that never came, for the intention was that the Division should go forward as the American tanks broke through, and while it was just possible for the infantrymen to advance over the pocked and pitted ground it was to be thirty-six hours before the bomb-craters could be patched up well enough for the tanks to go forward. And by then it would be too late. Meanwhile, well dug-in, in well-protected caves and cellars, and with carefully-sited machine-guns, the Germans were hitting back with stubborn fury, seemingly unshaken by the bombing.

Nevertheless, by nightfall most of the town was in the hands of the New Zealanders, and the Indians were on Castle Hill. The allied armies' leading troops were within 150 yards of Highway Six, the road to Rome.

It was as near as they were to get in this attack. The road to Rome would not be open until the dominating monastery had been taken, and the Indians' attack on the following day had to be halted because the lie of the ground made it almost impossible to prevent our own artillery fire from impeding the advance. On March 23 the attack was finally abandoned, without the Division having been engaged, and with only a few yards of blood-soaked ground to show for the dash and determination of the other two divisions. The Gurkhas, in spite of a belated flurry of snow, had got as far as occupying "Hangman's Hill", a rocky outcrop just below the monastery, but a German counter-attack forced the units below them to retreat and left them isolated; they were fed with supplies dropped by parachute.

The attack had failed largely because the tanks and, to a lesser degree, the infantry could not follow up the bombing as quickly as had been hoped; the very effectiveness of the bombing had churned the ground into impassability, all the worse for the torrential rain that had come down at a critical period of the battle. It was found, too, that the town of Cassino was built on a crust of earth above an underground stretch of the Rapido river. The bursting of this crust by the heavy bombs made the ground even more sodden than it had already been made by the rain. Added to these factors were the superb

(Opposite) Maj.-Gen. C. F. Keightley.

resistance of the German 1 Parachute Division under General Heidrich and its ability to filter reinforcements into the town and the monastery through underground passages. The New Zealanders had suffered 1,316 casualties in this operation, the Indians no less than 3,000.

After the abandonment of the attack the New Zealand Corps was ordered to consolidate and make a chain of forts along a line running across the south-eastern section of the town from Castle Hill to the railway station, and 78 Division, on March 26, reverted to XIII Corps. At the end of the month the position was that Fifth Army, on the left of the whole Italian front, was stretched from the sea to the Aurunci mountains, while Eighth Army was holding the line of the Gari and Rapido rivers, across which it had bridgeheads, with Cassino and the monastery still in German hands, but overlooked by 4 Indian Division on the high ground beyond. Seventy-eight Division occupied the sector stretching from the railway station at Cassino (held by the Buffs) to Monte Cairo in the heights above the monastery. At many parts of this line the two sides were only a few yards apart.

It was a miserable six weeks that followed. 36 Brigade held the left-hand sector—Cassino station and Cassino castle. Shelling and mortaring cost the Buffs at the railway station about sixty casualties, including a company commander killed, and 358 Battery of 138 Field Regiment, supporting them from Monte Purchio, to the south, was endlessly engaged in counter-battery work. The castle, taken over from an Indian battalion by the Royal West Kents (who found themselves fighting off a counter-attack as they were actually taking over) was held by 36 Brigade, with an O.P. from 138 Field, until April 26. The field regiment and its commander (Lt.-Col. Clive Usher, D.S.O.) distinguished themselves by their successful experiments in using the upper register in this mountainous territory, devising a drill for digging-in the guns on reverse slopes with their trails right down.

The castle stood on a precipitous rock, three hundred feet above the town. The Germans in the monastery looked straight down on to it; others in the town were only a hundred yards from the steep ridge of rock that led up to it; others again were on the hillside a hundred and fifty yards to the west.

It had been decided that the castle must be held at all costs as a jumping-off place for the next attack, and the cost was heavy. At first it was garrisoned by two complete companies of the Royal West Kents, but it was soon decided that it was as effective—and much more economical—to hold the castle with as small a force as possible. Eventually it was held by two platoons at a time, from each battalion in the brigade in turn.

The building itself consisted of a substantial tower, two-thirds of it still standing, and a courtyard to the west, facing the hillside. The whole was surrounded by a stone wall five feet thick and ten feet high. At the base of the tower was a well-protected cellar in which one platoon at a time took shelter; there was another small cellar where the other platoon lay by day, during the regular shelling from the monastery.

The men in the castle felt sometimes as though they were rats in a trap—that the enemy could reach the outer walls unseen and blow the whole building to blazes before the men inside knew what was happening. And there was no way of giving direct help to the garrison if it was attacked, for the slopes to the north-west were under observation from the Germans' supporting posts but the castle was ringed about by our own gun and mortar defensive fire tasks.

The only access to the castle for our own troops was up from the town by means of a precipitous ridge of rock, which a man had to use his two hands to climb. To the north was a narrow gorge, and beyond that again a steep spur on which battalion headquarters and two supporting companies clung precariously. Here the men lived in roughly-made hovels and holes, protected by clumsy stone breastworks. The fourth company of each battalion to take on the castle duty was in reserve half a mile to the north.

Near Battalion headquarters was an old quarry which served as a dump, the nightly terminus for a train of jeeps loaded with rations, water, and ammunition. Everybody lay low by day, under the constant artillery and mortar fire, but each night one of the two platoons in the castle was relieved—so that no platoon spent more than forty-eight hours there at a time—and supplies went up with each relief.

APRIL, 1944

More than once the cellars received a direct hit from a mortar bomb. On one such occasion Lt. Whitefoord and eight men of the Argylls were killed, and on another Capt. Lee and the whole of his O.P. party from 138 Field Regiment were casualties. One day a mortar bomb struck a petrol can; many men were badly burned, radio sets went up in flames, and the cellars were a whirling little hell of exploding ammunition.

The smell of death hung over everything. The hillsides around the castle were littered with the long unburied bodies of dead mules and dead men—the bodies of friend and enemy, Indian and European, all rotting in a brutally scarred, brutally indifferent landscape.

It is still a matter for argument amongst the old soldiers of the Division whether at this time 11 Brigade was worse off than 36 or better. There could have been little in it. On the night of March 26 the brigade had relieved two battalions of 4 Indian Division in the positions they had held for thirty-five days in the mountains north-west of Montecassino. Beyond them lay Monte Cairo, still occupied by the enemy, and a dominating eyrie for his snipers. At some points the enemy was less than fifty yards from our front line, and any movement in daylight was greeted with a salvo of mortar bombs. The men lived behind stone sangars, crouching under cover, during the hours of daylight, in cramped immobility. One company, relieved after six days in the forward area, could hardly march out for stiffness. In the forward sangars the only hot nourishment available was tea boiled over tommy cookers; rats abounded and, as the weather grew warmer, the air was heavy with the stench of corruption, and alive with flies.

The mortar platoons with the forward companies were splendid. At night they were hard at it, and by day they rested, in cramped and awkward watchfulness, just below the crests. The gunners were worked as hard, and in conditions even more frustrating. The whole area of battle was so tumultuously crumpled, the enemy positions and our own so scattered and yet so near each other, that it needed the utmost refinement of accuracy to avoid shelling our own troops. But they shelled the monastery continuously, and we were shelled in our turn: and three and four times a day, too, and a dozen times a night, there was a fresh outburst of mortar fire from the monastery.

The Irish Brigade after having relieved 11 Brigade on March 22 on the banks of the Rapido, moved on March 28 to relieve the French in the foothills of Monte Cairo, north of the monastery and north-west of 11 Brigade. The Inniskillings were nearest to the monastery, covering one of the few tracks from the hills into the German positions: the Irish Rifles held the key feature, Monte Castellone, 2,300 feet high; and the Royal Irish Fusiliers were in the valley running up from Monte Cairo to Cairo village. The Irish, like the men in the other brigades, lived like primitive men in caves, doggo by day and active, but murderously harassed, by night. The village of Cairo is said to have been the most heavily shelled pinpoint in Italy.

The village of San Michele, east of Cassino, was the Division's forward dumping area, overlooking the whole of the vast battlefield—a bleak and blasted landscape like a nightmare panorama of the surface of the moon. Every night trains of jeeps and mules left the village with supplies. Seven or eight hundred mules, driven by Arab, Italian, and Indian muleteers, massed and marched each night to the areas held by 11 Brigade and the Irish Brigade. Loads were divided as widely as possible among the mules in case of loss, and mail was carried in waterproof containers. The jeeps for 36 Brigade, loaded with rations and ammunition, would go along with the mules as far as they could, and from there, and from the points where even mules could go no further, the supplies went on the backs of Indian porters.

It was a dangerous journey for the patient brown men, and the convoys going furthest seldom arrived intact. But the administration was so good that the men in the sangars and in the castle cellars never needed to worry about their mail, their food, or even their cigarettes.

It was a journey of three or four hours for most of the muleteers, and as soon as they had dropped their loads they made the best speed they could back to base so as not to get caught by daylight. Between the quarry and the castle the Indian porters were protected and supervised by the anti-tank platoon of the battalion holding the castle—a horrible stretch of the journey, this, over which the porters ran the gauntlet of grenades, machine-gun fire, and mortar bombs. Colonel Tryon, the Division's A.A.Q.M.G., was often to be seen on the route at night, ensuring that everything possible was being done, as busy and as watchful as his junior officers and N.C.O.s. (It was rare indeed in the Second World War for a staff officer to be awarded a D.S.O., and Colonel Tryon's was felt by the whole Division to have been richly earned.) Major Pearson, the A.P.M., and his divisional police worked equally hard to control the hazardous supply routes and to keep them open. Models of smartness, and astonishingly patient, the M.P.s would be seen standing at the key points from first dusk until the last mule had passed on its way back, just before dawn.

It was even harder for the medical services than it was for the R.A.S.C. From the castle and the hillside sangars it was impossible to evacuate casualties by night, and although the enemy generally respected the Red Cross flag under which the daylight evacuations were conducted, not all his forward troops could be trusted to see it at all times. Sgt. Baldy, for instance, of 217 Field Ambulance, was wounded while carrying out his work and was awarded the M.M. for his courage and endurance in carrying on. Capt. Richardson, with the Northamptons, conducted an underground operating theatre for a fortnight; his cases were brought to him in daylight, and in full view of the enemy, by stretcher-bearers of 64 Anti-Tank Regiment, R.A., and of "A" Company of 11 Field Ambulance.

It was the end of April before the Division was withdrawn to rest—to the first real respite since it had landed in North Africa, eighteen months before. It handed over to the Poles, for whose reckless gallantry the Division soon learnt to feel an awed, yet amused, admiration. They exposed themselves with the most cheerful abandon, and one of 78 Division's brigade majors, R.A., has recorded how a Polish gunner subaltern, to whom he patiently and amiably refused a pass that would enable him to circulate in the forward areas in broad daylight, eventually exploded indignantly with, "I have been in Tobruk. I am not afraid. Give me ze pass!"

The Division handed over with no mixed feelings. Its two months in the Cassino battlefield had been perhaps the dreariest and unhappiest in its history, for the losses and the hardships it had suffered had been—it seemed—to no purpose. No victory had crowned its sufferings, and men had been lost not in a major battle but in nameless and apparently purposeless forays. Now, it was true, there was to be a respite in a green valley—a valley filled with the Italian springtime—but the Germans on Monastery Hill still barred the road to Rome.

CHAPTER V

THE ROAD TO ROME

WAR had by-passed the valley near Capua, but the brief Italian spring had seized and occupied it. The battle lines were thirty miles away, and the pall of smoke and dust that hung over them; the guns were out of earshot. The men attuned their ears now to birdsong, and the green fields, enamelled with flowers—how oddly English the clover seemed!—shone under a blaze of unbroken blue. It was as though the Division had stepped for a space from a Goya etching into a painting by Botticelli.

There were urban gaieties, too, not far away. Emlyn Williams had brought an E.N.S.A. company to Capua's Garrison Theatre, where it played "Blithe Spirit" to men who only a few days before had had walking-on parts, at least, in a more tragic and spectacular performance. There were cinemas in Capua, and canteens staffed by newly-arrived women welfare-workers, where many of the men heard Englishwomen's voices for the first time in nearly two years.

Serious training began for the Division on May 1—river-crossing exercises, street-fighting, and co-operation with tanks. The morale had been badly bruised by a series of hard and furious battles and heavy casualties. General Keightley's belief was that there was no better morale-builder than the most intensive training—training that would give the soldier in the ranks the certain knowledge that he knew his job so completely that he was necessarily a better man than the enemy. The divisional commander devised set schemes of his own and got each battalion commander to set others, so that there was a different scheme for each battalion every day. At the end of three weeks every officer and man had done an intensive spell of training such as he had never done before. Its value was soon to be proved.

Cassino Castle and Town

Beyond the Rapido. 214 Field Company R.E. making a bridge

Advancing in the Liri valley

38 (Irish) Brigade Pipes and Drums in Rome

THE ROAD TO ROME

Meanwhile, though, in spite of the emphasis on training, there was six days' leave for every man, spent at the rest camp at Maiori, or at other places on the Sorrento peninsula—Ravello or Amalfi. Day trips took the more enterprising to the fabled beauties of Capri, to the ruins of Pompeii, or to the squalid, cheerful, captivating bustle of Naples, where ragged urchins pursued them along the Via Roma with unnameable enticements, where the shops were full of gewgaws, and where many first fell in love with music at the newly-reopened San Carlo Opera House. It was not only music that pierced the armour of British complacency. Many a stolid soldier, wandering around the streets of Naples, felt a pang of pity as he saw the hard face of hunger mirrored in the patient eyes of some ancient Italian crone, or saw the need rather than the impudence in the unselfconscious pose of a begging child little bigger than a baby.

But the pathos of Naples and the charms of its surroundings were glimpsed only in the shortest of respites. The Monastery still barred the road to Rome, and the day of the final assault was at hand.

The enemy had reinforced and it had become clear that, for political as well as strategical reasons, Hitler meant to delay our liberation of Rome for longer than was possible by the fighting German retreat we had grown used to. The Germans had used the weeks during which they had denied us the Monastery to construct defences along the far bank of the Rapido, which ran here at right angles across Highway 6 and the entrance to the Liri Valley—a system of prepared positions known as the Gustav Line, running through the hill village of San Angelo and dominated, of course, by the Monastery. Six miles or so to the north was the similar Adolf Hitler Line, running through Aquino, on Highway 6, and the hill town of Piedimonte, north of Cassino. Between the two lines was close country, overlooked by the Germans in the mountains to the east; our axis through it was along a down-at-heel track which ran west of Highway 6 and parallel with it.

The time the Germans had spent on preparing their lines had been spent by us on photographing them from the air, and the attack was based on excellent overprints and photographs. This

APRIL-MAY, 1944

was merely one respect in which we benefited from our air superiority—the same kind of superiority that the enemy had enjoyed in the early days in North Africa. Throughout the battle that was about to begin the enemy never put up more than an odd reconnaissance plane, whilst we had not only our photographic reconnaissance to work from but also the massed softening-up onslaughts of the bombers and close support from fighter-bombers directed by a senior Air Force officer from Mount Trocchio, just south of the river.

The new plan left the Division in reserve during the first phase, which was an attack between the Monastery and the sea along a front of about nineteen miles. On the right, the Polish Corps was to attack the Monastery from the north-west, from the mountains where the Division had lurked in caves and holes in the ground, and also to swing across Highway 6, the road to Rome, north of Cassino. In the centre, 4 British and 8 Indian Divisions were to force a crossing of the Rapido while Fifth Army, on the left, with the French and the U.S. Corps, was to strike towards the north-west, capturing Mounts Maio and Ausonia so as to turn the southern bastion of the Liri Valley between San Giorgio and San Ambroglio.

At the appropriate moment in the battle the British and American divisions at Anzio were to break out of their perilous four-month old beach-head and cut off the German's retreat.

The rôle of the Division was that of the follow-through force. For that reason it was given an armoured brigade under command, and its task was to go through 4 British Division and swing right to cut Highway 6 west of Cassino. The Canadian Corps, in Eighth Army reserve, was to advance alongside, through the Indian Division's bridgehead.

* * * * *

"All round Hitler's Germany," ran General Leese's message to Eighth Army, "the Allies are closing in. . . . In the south the Eighth and Fifth Armies are about to strike . . ." and "you will be supported by overwhelming air forces," said General Alexander, the Commander-in-Chief, "and in guns and tanks we far outnumber the Germans." And the attack went in at midnight of May 11-12 supported by the enormous volume of bombing and of gunfire that the generals had promised.

Under this twofold barrage the assault boats of two divisions —4 British and 8 Indian—advanced to force the crossing of the Rapido. 78 Division was on a few hours' notice to move, and at first light on the morning of Sunday, May 14, the order came. The same troop-carrying lorries that had brought it from Cassino only two weeks before headed north again along Highway 6 to the Monastery.

But in those two weeks—in the few days that the Division had been lapped in Capua's springtime—winter had turned to summer. This was a familiar road enough—all too familiar— but now the sun was high and hot over Mignano, which had been a sodden island-village in a sea of mud, and everything and everybody was white with the summer dust.

Mignano had been made the main dump for the attack and the advance. Ammunition was piled high in its railway-cuttings, and two divisions had assembled in the ravines and gullies round it for the river crossing.

Now, two days later, the Division rumbled past the shattered village and into sight of the Monastery again, though "into sight" is not, perhaps, the precise phrase, for the Monastery itself was cloaked in a heavy pall of smoke that made our movements invisible. It was a relatively new development in our tactical scheme to hang a curtain of smoke-shells between our own preparations and the watchful eyes of the enemy in the Monastery, and three divisions—two for the river crossing and one for the break-through—had formed up unobserved and in relative safety behind it.

The Irish Brigade led the Division, and the Inniskillings led the Irish Brigade. The brigade was at full strength, with one squadron of the 16/5 Lancers from 6 Armoured Division, 214 Field Company R.E., and 152 Field Ambulance under command, as it advanced unopposed over the sappers' Bailey bridge on the hot afternoon of May 14. The two bridgehead divisions—4 British on the right and 8 Indian on the left—had swung out to the flanks to cover the breakthrough, and the tangled wreckage of battle on the far bank—shattered tanks and mangled corpses—was proof of the fighting that had already taken place to open the road to Rome.

MAY 15, 1944

At this stage the bridgehead across the Rapido varied in depth from 500 to 1,500 yards. Between the Gustav and the Adolf Hitler lines, about six miles apart, was a series of defended localities, very thoroughly prepared. Beyond the Rapido the country was a mass of minor features, or rather a seemingly endless vista of undulations, hardly worthy of the name of features, some a little higher than others—the bed, in fact, of what had been a vast lake in prehistoric times.

It was perfect country from a defender's point of view, crisscrossed by hedges, walls and ditches, and all the better for snipers and ambushes now that the trees and vines were in full leaf and the grass knee-high. Visibility was seldom more than 500 yards: the frequently heavy ground mist—often succeeded by a heat haze—was made thicker by the artificial smoke, by shellfire, by the smoke of burning bridges and buildings, and by the dust raised by tanks and lorries.

Across the proposed track of the Division a tributary of the Rapido, the Piopetta, which we had to bridge, ran in from the west; there was an indifferent track called Ace Route which ran more or less parallel with and to the south of Highway Six towards Aquino, and the axis of advance was cut from north to south by two main roads from Cassino, one to San Angelo the other to Pignataro, as well as by a number of small tracks, most of which were usually mined. The Division's first objective was the Cassino-Pignataro road.

Dawn of May 15 saw the first attack by the Division since the Sangro battle of six months before. The Poles, on our right, were still short of the Monastery, and the valley was filled with the smoke that spilled over from the shelling. The bridgehead was so narrow that the Division would have to advance on a one-battalion front, and it was impossible, as the battle began, to find out where precisely the flank formations were. The Hampshires of 4 Division had been ordered to guard the Division's right by taking the hill, Massa Vertechi, a mile or two ahead, and were said to be in precarious possession of it.

The Inniskillings had to begin their advance without the support of their attached squadron of 16/5 Lancers: one of the tanks attached to the Hampshires had stuck in the mud on the far side of the bridge over the Piopetta, effectively blocking it,

THE ROAD TO ROME

and the Division's sappers, working like beavers, could not promise their new bridge before dawn.

But by 4 a.m. the Inniskillings had got their two forward companies on to the Massa di Vendetti without having met any opposition; forty-five minutes later they came under machine-gun fire as they approached the Massa Tamburrini: and by dawn the two leading companies were in the standing corn about seventy yards from the enemy positions with a thick blanket of fog all round and enemy tanks nearby.

Meanwhile, the sappers had finished their bridge over the Piopetta; the tanks crossed at 8 a.m. and, lurching through the fog across the marshy fields, joined up with the waiting infantry. By nine o'clock the fog was lifting, the artillery concentration came down, and the infantry and the tanks charged together through the corn. Half-an-hour later Tamburrini had been taken after much tommy-gun work and tossing of grenades out of Sherman turrets. But we were still short of the Cassino-Pignataro road, and there was only the briefest of breathers before the next phase of the attack—against the high ground (Point 86) just short of the road itself.

For five minutes the artillery concentrated on Point 86, and the entire squadron of tanks battered the positions at close range with H.E. and machine-gun fire. Then "B" and "C" companies of the Inniskillings charged with the tanks, and had soon established themselves in the dug-outs and ditches they had taken, while "D" Company went through and were on the far side of the road by midday. Twenty Germans had been killed and sixty prisoners taken, along with five anti-tank guns; two self-propelled guns and a Mark IV tank had been knocked out.

Not, however, without casualties. Many of our own tanks had been immobilised as they blundered across a minefield— later to be destroyed by the enemy's self-propelled anti-tank guns. The enemy's harassing fire had been as heavy as anything the Division had experienced: two subalterns—Jackson and Milner—had been killed and two—Baxter and Philips— wounded; nine other ranks had been killed and fifty-seven wounded. The battalion had shot its bolt for the time being, and spent the rest of the day digging in against the expected counter-attacks.

While this action had been going on 11 Brigade had crossed the Rapido and were moving up on the right of the Irish Brigade towards the road the Irishmen had taken—the start line for the next phase. Like the Inniskillings, the Northamptons, who were leading the brigade, had to begin their advance without the support of tanks: they had to start at such short notice that the squadron-commander could not be found. They were met by a good deal of machine-gun, mortar and shell-fire as well as by sniping, but collected 126 prisoners as they moved forward.

There was, in fact, a good deal of incident for what was meant to be an advance towards a start-line. L/Cpl Allkin and Pte. McGill knocked out a self-propelled gun with a P.I.A.T. and Lt. Hillian earned an immediate M.C. by charging a German patrol which he saw moving towards a position overlooking his platoon. Firing a Bren gun from the hip as he ran, he drove off the patrol, killing and wounding five of its members. Major Reggie Cook—who had led "C" company with great dash from the first landings in North Africa—fell to a sniper's bullet and was buried where he fell. Even when they had reached the road, and joined up with the London Irish, the Northamptons, waiting in the ditch, were bombed by six Kittyhawks, astray from their target.

The full-scale divisional attack went in at nine o'clock on the next morning, May 16, with the Lancashire Fusiliers on the right, supported by 17/21 Lancers, and on the left the London Irish supported by 16/5 Lancers with heavy artillery support. The Division was to push forward between 4 Division on the right and 8 Indian Division, who the day before had captured the small village of Pignataro.

This meant that as the attack went forward each flank would become progressively more exposed. The London Irish, astride the road to Sinagoga, with three companies up, each with a troop of tanks, had their left flank across the River Piopetta open and under constant and heavy fire. The Lancashire Fusiliers, making towards Highway 6, about 1,200 yards from the start line, had their open right flank thinly protected by their attached tanks.

As our 400-gun barrage opened, the Germans concentrated

everything they had on the farms and groves to our rear, crammed with a concentration of trucks, tanks and supplies. Mortar bombs and nebelwerfers soon began to land on our forward troops. Early that morning it had been wet, cold and misty, but by the time the attack went in the sun's rays, growing warmer every minute, had cleared the last of the morning mist and once again the Monastery came into view, half-right and to the rear of the battle. Smoke-shells were poured on to the hill in a frantic effort to screen the battle from the German observers, but not with complete success—we were getting short of smoke-shells.

The two forward companies of the London Irish were almost immediately held up by fire from the cellars and houses at the other side of the road. But many of the enemy had fled to the dugouts during the barrage, abandoning their machine guns, and the Irishmen were on to them with their bayonets before they realised the barrage was over. In the centre "H" company broke into the village of Sinagoga, where for an hour there was a tough little battle, hand-to-hand and house-to-house. Cpl. Barnes distinguished himself by going forward alone, covered by his Bren gunner, against an active self-propelled 75. He killed one of the crew before he was killed himself. Shortly after this the garrison in the village surrendered and by noon all the objectives were taken.

Meanwhile, the Lancashire Fusiliers had advanced on the right with two companies up supported by the Lancers' Shermans. It was tough going over the ridged fields and through the farm buildings: every inch of ground was defended. The right-hand company, for instance, suffered heavily in taking a farm-house, which fell only when we could get our tanks up to it. "C" company then passed through but before they were able to consolidate they were counter-attacked by tanks. Our own tanks were hampered by the close wooded country and a sunken lane, while the enemy infantry edged forward under cover of their tanks. It was a tank deadlock—the rival tanks were close on opposite sides of the same rise in the ground. When any of our tanks ventured a move it was fired on as soon as its turret appeared above the crest. The Germans could not be outflanked because of the sunken lane.

It was here, in breaking up the deadlock, that Fusilier Jefferson won the Division's third V.C., and one worthy to be ranked with Major Anderson's and Major Le Patourel's. His citation reads:

"On 16th May, 1944, during an attack on the Gustav Line, an anti-tank obstacle held up some of our tanks, leaving the leading Company of Fusilier Jefferson's battalion to dig in on the hill without tanks or anti-tank guns. The enemy counter-attacked with infantry and two Mark IV tanks which opened fire at short range causing a number of casualties and eliminating one P.I.A.T. group entirely.

"As the tanks advanced towards the partially dug trenches Fusilier Jefferson, entirely on his own initiative, seized a P.I.A.T. and running forward alone under heavy fire, took up a position behind a hedge; as he could not see properly he came into the open, and standing up under a hail of bullets fired at the leading tank which was now only twenty yards away. It burst into flames and all the crew were killed.

"Fusilier Jefferson then reloaded the P.I.A.T. and proceeded towards the second tank, which withdrew before he could get within range. By this time our own tanks had arrived and the enemy counter-attack was smashed with heavy casualties.

"Fusilier Jefferson's gallant act not merely saved the lives of his company and caused many casualties to the Germans, but also broke up the enemy counter-attack and had a decisive effect on the subsequent operation. His supreme gallantry and disregard of personal risk contributed very largely to the success of the action."

When the counter-attack had been broken and the final objectives reached, the Lancashire Fusiliers had heavy losses to count. In "C" company, for instance, forty men out of ninety had been killed or wounded. But the enemy's losses had been even heavier, and the battalion was consolidating now in the Germans' old defences, the lucky ones in the famous new steel pill-boxes each of which consisted of an underground three-roomed flatlet with a well-stocked larder.

THE ROAD TO ROME

That was at midday, and by nightfall the London Irish were beyond the objective among a group of houses overlooking the river Piopetta. An afternoon counter-attack from the south had been broken up with the aid of the artillery, who had one of their 17-pounders destroyed with all its crew wounded or killed. The London Irish had lost two of their support Vickers—with their crews, five officers and sixty other ranks killed or wounded. Five of the anti-tank troop and eleven from the support group had been killed, and the supporting tanks had also suffered. But they had taken 120 prisoners, killed at least 100 Germans and knocked out 9 tanks or S.P. guns.

The Northamptons, through whom the Lancashire Fusiliers had passed in the morning, had also experienced very heavy shelling and mortaring all day but had managed to improve their positions along the Pignataro road, in spite of the shell that destroyed battalion headquarters, killing one signaller, burying six—later extricated—and destroying all the radio sets. It took an alert and efficient Brigade H.Q. no more than an hour to restore communications.

The Gustav Line, though, was pierced, and it was clear by dawn of the next day, May 17, that it was on the edge of breaking completely—that it could not be long before the Monastery was encircled. The enemy's defensive fire began to die down, as our counter-battery work took its toll of his guns. In his sharp counter-attacks with tanks, he had discovered how vulnerable a tank is on a narrow front against determined infantry with P.I.A.T.s and anti-tank guns.

The Monastery, moreover, was becoming an exposed salient as much as a strong-point. The Poles put in another attack from the north, dislodged the Germans from their positions, and held their gains against repeated counter-attacks, while to their south 4 British Infantry Division drove across Highway 6, thus practically surrounding Cassino, and defeated all enemy attempts to regain the road.

But although the fighting was more clearly going our way it had not yet died down. The battle was swinging now around the little town of Piumarola, half-way between the Gustav and the Adolf Hitler lines. The position was obscure still, and conflicting messages came from Piumarola to Brigade H.Q.: now the town had fallen to the Lothian and Border Horse, now the news was that the tanks had run into a trap short of the town.

The Royal Irish Fusiliers had met little opposition in advancing to the high ground east of the town, but the Inniskillings found that the Lothians, sure enough, had been held just short of Piumarola by anti-tank and self-propelled guns.

Accordingly, a three-company encirclement and attack was put in, in which a squadron each of the 16/5 Lancers and the Lothians also took part. There was an afternoon and evening of confused fighting, with the tanks cramped in a sunken lane and the infantrymen playing a lethal game of hide-and-seek in the houses and the rubble-strewn streets, before the little town was ours and secure against counter-attack. The Inniskillings lost four killed and thirty-one wounded, but their hundred and more prisoners (along with three self-propelled guns) turned out to be men of the German 1 Parachute Division—withdrawn from Cassino and the Monastery, and caught at their checkpoint. It was the first indication of what was happening on our right, our first news of the Poles.

To the left of the Inniskillings that evening the London Irish, still under heavy shell-fire on the river banks—they lost twenty-five men that day—were also interrogating German parachute troops withdrawn from Cassino. Could the Monastery have fallen?

That night, in the warm still darkness of May 17, even the Lancashire Fusiliers did not know—and they were on the extreme right of the line, only a couple of miles from the Poles around the Monastery. They were overlooking Highway 6 as darkness fell, and the London Irish patrols had crossed the valley to join them, but the orders were not to cross the Highway to Monastery Hill: "the exact position of the Poles is not known."

It was on the morning of Thursday May 18 that a hand-picked patrol of three corporals of the Lancashire Fusiliers, all holders of the M.M., crossed the Highway in what was more a formal ceremony—as Major Majdalany observed—than a military feat. The cutting of the Highway by 78 Division had turned the Monastery from a fort into a death-trap for its occupants, and as day broke—the first day on which our gunners had not hung the Monastery with smoke—the red and

white flag of Poland could be seen flying from the grey ruins.
A week of confused, scrappy, and bloody fighting by the
Division had ended in the breaking of the Gustav line. Congratulatory messages from the Commander-in-Chief, General
Alexander, and from General Leese, the Army Commander,
were passed on with pride by General Keightley to a Division
that had "formed the left pincer in the attack on the Monastery"
and whose "successful and rapid advance was largely responsible
for its capture". The Division had taken more than four
hundred prisoners, killed or wounded over four hundred more,
and knocked out or captured forty tanks and self-propelled
guns. "It can only be guessed", said the Divisional commander,
"what effect this advance had on loosening up the French and
Polish fronts."

The cost had not been light. The Irish Brigade in particular,
which had set the pace of the attack against the Gustav Line,
had lost Lt.-Col. Ion Goff, commanding the London Irish, on
the first day of the battle and Laurie Franklyn-Vaile, commanding "C" company of the Irish Fusiliers. Lt.-Col. Bala Bredin,
commanding the Inniskillings, was badly wounded in both legs
but refused to be moved—until he fainted and could no longer
register his protests. The death of John Loveday, commanding
the 16/5 Lancers, was felt almost as keenly by the infantrymen
who had been supported by his tanks as if he had been a longstanding member of what General Keightley was proudly
referring to as "this great Divisional team of ours."

"Team" was the word. In Italy as in the other theatres the
infantrymen of 78 Division were served as nobly as infantrymen
could ever hope to be by their gunner and sapper comrades,
and by the men of the R.A.S.C., R.A.M.C., R.E.M.E. and the
rest. In this particular advance it was the signallers who earned
especial praise: in a constantly shifting battle they stuck to their
radio sets, or set off to repair lines, under unusually heavy shellfire, and the advance could not have been as fast as it was had
it not been for their coolness and skill.

* * * * *

As the Germans fell back on to their Adolf Hitler line, six
miles away, 11 Brigade and the Irish Brigade consolidated the

ground they had won, and 36 Brigade took over the lead.

As dark fell on May 18, the day the Monastery had fallen, the Argylls and the Buffs moved up towards the aerodrome just short of the town of Aquino. It was a moonless night, lit only by the whirling fireflies and by the flash of guns from the left, where the tanks of the Derbyshire Yeomanry were already engaging the occupied houses at the edge of the town.

An over-optimistic message from the Derbyshire Yeomanry, that night, that they were in the town, was the basis for the plan of the next day's attack: 36 Brigade was to occupy Aquino, covered by the fire of three field regiments of Royal Artillery, and supported by the Canadian tanks, while the Derbyshire Yeomanry and the lorried troops of the Rifle Brigade were to swing round the town and through the Hitler Line.

But beyond the town and to either flank was a deep ravine impassable to tanks except at one or two narrow tracks—a ravine that had not shown itself either in air photographs or to the leading troops at night. So the tanks were held up, and so were the Argylls and the Buffs, checked by the wire just short of the town proper and raked by fire from the concrete emplacements beyond. They were there for a long, hot day before they were withdrawn, covered by 11 Brigade.

The Argylls had lost two killed, twenty wounded and six missing in this gamble that failed to come off. Among the wounded was the battalion commander, Lt.-Col. Taylor, M.C., who refused to leave his men in spite of the wound in his leg. Among the Buffs' thirty casualties was their C.O., Lt.-Col. Monk, M.C., killed after leading the battalion since November 1943, after the battle of the Trigno.

But in spite of this check at Aquino, the Adolf Hitler line was to crack quickly. The line was nothing like as strong as the abandoned Gustav positions. It ran straight across the Liri valley for several miles in country more open than the Division had seen for a long time. The enemy had not the gun-power necessary to man the pill-boxes and his men were in no condition to put up a full-scale resistance, as was shown in a captured letter—intended by a German officer for his wife:

"May 18. . . . You have no idea of the rigours and horrors

of this retreat. . . . We will not let ourselves become downhearted, but people are tired and have had nothing to eat for three days. Our Free French and Moroccan enemies are remarkable fine soldiers. My heart bleeds when I look at my fine unit, after five days' fighting: 150 men lost. The echelons are already far to the rear, three recce cars are in pieces, my armoured command vehicle and all its wireless equipment has been destroyed by a French AFV. Since April 26 weapons, paper and food have been lacking completely.

"To-day it looks as if things are a little better. Perhaps we shall manage, after all, to avoid the crumbling of the whole Italian front, but that appears to be a small hope. . . ."

Small hope, indeed. The French had broken through the mountains to the south and were threatening to get behind the whole line. The Canadian infantry attacked Pontecorvo, south of Aquino, where the Germans had to give up without a fight, and the Canadian tanks swept through the gap up the valley of the Liri to its junction with its tributary, the Melfa. The Poles were battering at the hill-top town of Piedimonte on May 20—the fortress which had linked the Gustav and the Hitler Lines.

The men in the Anzio pocket broke out and joined hands with the Americans advancing up the coast. The Hitler Line was gone, and the Germans were falling back on Rome.

Apart from the battle at Aquino, the Division had had little hand in the breaking of the Hitler Line, save that its artillery had hung a curtain of fire over the Canadian break-through in the centre. Its task now was to cross the River Melfa and push along Highway 6 to Arce, as the right wing of the advance on Rome.

Eleven Brigade was the first to move off, in the wake of the Canadians and the 6 Armoured Division. A squadron of tanks from the Warwickshire Yeomanry was with each battalion—the Canadian Armoured Brigade had been relieved by 9 Armoured, and its 3 Hussars were with the Irish Brigade, its Wiltshire Yeomanry with 36.

The Lancashire Fusiliers and the East Surreys passed unopposed through Aquino—a ruin and a graveyard—on the morning of May 25, and May 27 saw the Division in the steep, broken hill-country where Highway 6 takes a sharp left-handed turn from Arce, through the river town of Ceprano, to turn eventually right again through Frosinone and on to Rome.

The Irish Fusiliers led the advance towards Ceprano with their first objective the Arce–Ceprano road. The Guards of 6 Armoured Division were fighting for the twin peaks, Piccolo and Grande, on their right and the Division was held up until these dominating mountains were taken, on May 28. The Irishmen found that the Canadians had already captured Ceprano, but the going had been very difficult and the Fusiliers had sustained twenty-five casualties from heavy shelling. They continued the advance the next day and crossed the river Liri to the north of Ceprano, meeting no opposition other than mines.

The task of the Irish Brigade the next day was to capture the village of Strangolagalli about three miles north of Highway 6, and to the west of Arce, which was just being cleared by the Guards. The country which the Division was passing through now was about the most difficult tank country it had met—impossible, indeed, for almost any kind of vehicle. The engineers bore the heaviest burden of the advance, the speed of which depended on how quickly they could push roads through.

The Irish Fusiliers moved forward slowly with the 3 Hussars in support, heavily battered by nebelwerfers and mortars. With the London Irish, but helped chiefly by the speed with which 17 Field Regiment, R.A., got into action and put down a concentration, they took an enemy-held hill across the Liri that was protecting Strangolagalli, which the Inniskillings entered unopposed, and 36 Brigade pushed along on the left of the Irish Brigade up Highway 6 towards Frosinone.

During this phase the enemy withdrawal was particularly skilful. The Germans slipped from one good position to another at night, leaving roads, verges, villages and bridge-approaches mined and booby-trapped, and all the avenues of advance covered by observed artillery and mortar-fire. The mines and the booby-traps were especially troublesome at night, but the Division, showing not only its usual determination and guts but a growing skill and familiarity with the deadly obstacles left behind, pressed hard on the heels of the enemy, giving him no respite.

The Argylls, supported by a troop of Wiltshire Yeomanry and a pioneer platoon whose duty it was to clear the mines, were now leading. Progress was slow. All the bridges on Highway 6 were destroyed, so diversions had to be found and the mines lifted. The tanks got ditched and bogged and the infantrymen helped their crews to shove and heave at them over the streams and gulleys and through the thickly planted orchards and olive groves. There were snipers in the woods and the troops were being continually mortared. In one morning the Argylls lost two men killed and twelve wounded from mortar-fire.

The Royal West Kents, meanwhile, working through the rough country to the north, were meeting fairly stiff opposition from rearguards supported by self-propelled guns, and when the Buffs took over the lead next day, May 30, their supporting tanks found it hard to keep up with the infantry. Near Ripi they encountered opposition from rearguard troops and six tanks were dealt with by our guns. The enemy artillery fire at times was intense and the Buffs suffered casualties including one company commander wounded, but during the night a patrol was able to report that Ripi was clear of the enemy. The Irish Brigade, operating on the right, was ordered to take San Giovanni and link up there with 36 Brigade. San Giovanni was strongly held and there were two hours of fierce street fighting for the London Irish and 3 Hussars before the village fell, along with almost a hundred enemy dead and a brace of tanks.

But along the whole front the Germans were now in full retreat. The Fifth Army was far ahead, advancing up the coast with the Anzio forces. By June 1 they had broken through the Valmontone–Velletri line north of Velletri and were in the Alban Hills, between a dozen and a score of miles short of Rome, and had cut Highway 6 east of Valmontone. This break-through had made it impossible for the enemy to counter-attack with any hope of success on the southern front.

On XIII Corps's front the enemy was falling back with very little attempt to delay our advance apart from mortaring and demolitions. It was thought he might try to hold us up—the right wing—once we had reached the very hilly country north of Alatri but he could do little to stop us for any length of time until he reached the Pescara–Rome lateral—the most important road in central Italy. The Canadians had taken Frosinone on Highway 6 on May 31 and the Indians were in process of taking Veroli on the right flank.

It was largely a matter now of clearing up and hurrying on, and in the afternoon of June 1 the Argylls were carried forward in R.A.S.C. trucks and unloaded just west of Frosinone with orders to advance north and clear the road to Alatri, then to capture the town, six miles away. The scout cars of 56 Recce were already skirmishing up the road and "A" squadron of the Wiltshire Yeomanry was to give support to the Argylls.

At first light on June 2 the Argylls advanced and had soon captured Monte San Angelo and Monte Caprara to the left and right of the road. They were now a mile from Alatri which, like many a small Italian town, was at the top of an olive-clad hill looking from beneath both attractive and tempting. And yet forbidding, for its ancient walls—the walls of the city of Aletrium—were miraculously well preserved, thirty feet high in places, and built of massive many-sided blocks.

From the town the enemy could watch the whole of the road below and had complete command of the bridge at the foot of the hill. A direct assault was impossible, so Lt.-Col. Taylor decided to surround the town. "B" company was ordered to move west on to Monte San Francisco and "Y" company to seize the monastery on a hill to the north of the town. It was a hot day and the hills were steep and rocky, the valleys deep. "Y" company had to make a long advance over exposed ground. The tanks had not yet arrived so the company, commanded by Capt. Davies, advanced without them. A platoon was sent up to the monastery walls from where an assault would be made. They climbed 300 feet up the steep hill and half-way up came under machine-gun fire which they were soon able to silence, and they reached the top to find a solid stone wall eight feet high, its gate the only entrance to the monastery. In the absence of tanks, a hole was blown in the wall with a Piat, large enough for Lt. Stephan and his patrol to crawl through, finding the monastery unoccupied, the town in full view, and the enemy's way of escape to the north in easy machine-gun range. The enemy was directing accurate shell-fire on the road to the south but the tanks below secured sixteen direct hits on the clock-tower which the enemy was using as his observation post. At 4 p.m. two companies of the Royal West Kents attacked the town, and the Germans robbed the watching Argylls of the cream of the victory by slipping away down the road to the west—the one road which was not overlooked by the monastery.

To the left of this little battle 11 Brigade was clearing the hills, in isolated little actions such as that in which R.S.M. Surkitt, D.C.M., of the Northamptons, with his batman and a group of Italian partisans, destroyed a German self-propelled gun by grenade, while the rest of the battalion took its ease for a couple of days in Fumone, imprisoning Fascists and enjoying the welcome due to liberators.

* * * * *

The more glamorous welcome was awaiting the Americans of Fifth Army, now only eight miles from Rome, at the centre of the advance. To help to get them there the Division, on the right flank, had marched and fought thirty miles across broken country in five days. They were put into Corps reserve, and 6 Armoured Division took up the pursuit over the easier stretch, for tanks, of what was left of Highway 6.

As the Division left the line General Keightley passed on to all its units the letter he had had from General Leese:

"Now that 78 Division is out of the line, I should like to send my best congratulations on the tremendous energy and drive your Division showed throughout its successive fights.

"The excellent training of the Division has more than proved itself on the day. Its excellent attacks towards Highway Six, supported by tanks and artillery, were admirably organised and carried out and led decisively to the fall of Cassino and the Monastery Hill.

"I am very grateful for the quick contact your troops

gained along the Hitler Line, and for your flank march from Arce, as well as the general speed of movement achieved. The many physical difficulties of the ground were admirably overcome and throughout the hard fighting in the mountains the spirit and toughness of the troops was beyond praise.

"All this I expected from the great traditions of your Division with its fine record in North Africa, Sicily and Eastern Italy."

A little after dawn on Sunday, June 4, American cars and tanks entered the suburbs of Rome to the wild ringing of church bells, and under a bombardment of flowers. The enemy had withdrawn to the north and left it open. In twenty-four days the forces of General Alexander had advanced eighty miles, broken through three defensive lines, and shattered the German Tenth Army. Rome was ours at last, but the triumph had been so long delayed, and the cost so heavy—at Anzio, Cassino, and in the Liri valley—that as the Division rested near Alatri it could think of Rome only as a leave-town for a happier future, and a rueful and erudite *Daily Telegraph* correspondent was quoting in his diary the disillusioned words that C. E. Montague had written of an earlier triumph:

"What a victory it might have been—the real, the Winged Victory, chivalric, whole and unstained! The bride that our generous youth had sought and not won ... had come to us now; an old woman, she no longer refused us."

Two days later the allied armies landed in France.

CHAPTER VI

HANNIBAL'S BATTLEFIELD

THE battle swept on beyond Rome, and the R.A.S.C., alone of the Division, was vouchsafed no rest but was kept busy supplying the two armoured divisions that were leading Eighth Army's advance—6 British and 6 South African. When the time came for the Division to go forward, on June 8, after less than a week's rest, it was an exhausted R.A.S.C. that lifted it to Rignano, its concentration area, fifteen miles north of Rome.

The roads were littered with the debris of a retreating army, a retreating army that had been harried and hounded from the air—burnt-out vehicles and tanks, and slit trenches by the roadside strewn with charred and broken equipment. (One staff officer of the Division was to write later that "at no stage of the campaign did we get clearer evidence of the support we were getting from the air. It was most encouraging to see the results of air attack on the retreating Germans, whose casualties at this stage must have been enormous.")

There was a tantalising glimpse of Rome itself, its domes and roof-tops silvered by moonlight, and then a sharp reminder that there was a new battle ahead when, at Rignano, Divisional headquarters was heavily shelled and two of its oldest hands— two despatch-riders of Divisional Signals—killed outright.

General Alexander, impressed by the scope of the victory at Rome and by the extent to which the enemy was disorganised, had already signalled new objectives to his army commanders. Fifth Army was to make for Pisa, Eighth Army for Florence: the enemy, it was considered, was too weakened to delay them long, let alone to make effective counter-attacks.

Thirteen Corps was astride the Tiber, with 6 British Armoured Division on the east of the river, 6 South African and 78 Division on the west, the Division screening the South

Africans' right. For a time the Division had under command 66 Medium Regiment, R.A., whose longer range and heavier shell were to prove useful in the battles immediately ahead. It was commanded by Lt.-Col. Thuillier, D.S.O.

The rate of advance to Orvieto and beyond was conditioned only by the congestion on the roads and the cluttered wreckage left behind by the Germans. The London Irish had a brush with the enemy at Pianicciale, but most of the way the Division was entering towns and villages already taken by the Americans and South Africans. For many units it was something of a triumphal procession again—flowers, wine and cheering Italians—as it had been in the early days in Southern Italy.

56 Recce Regiment, especially, was having a spectacularly successful run. For the time being it was operating as an independent task force, and Lt.-Col. Chavasse had under his command a squadron of Warwickshire Yeomanry, "A" Company of the Royal Irish Fusiliers, two troops of 315/105 Anti-Tank Battery, a battery of 17 Field Regiment, and a detachment of 237 Field Company, R.E. The main body protected the right flank of the advancing South Africans, along the west bank of the Tiber, while "A" Squadron, on the extreme right of the regiment, kept in touch with the British armour on the other side of the river, where the advance was slower.

In its advance from Orvieto to the shores of Lake Trasimene the regiment killed 145 Germans, took 121 prisoners, captured or destroyed 26 guns of over 26 mm. calibre, 55 machine guns, and 37 assorted vehicles including—of all things—one lorry-load of French brandy and sweets.

Such prizes must, in fact, have given a buccaneering flavour to the regiment's customary dash: this was a rich country of castles and villas, all with well-stocked cellars and the contents of which could either be looted with a light heart as having been left behind by the Germans or were freely dispensed by welcoming Italian landlords.

It was an exciting chase while it lasted, but it had its risks and even its horrors, as Lt. Foster of the Inniskillings discovered. Reconnoitring alone, on a motor-bicycle, a village near Orvieto that had been reported clear, he was taken prisoner by a German platoon commanded by a nineteen-year old officer. He travelled with them as they retreated to the north-east, avoiding all roads. The Germans had no rations and lived on the country, but they were in good heart. The day after Foster's capture the platoon was fired on by Italian partisans from a farm, some of the Germans being killed. Foster had to watch them counter-attack and kill all the inhabitants of the farm, including the women and children. Later that same day they ran into the British and Foster escaped in the confusion, having covered fifty miles in his couple of days as a prisoner.

On June 15, 11 Brigade had passed through the Irish Brigade, crossed the River Paglia, and continued the advance. By this time the forward troops of the Division were a hundred miles north of Rome and half-way to Florence. But it could not be expected to go on at this rate. The Germans were bound to make some sort of a stand before we approached Florence so as to delay us, cause what damage they could, and save as much of their own armies as possible.

It was necessary, too, for the Germans to bolster up the morale of their troops, which was suffering as a result of the disorganised retreat from Rome. A diary captured with an officer of the 3 Parachute Regiment gives an indication of what a long retreat does to discipline:

"June 13. It is daylight and the trucks still stand in convoy on the road. They will again become victims of the fighter bombers no doubt. . . .

"June 14. The corn is ripe but there is nobody to reap it. The Italians don't bother about anything. Young fellows are wandering about everywhere. The 'niggers' have no organisation. The German soldier is disgusted with this behaviour. No German soldier can go anywhere alone because the instances of guerrillas surrounding them are multiplying. . . .

"June 16. We need every man. . . . The nerve strain grows and sleep is lacking. The present inferiority in both men and material is hard on morale. Above all our Luftwaffe is lacking. We have to burrow like moles. . . .

"June 18. An all-day battle. The enemy (from North

Africa) attacks company positions. According to orders I conduct a fighting withdrawal from one line to another. . . . In spite of instructions about march discipline the men are impossible on a night march. The moral I draw from it is that in training first of all one must accustom oneself to hardships. I myself carry a typewriter on this march.

"June 19. . . . We caught a couple of geese but nobody enjoys them because the fellows are so exhausted and worn out. Everybody is waiting for the mail which we have not had for a long time. Enemy is attacking the battalion sector supported by tanks and manages to break through: situation is critical. . . ."

At midday on June 16 the Northamptons launched an attack on Monte Gabbione, mid-way between Orvieto and Lake Trasimene, supported by artillery, by the Wiltshire Yeomanry, and support-group mortars. They met stiff opposition and the capture of this little town proved to be one of the best actions ever fought by the battalion. The town stood on a hill and completely overlooked our approach. The battalion formed up in a wood—the country was close and co-operation with tanks therefore difficult. After an initial concentration "A" company, whose task it was to capture the town, advanced. The first 2,000 yards were simple, under the cover of the trees, but as soon as they reached the open they were greeted with volleys of rifle fire. 8 platoon, led by Lt. Terry, advanced to the school, one of the key points of the town, whilst 9 platoon, led by Lt. Pulleyn, soon to be wounded in both arms, advanced to a large building on the right and 7 platoon remained below as fire platoon. After a brief skirmish the school and the building were taken; and the platoons were joined by Company Headquarters in the school where for several hours they were under rifle and machine-gun fire from houses opposite. Meanwhile, "C" company, led by Major Newby, had entered the town and the men of 7 platoon, occupying a house near by, had to leap thirty feet from the veranda, one by one, when the building went up in flames. Major Crocker, of "S" company making his way back to battalion headquarters, below the town, was led by the padre, Captain Elworthy, and was able to direct the fire from the Wiltshires' tanks on to the points still in enemy hands. The expected counter-attack never came, and when "C" company entered the town next morning they found the enemy had withdrawn during the night.

That same afternoon saw the East Surreys, on the left of the Northamptons, and at this time under command of 9 Armoured Brigade, heavily engaged at Citta della Pieve, a little hillside town nearly two thousand feet above sea level, where the enemy's 1 Parachute Division was covering the withdrawal of the battle groups of 334 Division, on their left. It was over Citta della Pieve that Capt. Cowan, commanding the Division's Air O.P. flight was killed. He was shot down while reconnoitring forward landing grounds near the town. Thirty men of the Royal Irish Fusiliers, under Lt. Manson, were also supporting 9 Armoured Brigade as lorried infantry. Two thousand yards short of the town they met heavy resistance but this was overcome partly by the daring of Cpl. Patton and Fusilier Bell, M.M., and thirty of the enemy were captured. They reached the centre of the town but were ordered to withdraw and the enemy at once recaptured the position. 36 brigade was sent forward, therefore, to by-pass the town and, after meeting opposition from snipers and machine-guns, by dark of June 18 was well to the north of it. For the first 500 yards they advanced along the crest of a ridge in full view of Citta del Pieve, before turning on to the main road through the thick—and welcome—woods that surrounded the town. That evening we intercepted an enemy wireless message giving their time of withdrawal. At that time, plus five minutes, the whole divisional artillery plastered the exits from the town for two minutes. Next morning, the Buffs, taking over from the East Surreys, found the outskirts littered with the bodies of German paratroopers. The few who remained alive subjected us to what General Keightley afterwards described as the deadliest sniping he had seen in the war (he had a narrow escape himself when his field-glasses were shattered by a sniper's bullet) but their final opposition was overcome by the Buffs and the Royal West Kents, who pushed through the town and on to the high ground beyond.

It was now, just when the time had come for the enemy to make a stand, that rain came to hamper our advance and our air cover and to give him the opportunity he needed to strengthen his defences. The Argylls, leading 36 Brigade towards Vaiano over rugged country, had a thirty-six hour march in heat and heavy rain, with only four hours' rest and a sharp skirmish in the village of Strada on the way.

The Argylls attacked Vaiano as night fell, under artillery fire, and were engaged until midnight in close fighting among the scattered houses and gardens on the outskirts of the town. At 2 a.m. an enemy counter-attack overran the outlying platoon and the Argylls were forced to withdraw, with one man killed, sixteen wounded, and thirty-six missing. The town was held by a full enemy battalion, who put up the stiffest resistance the Argylls had met since Alatri.

On June 21 the Buffs passed through the Argylls and attacked positions between Strada and Vaiano intending, but failing, to take Vaiano.

36 Brigade was now relieved by 28 Brigade from 4 Division (the Argylls by a battalion of Hampshires whom they had relieved during the battle for Hunt's Gap in February 1943 and to whom they were able to hand back their telephone exchange which the Argylls had salvaged). Orders had been received for the Division to be withdrawn completely from the line and to go to Egypt for a rest, and the advance parties were already on their way, but the enemy was settling himself strongly south of Lake Trasimene, our advance was halted, and it was clear that the Division had some fighting to do before it could leave the line.

The leading troops were in sight now of Lake Trasimene, vast and placid, its surrounding slopes thickly wooded. It was here that Hannibal had destroyed a Roman army in his march from the north; what was in store for the invaders of 2,000 years later, advancing from the south? The first success, at any rate, went to the Germans: the Lancashire Fusiliers, advancing towards the lake with the East Surreys on their left and the Northamptons on their right, and supported by tanks of the Warwickshire Yeomanry, were thrown back from the strongly held village of San Fatucchio on June 20.

At eleven that night a strong fighting patrol of the Lancashire Fusiliers tried to force their way into the village, which overlooked our line of advance. The forward troops were shelled, mortared and sniped at, and the three companies to the south of the village failed to make much headway. The next day the Fusiliers supported the London Irish in still another and, this time, stronger attack on the village, supported by tanks of the Canadian 11 Armoured Brigade (who had just replaced the 3 Hussars). The guns of 17 Field Regiment, supporting the London Irish, were unable to put down adequate cover as the forward troops were too close to the target area, but the Canadian tanks got behind the town and tipped the scale. An hour later "E" Company of the London Irish blasted their way into the first block of buildings after bitter hand-to-hand fighting, while "F" Company was having a bloody battle at close quarters in the cornfields. By midday the resistance in the town collapsed and we entered the town to find fifty dead Germans in the streets, many of them the victims of the final charge by the London Irish, who for the second time in six weeks had fought a successful battle that had cost them a hundred casualties. But the success was due primarily to the enterprise and spirit of the Canadian tank men, who had found ways round the town that the Warwickshire Yeomanry, by sticking to the roads, had not suspected.

There was to be no let-up for the Irish Brigade. The artillery switched on to the cemetery at San Felice, just beyond San Fatucchio, and the same afternoon the London Irish assaulted the cemetery and after half-an-hour's tough fighting entered the church. An hour later the Germans counter-attacked the cemetery but were caught by the 17 Field Regiment and by our mortars, and thrown back. By now all companies of the London Irish were down to a third of their strength and the tank losses, too, had been heavy. After two hours' fighting in the ripe corn and orchards, the cross-roads were captured and yet another counter-attack was broken up by artillery and mortar-fire. Meanwhile the Inniskillings had advanced on the right and attacked the village of Pucciarelli. After three hours of hard fighting, during which Capt. Roy Irwin, commanding "A" Company, was badly wounded, they reached their objectives. That night there was still an enemy pocket between the Inniskillings and the London Irish. Next morning the

Inniskillings were counter-attacked by forty infantry and a self-propelled gun which did a good deal of damage, but the London Irish were attacking towards them and clearing the ridge between them with the help of tanks and artillery. House after house and room after room was blasted until every German had escaped, been wounded or taken prisoner. But it took all afternoon and the whole of the next day before the London Irish were firmly established in San Fatucchio and the Inniskillings in Pucciarelli.

It was necessary now for the Eighth Army to prepare a fully organised attack to break through past Lake Trasimene. The attack was to be delivered by XIII Corps, strengthened by 4 British Infantry Division, with 78 Division on the right advancing along the western shore of the lake, 4 British Division on their left, and further left again the South Africans who were having a hard battle for Chiusi.

The attack opened on June 24 with an artillery concentration half of which was provided by the Division's three field regiments. The Irish Brigade was to take the village of Pescia and Ranciano, just inland from the lake and south of the tiny river Pescia, not much more than a narrow ditch at this time of the year, but still an effective anti-tank obstacle, and with the enemy dug in on its far bank. The actual crossing was to be the task of 36 Brigade, which was to pass through the Irish Brigade once the villages had been taken. Eleven Brigade was on the right, along the shores of Lake Trasimene itself.

At half-past five in the morning the Royal Irish Fusiliers attacked in the centre, supported by 11 Canadian Armoured Regiment. The Inniskillings, on the right, were on high ground, and the London Irish on the left. It was slow and hard fighting for the Fusiliers against heavy artillery and mortar-fire and concentrations from nebelwerfers, but the Canadians did magnificent work, knocking out one Mark V Panther and two Mark IV specials. By late afternoon one company was in Ranciano and another in Pescia. They had taken eighty-five prisoners at a cost of forty casualties all told. No officers were killed, but the battalion commander, Lt.-Col. James Dunnill, was taken prisoner the next day when, visiting the forward companies in a tank, along with Major Anderson, of 17 Field

Regiment, and Lt. Gamble, the battalion's acting Intelligence Officer, the tank driver took the wrong turning and drove into the midst of the enemy.

For the time being the Northamptons came under command of the Irish Brigade and by that evening, with tank support, they were clearing the mouth of the Pescia.

But it was the turn now of 36 Brigade to come through and cross the stream, and at six in the evening the Buffs were over, digging themselves into a small bridgehead; the Wiltshire Yeomanry's tanks had been unable to make the crossing. There was heavy shelling of the Buffs in the bridgehead, of the Royal West Kents on the near side of the river, and of the sappers erecting a Bailey bridge. This, together with heavy rain now beginning to fall, and with the failure of the tanks to make the crossing before the bridge had been built, all combined to slow down operations for the night. But the beginning had been made, and the Division had already taken 210 prisoners.

The German shelling seemed to be directed from O.Ps. at Castiglione del Lago, a village on a small promontory jutting out into the lake, a little to the north. At seven the next morning, June 25, the Royal West Kents crossed the Bailey bridge that the sappers had erected under the heavy shelling and in the heavy rain, and an hour later the Argylls and the Northamptons followed.

The crossing was hazardous and the shelling was among the heaviest the Division had experienced. There was no slackening on the far side of the stream, either, and the many casualties included Major Neil Webster, commanding "B" company of the Argylls. At 10.30 that morning "Y" company drove the enemy section from one farmhouse, and an hour later one of its platoons, only eighteen strong, led by Lt. Stephan, killed eleven Germans and captured three in taking yet another farm. The Argylls had two killed that day and fourteen wounded, among them Major Pat Spens. The Royal West Kents had passed the Buffs in the morning but had been unable to enter Castiglione del Lago in face of the heavy mortar and machine-gun fire under which they had suffered heavily. It was a grim day for the Northamptons, too. After crossing the Pescia they occupied a house where they were shelled and mortared all day and all night, and had to be withdrawn the following day.

That night two Italians volunteered to reconnoitre Castiglione de Lago. They set off at midnight by boat and returned at 3 a.m. to say that there were only patrols in the town, not a full occupying force, though there was a battery of guns in action. But 36 Brigade was not to reach Castiglione yet: they held their ground throughout the next day while the other two brigades straightened the line to their rear. The Germans were reported to be reinforcing and had brought over the 104 Panzer Grenadier Regiment from Perugia. The Argylls were on the left, furthest from the lake, and that day suffered nine casualties from shelling. Just behind them and on the right the Royal West Kents were particularly heavily shelled and mortared; their considerable casualties included Brigadier James, commanding 36 Brigade, killed by gunfire ahead of the Royal West Kents' positions. He had been commanding the Brigade since April, and was succeeded by Brigadier Packard, D.S.O., O.B.E., who had been commanding the Divisional Artillery, which he now handed over to Brigadier Hollbrook, M.C., the commander of 6 Army Group Royal Artillery, who was lent to the Division for the few days' action, before the move to Tivoli, near Rome.

That night 56 Recce, now under command of the Division again, relieved the two right-hand companies of the battle-scarred Royal West Kents, and stopped the gap as infantry, spread out in various shells of farm houses and stables, to be ready in the event of a counter-attack. It never came because the whole strength of the Trasimene position had rested, as in Hannibal's day, in the Fatucchio feature. Once that had gone the position was bound to crumble. Even so, the regiment took three days and three nights of heavy shelling and mortaring in not particularly well-protected positions: the ruins offered only flimsy protection, and the ground was solid rock into which it was impossible to dig.

What loosened the German defence was the British advance on either side of the Division's salient. On the left the South Africans cleared Chiusi on June 26 and were now on their way to Montepulciano, level with the Division (though it was June 30 before they took the town). To the right—east, that is, of the lake—6 Armoured Division, of X British Corps, reached the Division by June 27, when it entered the outskirts of Magione.

That same day the Lancashire Fusiliers went forward, through summer showers and against heavy shelling, but without making any contact with enemy infantry.

Four Division advanced on the left the following day, but it was 56 Recce, leading 78 Division, that reported the first signs that the enemy was withdrawing, after having held us for a week in front of Castiglione del Lago.

A patrol from "B" Squadron, under Capt. Lampard, was ordered forward to capture a house just short of the town proper. They had only lifted a few key mines from the mine field surrounding the house before they were fired on, but the troop which followed them found that meanwhile the enemy had evacuated the house. Next morning "B" Squadron went forward on foot to Castiglione del Lago to reconnoitre the town and lift the mines from the road. They found the town clear and "A" Squadron, now on wheels, moved forward, by-passing the town, and continued the journey north. By the afternoon of the hot June day they were well north of Castiglione with 7 Troop operating on the right, and 8 Troop, under Lt. Ridley, took an enemy platoon by surprise, killed eight of them and wounded half-a-dozen before the rest took to their heels and disappeared into the corn. The next village had been evacuated by the Germans only half-an-hour before, and Ridley's men stopped only long enough for a glass of wine at the big house and, four miles beyond it, found themselves in the middle of a German company area. Here a small battle developed whilst the two armoured cars blasted the farm occupied by the German headquarters. A British sergeant was badly wounded in the leg from twenty yards' range when calling the Germans to battle. His car had been rendered powerless by Schmeisser fire from a top-floor window of the farm, and the driver could find no way of getting his car out of the farmyard. He was rescued by the driver of the other car who came forward and silenced the man at the window, gladdened meanwhile to hear the heavy rumble that meant that the tanks of the Warwickshire Yeomanry were moving up to the rescue. The tanks cleared the farm and the Germans guns and vehicles in the wood beyond.

By the last day of the month the Buffs and the Royal West Kents were resting in Castiglione del Lago and the Argylls on the left of 56 Recce, were already in the village of Piana, a mile or so north of Castiglione, mopping up the sniper posts. The shelling and mortaring were slackening now, and the East Surreys, ahead of 36 Brigade, were up to the River Spina, which runs into the north end of the lake, before they made contact with the enemy. The Northamptons had been moved forward to Piana by the R.A.S.C. along bad, hot and dusty roads. From there they attacked, after a heavy artillery concentration, and found the land ahead clear of the enemy, though littered with the victims of our artillery fire. On the morning of July 1 they moved forward, supported by a squadron of Wiltshire Yeomanry, occupied Gaggla and Padre il Monelli without opposition, and sent out patrols as far as the River Spina.

The battle for Hannibal's lake had come to an end in the sticky July heat, the enemy obliged to give way before the weight and accuracy of the artillery concentration and by the dovetailing of the attacks of each division, on both sides of the lake.

Now the Division could leave for the rest it had been promised before the battle for Lake Trasimene had developed: the Irish Brigade, which had been in reserve for several days, had already begun to move back south, and when, on the night of July 1, the Royal West Kents and the Buffs relieved the Northamptons and the East Surreys, 11 Brigade moved back to Panicarola.

For two days the Buffs and the Royal West Kents continued to advance against decreasing resistance and eventually abandoned the pursuit at Cortona, well to the north of the lake. 56 Recce was advancing along the railway line, hammered by self-propelled guns all day and most of the night, and having continually to make diversions as the Germans had blown up all the bridges in their retreat. They were the last to be relieved, but by July 4 the whole of the Division was out of the line, the pursuit handed over to 6 British Armoured Division.

CHAPTER VII

EGYPTIAN INTERLUDE

THE Division's first halt on its way to Egypt was at Tivoli, in the Sabine Hills, a few miles east of Rome—a town where the ruins, such as those of Hadrian's Villa, were the work not of gunfire but of time, and where the cicadas' chirping replaced the intermittent crackle of small arms that had provided the daily obbligato further north. There were visits to Rome itself, shrill with G.I.s and shoe-shine boys, but still capable of charming the descendants of those who had marched as captives in Caesar's triumph. And for the faithful, the pious, and the merely curious—4,000 of them—there was an audience with the Pope.

Then south to Taranto, past the scene of hard-won victory at Cassino, the men crammed in dusty insanitary trains, baking in the summer heat, and then a blessed interval at sea, the Mediterranean a sparkling blue and Sicily, once a battlefield, now a grey and green memory on the starboard horizon.

The Division disembarked at Port Said, and took up its new quarters at Qassasin, twenty miles from Ismailia, seventy from Cairo. The rest-camp was in the middle of a desert, a serried mass of white tents seeming to extend for miles in every direction. The thermometer seldom fell below a hundred degrees Fahrenheit in the shade—too hot during the day to do anything but lie sweating on a bed waiting for the cooler evenings. But the camp was well-organised, there were running-water and shower-baths, a very well stocked N.A.A.F.I., clubs and cinemas. From here every man had five days' leave to Cairo, Alexandria, or Ismailia. The senior officers stayed at Shepheard's or the Continental in Cairo, or at the Cecil in Alexandria—for the junior officers there were the Grand and the Royal Oak at Cairo and the Méditerranée or Claridge's at Alexandria. Sergeants and below could stay on a house-boat moored near Gezirah Island and the Gezirah Club was open to all officers; the pavilion and part of the grounds to other ranks.

It seemed a treat merely to be able to walk on pavements again and to buy the absurd semi-necessities of townsfolk—a pleasure that many in the Division had not experienced for two years. But the prices were appalling and many a man learnt the provenance of the verb "to gyp".

It had been intended that the Division should first of all rest and refresh itself in Egypt, and then move to Palestine for two months' training, but after only a fortnight in Egypt orders were received to return to Italy as soon as possible. It was guessed, rightly, that the unexpectedly tough resistance on the Gothic Line and the transfer of many of the allied troops from Italy to the Second Front was the reason for this recall. However it was still another month before the Division left, and, as it was not worth while going to Palestine, training and re-fitting was carried out in the desert. Special attention was paid to co-operation with tanks—chiefly by lectures and discussions—and the men were drilled in the quick consolidation and reinforcement of platoons and companies that had captured objectives. The 56 Recce Regiment took over the Greyhound armoured cars that were to replace its Humbers, and R.E.M.E. found itself busy with modifications.

But there was still plenty of time for recreation. The Irish Brigade moved to Sidi Bishr, near Alexandria, in a camp near the sea which had good facilities for bathing and plenty of opportunities for trips to Alexandria, where there were balls and parties, race-meetings and luxurious restaurant meals. 11 Brigade moved to Beni Yusef, near Cairo, in a camp which boasted wooden huts and a view of the Pyramids. 36 Brigade remained in Qassasin.

It was while the Division was in Cairo that, smarting under the insolent profiteering and open contempt of the tradesmen and hangers-on of this typical "back area", the British troops broke for once out of their tradition of discipline, and lost the patient good-temper which distinguished them from the perhaps less tolerant Dominion and American units. A night of inexcusable but easily understandable riot in Cairo cost the shopkeepers some three thousand pounds' worth of damage and more than a hundred men from the Division nursed their hangovers overnight in jails and guardrooms.

Towards the end of August the transport began to go back to Italy: by mid-September the whole Division was back at Taranto, and after a few more days' training set off north again with another winter campaign in Italy to look forward to, but this time better equipped—especially in the way of extra blankets and heavy clothing—than it had been in the Sangro valley and the Southern Apennines. The battalions had been brought up to full strength—mostly by large drafts of men from anti-aircraft and anti-tank units and by R.A.S.C. officers, many of whom had not been in action in forward areas before but who were soon to prove their worth.

While the Division was in Egypt it received a signal from Eighth Army ordering all U.K. infantry battalions to re-organise on a three-company basis. This was most unpopular with all battalion commanders, whose experience was that the fourth company had often turned the day in previous battles and who said they would rather fight with four companies of two platoons each than with three companies of three platoons. It was eventually decided that each battalion would continue to fight at the existing war establishment until reduced below 33 officers and 701 other ranks, including the first-line reinforcements; only then would a battalion be reorganised on a three-company basis.

It was also while in Egypt that the Division was brought up to the full scale of G.1098 equipment—including transport—for the first time since its formation in Scotland. In Africa, Sicily, and the first Italian campaign it had been on light scales, largely to give greater mobility. Even now the Division's A/Q decided to keep the extra vehicles and equipment in a divisional reserve: the Division remained, therefore, as mobile as ever but with a reserve that was to prove of great benefit in the coming campaign in Italy, when fast-moving items of clothing, for instance, were replaced by the Division itself in a matter of days—replacements that otherwise might never have been possible.

Just before leaving for Egypt the 6 Inniskillings had been disbanded by orders from the War Office. The Irish Brigade lamented the loss of a fine fighting battalion which had landed with the rest of the brigade in November 1942. The same regiment's second battalion (already in Egypt) took their place —transferred from 5 Division, in which it had fought with great distinction in France and later in Italy, on the Garigliano and at Anzio. It was possible, fortunately, to keep most of the men of the 6 Inniskillings in the brigade. Lt.-Col. Scott, commanding the 2 Inniskillings was to remain in command; Lt.-Col. Bredin, just back from hospital, was to command the London Irish, and Lt.-Col. Horsfall the Irish Fusiliers.

While in Egypt, General Keightley was ordered to relinquish his command of 78 Division and to take command of V Corps. He had commanded the Division since December 1943, before which he had been in command of 6 Armoured Division in North Africa.

The departure of General Charles Keightley from the Division was a loss and a disappointment. During his command he had always stressed the importance of close co-operation with tanks. He had had a good deal of experience in dealing with armoured formations, and so his direction and advice were readily accepted. There is no doubt that this was directly responsible for lessening the casualty rate in the heavy fighting which fell to the lot of 78 Division.

General Keightley had a quick sense of humour and was well liked and respected by all ranks. He was a good judge of men, and rightly had no scruples about removing officers and other ranks if their efficiency was in question.

He had seen his Division through the heavy fighting at Cassino and in the exploitation which followed. Throughout his period of command of the Division he had shown balance and judgment, and it would be fair to say that he had never missed a chance of taking advantage of the enemy. Under him the Division had maintained its high reputation and had even enhanced it.

Naturally, therefore, all ranks saw him leave with genuine regret. He had served them well and had fought the Division with courage and skill. The blow was lessened by the fact that it was known that he was going to V Corps, and it was fairly certain that their ways would cross again in the future.

EGYPTIAN INTERLUDE

General Keightley left in July and Brigadier R. K. Arbuthnott, D.S.O., M.C., commander of 11 Brigade, took over the Division until the arrival in August of Major-General Butterworth, D.S.O., who held the appointment only until October, when he left owing to ill-health. Once again Brigadier Arbuthnott took over and after a month he was confirmed in the appointment and promoted Major-General.

Major-General Keith Arbuthnott was one of 78 Division's most faithful commanders, having taken command of 11 Brigade in the middle of the battle of Termoli and having commanded it in all the hard fighting at Cassino, through Rome and northwards.

Major-General Arbuthnott is a Scotsman by birth and he demonstrated all the characteristics which make them such tough fighters. He had been an instructor at the Staff College and so he combined a sound knowledge of the ethics of war, a quick eye for country, great energy and a steady nerve.

Both as a Brigade Commander and a Divisional Commander he had an immense number of extremely tough battles to fight and these he always undertook with complete confidence and invariably with the greatest possible success.

His ability to stage and fight infantry and tank attacks in quick succession by day and night, especially in the Argenta Gap fighting, was an achievement to be justly proud of.

In this fighting particularly he showed how quick decisions by the commander combined with well trained gallant troops can achieve outstanding success if the enemy can be kept off his balance by a series of quick blows. The enemy was never really able to recover himself at this stage chiefly due to Keith Arbuthnott's skill and determination.

He always watched his men's welfare and in the phases of operations when 78 Division was battling in snow and mud he never ceased to do all in his power to ameliorate the discomfort of the men of the Division, never sparing himself in the effort.

He possessed all the typical fighting qualities expected of a Commander of 78 Division and that is probably as great a compliment as it is possible to pay a commander in the last war.

He remained with the Division until nearly the end of its career—a much loved as well as a most successful commander.

The command of 11 Brigade was temporarily taken over by Lt.-Col. Mackenzie, who had a bar to both his D.S.O. and his M.C., and who had been commanding the Lancashire Fusiliers, leaving Brigadier Scott and Brigadier Packard in charge of the Irish and 36 Brigades respectively.

CHAPTER VIII

THE NORTHERN APENNINES

DURING the Division's three months' absence from the line Fifth and Eighth Armies had been plodding steadily but slowly up Italy, and after a good deal of hard fighting had broken into the Gothic Line. Into it, but not through it, for the so-called Gothic Line was not so much a line as a series of defences which made skilful use of the high broken northern Apennines north of the line from Pisa on the west to Pesaro on the east, below Rimini, and almost as far north as Bologna. Bologna, in fact, was the gateway to the plains of Lombardy, watered by the Po and its tributaries, and whilst the Germans, on the one hand, proposed to keep the allies in the mountains until the winter broke, it was the allies' intention to deploy their armour in the plains. Meanwhile they were faced not only with infantry positions and machine-gun and mortar emplacements but also—where the natural defences were weakest—with concrete pillboxes some of which had been fitted with tank turrets mounting anti-tank guns.

Nevertheless, by September 25, the day the Division began to move north from its assembly area at Taranto, Eighth Army had taken Rimini and begun to push slowly along Highway 9, the great Rimini–Bologna lateral, while Fifth Army was advancing on Bologna through the mountains to the north of Florence.

In Taranto the weather was already beginning to turn colder, and the Division got into battle-dress again for the move to the north, headed by 56 Recce in its new Greyhound armoured cars and by the Irish Brigade. The three-day journey along the Adriatic coast took the Division over three of its own chief battlegrounds—Termoli, the Trigno, and the Sangro—as well as past many a scene of minor brushes, often as memorable and perhaps as moving to this or that platoon or individual infantryman as that of a major battle.

The Division waited five days at Fano, forty miles south-east of Rimini on the Adriatic coast, in Eighth Army reserve, while its senior officers went ahead to visit V Corps' section of the Eighth Army front, or viewed it from the gigantic rock on which the tiny republic of San Marino is perched.

From here the Eighth Army positions from Savignano to Sanarchangelo could be seen—still only a little way along the Rimini–Bologna road. Here Eighth Army was already on the edge of the Lombardy plain, and finding that the endless succession of rivers, canals and ditches were even worse obstacles than the mountains and valleys through which they had previously forced their way at such a cost.

The first orders for the Division were to move forward on October 4 and to come under V Corps, now commanded by General Keightley, its old commander of only a few weeks before, but twenty-four hours before they were due to move up from Fano there was a sudden change of plan: they were to come under command of British XIII Corps, occupying the right sector of Fifth Army.

Fifth Army was in the central mountains, and preparing to make a determined effort to break into the plains of Bologna before winter came to make the mountain tracks impassable. XIII British Corps, right of Fifth Army, had been ordered to extend its front westward and take over the Firenzuola-Imola road, thus enabling II U.S. Corps to concentrate all its forces on the direct route to Bologna. As General Alexander, the Commander-in-Chief, pointed out to General Maitland Wilson, the Supreme Allied Commander, "... it is a slow and costly process and my fears now are that we may not be just strong enough to carry it through. I am reinforcing Fifth Army by giving them 78 Division for XIII Corps. It is my last remaining fully fresh division."

The Division moved from Fano at a few hours' notice and set off in trucks on its long journey south-west through the mountains in the pouring rain. The move was carried out entirely under verbal orders, and the Division's Military Police, as unobtrusively efficient as ever, proved to have done an excellent job in moving well ahead and signposting the route. It was thanks to them that "Follow the battle-axe" was as much in the way of orders as anyone needed. It meant thirty-six hours of continuous driving, and virtually everybody in the Division who could drive—officers, N.C.O.s, batmen—took a turn at the wheel so as to give the regular drivers a rest, and keep the vehicles moving.

After a pause at Assisi, the Division was halted at Figline, twenty-five miles south of Florence. The Irish Brigade was the first to move forward and by October 5 was concentrated in the Firenzuola area and that night began to relieve 351 Infantry Regiment of 88 (U.S.) Division astride the Imola road, just north of Castel del Rio. South of this village a long viaduct over the River Santerno had been demolished by the retreating Germans. The Americans had constructed a precipitous and muddy diversion which after two days' heavy rain had become almost impassable for the British transport, though the Americans with their superior vehicles were still managing to negotiate it. Virtually the whole of 64 Anti-tank and 49 L.A.A. Regiment were put to working with the sappers on road maintenance, largely in digging ditches meant to drain the road of liquid mud.

Until the bridge had been built over the destroyed viaduct, it was impossible for the Division to move towards Imola, where the axes of advance of Fifth and Eighth Armies would join. A bridge was put under way immediately, and what proved to be one of the highest Bailey bridges in existence was built—but even then it was impossible to pass more than one battalion a day over it. The chief reason for this was that all vehicles, on reaching the bridge, had to remove the chains needed for the muddy roads: they would have set up so much vibration as to endanger the bridge.

Like so much of the Italian countryside that the Division had fought over, the northern Apennines proved bad country for the attackers. Running northward from the mountains into the Lombardy plain are a number of fast-running rivers, the Senio, the Santerno and the Sillaro amongst them; near the sources they run fast over rocky beds and through deep gorges. By the sides of these rivers are the few main roads of the area, but they had never been intended for military traffic and in no time had disintegrated into muddy tracks, impassable

OCTOBER 5-7, 1944

for all wheels other than jeeps and soon not even for those. At this period 78 Division, the Guards Brigade and, for a time, 88 U.S. Division were all maintained along one of these roads which crossed and recrossed the River Santerno, at times climbing up the mountain side. There was barely room for two-way traffic along it and only room for one-way traffic over the Bailey or timber bridges. The forward troops and observation posts in the heights had to be maintained by mule from the beginning and as the roads deteriorated and the line advanced the mule-routes became longer and longer. Between the rivers mountain spurs ran down to the plain, all of them bleak and bare. The mountains consisted of clay, shale and loose stones and presented enormous precipices of slippery grey mud; many of the slopes were 300 feet high and in wet weather movement on them became almost impossible, deep as they were in sloppy, cloying mud. Into the sides of the spurs were cut deep gorges that carried tributaries to the main rivers. Any flat place there happened to be in this country was bound to be boggy, and the gun positions were individually chosen at hairpin bends, in river beds, along any flattish piece of road or on the hillside. The gunners found it prudent before occupying a position to see if it would be possible to get out again, when conditions might well have worsened under rain or heavy traffic. During this phase of the campaign many of the gunners' targets were fixed by means of air photographs. The country was badly mapped and, because of its steepness, unusually difficult for gunners entrusted with the close support of infantry. All the gunners who fought through the rugged Italian mountains at this time acknowledge a special debt of gratitude, too, to an Air O.P. flight commanded by Capt. Bernstein, D.F.C., R.A., whose small aircraft took off from crazy little landing-strips, never knowing whether they would be obscured by fog or mist when they came back to land.

The only buildings in the area were scattered farms of poor quality and here and there a hamlet of a dozen or so houses, all damaged. The only village of any size was Castel del Rio, which became the location first of Main and then of Rear Divisional H.Q., always—until the capture of Penzola in December— under the enemy's observation and often under shell-fire.

Bailey Bridge at Valsalva near Castel del Rio

Bridge near Castel del Rio

It was near here, just to the right of the road to Imola, that the Division went into the line. About five miles ahead of it was a forbidding cliff called the Vena del Gesso which stretched across the front for about eight miles from Monte Mauro to Monte Penzola with only a narrow gap at Tossignano through which the Castel del Rio–Imola road passed. A sheer face of cliff was facing the Division and the only possible way to overcome it seemed to be to turn the western end by capturing Monte del Acqua Salata, about four thousand yards west of Tossignano. To the right was 1 Guards Brigade on Monte Battaglia, the scene of bitter fighting for the last few weeks. Here the Guards, still harassed by raids, shelling and mortaring, were cut off from 1 Division, to whom they normally belonged. For the time being, therefore, they came technically under command of 78 Division but were not available for offensive operations. To the left 88 (U.S.) Infantry Division was advancing towards Sassoleone and Gesso.

The enemy, determined to prevent the Americans breaking through the mountains to Bologna, was heavily reinforcing his troops; the elements of seven German divisions were aligned between Monte Battaglia and the Sillaro river.

The plan was for the Division to advance along the line of the Imola road, safeguarding the right flank of the Americans' advance. The Americans, who had captured Monte Capello after a stiff fight, feared that it was being held too lightly, but it soon became apparent that the enemy was more interested in Monte Battaglia, to the east.

The Irish Brigade had two battalions in the line east of the Santerno by the night of October 5-6 and on the evening of the 6th the Royal Irish Fusiliers took over the Codronco spur, on the left of the Santerno and the Imola road. The Germans were still holding the eastern end of this spur, and on the next evening the Fusiliers made the first assault. Their object was to clear the enemy from the hill on the left of the spur (Point 382), and so help the Americans on. Three times that night "D" company tried to get among the houses on the hill, up the steep, slippery slopes of mud, and three times they were held up by fierce machine-gun fire. The company fought their way to within 400 yards of their objective and there consolidated around the

(Opposite) Maj.-Gen. R. K. Arbuthnott.

church throughout the day, whilst heavy shell-fire was brought to bear on the enemy's positions. At eight the next evening they attacked again and found that the enemy had withdrawn, leaving twenty dead behind.

The Division now had to take over another sector from 88 (U.S) Division. For this 11 Brigade was used, the Lancashire Fusiliers taking over the Montemorosino sector on October 10 and the East Surreys La Morea the following day. 56 Recce took over from the Royal Irish Fusiliers allowing the Irish Brigade to concentrate east of the Santerno.

The Division was ordered to advance astride the Imola road, down the Santerno valley on Imola. South and east of the river, the Irish Brigade was to advance towards the Vena del Gesso by taking a series of objectives up to Taverna. North and west of the river 11 Brigade was to take Point 508, Spaduro and Acqua Salata.

The Irish Brigade's operations were to depend on a considerable advance by the Division on the right, but as this did not take place the brigade's move was cancelled and the plan for 11 Brigade was put to the test.

By the time serious fighting began on October 13-14 the Americans had taken Gesso and Montes Falchetto and De la Tombe. They were fortunate in having a reasonable road to Sassoleone and were able to use tanks to get them to Gesso and De La Tombe. When we took over we had no metalled road beyond Sassoleone and the mud cart-tracks soon became impassable to vehicles, owing to rain, and tanks could not be used.

This, therefore, was the position on 11 Brigade's front: our line ran from the Filetto spur 4,000 yards north of Castel del Rio up the spur to La Morea on the west side of the Ravine de Madonna del Rio to Gesso. This hamlet, seized by the Americans after a fierce and prolonged struggle on October 12, was taken over by the Northamptons on the evening of October 13.

11 Brigade's first objective was Monte Pieve (Point 508) as a first step to moving on to Spaduro, Acqua Salata and beyond. Spaduro was now of particular importance as its possession by the Germans was a thorn in the side of the U.S. 11 Corps in their operations against Monte Grande.

But first Point 508 had to be taken—a difficult proposition, protected as it was by the formidable ravines of Madonna and Filetto. The only reasonable approach was along the narrow neck from Gesso. This allowed for the deployment of one battalion at most on a one or two company front. But it was thought that it might be possible to gain a footing at the southern and lowest tip of the feature across the Filetto Torrente.

Both were attempted in the night of October 13-14 by 11 Brigade (commanded since about the 11th by Lt.-Col. John Mackenzie of the Lancashire Fusiliers. It was unfortunate that this change of command in the brigade, caused by the promotion of Brigadier Arbuthnott to command the Division, happened at this particular moment.) At nightfall the Northamptons moved to a valley behind the East Surreys, who were holding the ground beyond San Apollinare, known as the "Twin Tits", to the west of Monte Pieve. From there they were to advance over open plough-land with little cover. The route was along the ridge running north-east through Gesso, turning eastward to Point 462, and then up the steep slope to Point 508. The plan was for "A" company to relieve the Americans on Point 462 and then for "D" company to pass through "A" at four in the morning and capture Point 508. "B" company would then follow supported by a squadron of Canadian tanks and capture Point 473 beyond. "A" company moved off at last light towards Gesso. Just short of the village many of the company were killed and wounded by anti-personnel mines. By the light of a burning haystack the rest of the company moved forward to Point 462, where they relieved the Americans, who climbed out of their fox-holes and silently withdrew. At 2 a.m. "D" moved to join "A" company, passing on the way the padre, Capt. Elworthy, who was evacuating casualties from "A" company, and by a quarter to four were on the start line waiting for the attack to go in. Then came the second disaster. The opening barrage fell short, killing six men, wounding seventeen, and smashing four Bren guns and two wireless sets; by the time the company had been reorganised, day was breaking, it was impossible to open the attack and the battalion withdrew.

Meanwhile, on the right, the Lancashire Fusiliers were making slow progress from the south. At the same time as the

Northamptons had been about to attack, they had taken their first objective, Rivaldino, against heavy machine-gun fire and after stiff fighting at close quarters. Handing over Rivaldino to a supporting company and a troop of 56 Recce, the Fusiliers pushed northward towards Casa Filetto and Casa Casino taking twenty-one prisoners on the way.

All through that early morning the Lancashire Fusiliers pressed forward against heavy machine-gunning and mortaring, and by 9 a.m. platoons of "B" Company had gained Point 328 but opposition was strong and the battalion was cramped in the deep wadi. It was therefore decided to give up the attempt. At eleven that night the whole battalion was withdrawn to its original positions. During the day one officer and six other ranks had been killed and three officers and forty-nine other ranks were wounded or missing.

As the Lancashire Fusiliers were withdrawing the Northamptons were making a freshly-planned attack. As soon as the barrage had lifted, "A" Company moved forward and were immediately involved, suffering fifteen casualties and by 2 a.m. it was decided that the attack had failed and the company withdrew. "C" Company was luckier and managed to get thirty-six men up to the building on Point 508. They dug in where they could—on the sparse, steep side of the peak, or among the piles of massed rubble that had once been houses. Two platoons of "B" Company were ordered up the hill to help them but they too met such strong resistance that before reaching the summit they had run out of ammunition. The two platoons had to withdraw, leaving only twenty-five men on Point 508—and an hour later they too were forced to return, after having been strongly counter-attacked by flame-throwers.

At dawn the next morning, October 15, the Northamptons attacked for the third time, this time with the support of Canadian tanks. The attacks on Points 508 and 401 by "D" and "A" Companies were to be put in simultaneously behind an artillery smoke screen. It was impossible for the infantrymen to keep in contact with the tanks, which in any case came under intense fire as soon as they appeared. "D" Company was soon held up by machine-gun fire at the foot of Point 508, while on the left "A" Company was forced into broken ground on the left and lower sides of the valley. Each man was fired on as he sprinted down the hill and the depleted company made quick dashes from cover to cover towards the farm on Point 401 and reached their objective successfully. Meanwhile the tanks went to the rescue of "D" Company with their 75 mm. guns and machine-guns blazing—a heartening racket to the men on the ground. But engine trouble halted the leading tank and the others were unable to pass it on the narrow track.

There was no wireless link between the tanks and the infantry, and communication had to be maintained by battering with a shovel on the tank's side until somebody put his head out to see what was the matter. The company tried again to advance over the mere 200 yards interval that separated them from their objective, but the casualties mounted and again they had to withdraw. "A" Company remained on their objective throughout the day within a stone's throw of the enemy; but their casualties had been too great and at night they too made their way back to the main positions around Gesso. At nightfall the battalion were all together—the 165 of them who were left of the fighting echelon; there had been ninety-three casualties.

It was now the East Surreys' turn to attack, their zero hour being midnight of October 15-16. It was hoped that there would be more chance if the attack was made later as it would give the enemy less time to mount a counter-attack before dawn. The attack went in under a heavy barrage with "B" Company on the right, "C" on the left. The companies gained the upper slopes of the hill under intense fire. But from here the ascent developed into a sheer cliff, making cover from mortar fire impossible. The enemy dropped grenades on the attacking troops and raked them with small-arms fire. A small party did reach the top only to be forced to withdraw after heavy losses. The attack had failed again.

On October 16 a new army plan was issued. 88 U.S. Division was to operate north of the Sillaro, 78 Division between the Sillaro and the Santerno and our positions south of the Santerno were to be taken over by 6 Armoured Division. On our right flank the other divisions of XIII Corps, 8 Indian, 1 and 6 Armoured, were echeloned back far behind us, on wide fronts with poor communications. The first two had been

OCTOBER 16-19, 1944

in action continuously for a long time. There was now, therefore, no question of any advance south-east of the Santerno, which meant that we could not use the Santerno valley for operations.

On our own front were two main ridges running from south-west to north-east but joined together at Monte Pieve, Point 508. From there north-eastward they were divided by the Sallustra valley.

Both ranges consisted of a series of peaks joined by a narrow ridge, dotted with stoutly constructed buildings, sometimes a farm, sometimes a church.

Running at nearly right angles from these main ridges, subsidiary spurs ran out. These were invariably extremely steep on their south-west face, often sheer cliffs of hard clay, but much more gentle on the north-east. Our communications were very poor. The enemy had a network of roads based on Highway 9—many good roads running into the hills behind their forward positions. They also had good billets.

It was obvious that we would have to force our way along both the two main ridges, as one could not be taken and held without the other, but before that could begin we should still have to seize first Point 508 and secondly Monte Spaduro.

By now 36 Brigade was available and while 11 Brigade sidestepped to the north-west 36 took over the Pieve sector with the task of continuing north-east to take Monte Acqua Salata and Monte Verro; 11 Brigade was to form a firm base for this attack and the Irish Brigade, after the capture of Monte Pieve, was to advance and capture Monte Spaduro.

The attack by 36 Brigade was launched on the night of October 18. The Buffs were to attack down the causeway from Gesso, the Royal West Kents across the Filetto at Madonna del Rio and the Argylls to clear the ridge to the north and capture Points 401 and 416.

A particularly heavy barrage was put down, and the infantry moved forward with the utmost caution, mindful of the punishment their sister brigade had taken over this bare and exposed approach. But all was anti-climax, for there was no opposition, and it was clear, as the men reached their objective, that the Germans had withdrawn—and only a few hours before.

It is impossible even now to understand why. Monte la Pieve was far the best observation post in the area and 11 Brigade's costly failure was proof of its immense strength. The only possible explanation seems to be that 11 Brigade had in fact taken such a toll of the defenders, and shown such determination, that the German commander, realising that a much heavier assault would follow and would prove too much for him, decided to shorten his line.

From the top of Monte la Pieve 36 Brigade could see its next objective—Monte Acqua Salata, a thousand yards away to the east, at the end of a narrow causeway. This lay 300 feet below the hill summits; it was not more than ten yards wide in several places and both of its sides fell away in precipitous clay for yet another 300 feet. Acqua Salata with its subsidiary features, Monte del Verro to the north and Monte Penzola to the south, formed an approach to the Vena del Gesso on the other side of the Santerno river.

Patrols from the Argylls reported that the enemy was still holding the hill, and plans were made for its immediate capture by the Buffs. A two-company attack was arranged that night (October 19-20), to capture a group of farm buildings to the northern end of the Acqua Salata ridge. The men were tired after their advance of the night before and made slow progress through the muddy clay against heavy fire. There was no room to deploy, the causeway was mined, and as dawn broke the farm was still in the enemy's hands. The battalion had to retreat to its original position, having suffered fifteen casualties.

The Royal Irish Fusiliers had already taken over the Argylls' newly-won positions on Points 401 and 416, preparatory to an atttack on Monte Spaduro farther on. Monte Spaduro ran north from Monte la Pieve; it was a massive feature stretching north and south for two miles, shutting off—as long as it was in enemy hands—all progress towards the Lombardy plain and the town of Castel San Pietro, between Imola and Bologna on Highway 9. It presented to the south a front shaped like a horse-shoe, with a re-entrant in the centre seamed with deep ravines and gulleys. Between it and Monte la Pieve were smaller hills, among them Point 387, the approach to which was along a narrow neck guarded by a house called Casa di Spinello, which proved to be the key to the capture of Spaduro. North of Spaduro on the other side of the Sillaro was another important hill, Monte Grande, which the Americans were now attacking and were shortly to capture.

The Irish Fusiliers attacked at nightfall towards Monte Spaduro, at the same time as the Buffs were attacking towards Acqua Salata. "A" Company led in the darkness followed by "B" Company. An hour later "A" Company had a foothold on 387 ridge, having taken the enemy by surprise. They soon overcame the opposition there and a number of Germans were killed or taken prisoner. "B" Company then passed through and attacked towards Point 396, the peak of Monte Spaduro. They soon ran into trouble in a group of buildings which was strongly held; having overcome that they then found themselves faced by an almost impassable cliff. For an hour in the darkness patrols tried to find a place where this cliff could be scaled and, having found one, it took another hour to haul the men up on the ridge above—but by dawn the battalion had attacked and captured the height. However, as the mist lifted the enemy machine-guns opened up and at six o'clock a strong counter-attack came in against both companies. Casa Spinello, which the Irish Fusiliers had by-passed during the night, turned out to be strongly held by the enemy. The Irishmen fought stubbornly but they were outnumbered; when they ran out of ammunition they flung rocks at the advancing Germans, battered at them with rifle-butts, or grappled with their bare hands. Only a few got back from each company. The bare rocky hillsides were littered with dead from both sides; forty Fusiliers were taken prisoner; and Capt. Graham, commanding "A" Company, was found on the battlefield in the middle of a litter of German and Irish dead, all riddled with bullets. A smoke-screen had to be put down at midday so that "C" Company, who had been trying to go forward to help, could be withdrawn to safety.

It was now decided to make no further attempt on Spaduro until Acqua Salata had been taken, so the Argylls were ordered to attack and capture Acqua Salata on the evening of October 20-21. The artillery fire began at 6.40 and twenty minutes later "R" and "B" Companies moved forward in the evening dusk.

Some shells landed on the companies as they were crossing the causeway, causing casualties, but the Argylls were soon fighting their way up the hill. They set on the Germans with Tommy guns, bayonets, and bare hands, hurling some of them down the hillside in the darkenss. By eight o'clock the first objectives had been taken. "X" Company, under Capt. Charters, was then sent forward through "R" Company to capture the farm at the foot of the ridge. They paused within fifty yards of the farm while a section under Cpl. George and L/Cpl. Kaminsky, M.M., a fluent German speaker, was sent forward to reconnoitre. A wounded German by the side of the track willingly told them the way, but a few minutes later a German patrol opened fire at five yards' range. It was plain that the farm's defences would have to be cleared methodically, and one platoon, under Sgt. Bell, M.M., killed three Germans, took four others prisoner, and knocked out two machine-gun positions, and by 10.15 "X" Company was able to fire its success signal. "Y" Company went forward with reserves of ammunition and by midnight Acqua Salata was in our hands.

The one factor, more than any other, that had made this small but fierce little attack successful was the co-ordination between infantry and artillery. The Argylls went in as soon as the barrage, put down by 138 Field Regiment, had lifted, and were on to the enemy before he had realised the barrage was over.

As soon as the Division knew that Acqua Salata was ours the London Irish began the Irish Brigade's second attack on Monte Spaduro. Once again the leading companies swung to the left of the Casa Spinello, where there was still a pocket of enemy, and found themselves in the gulleys. It was there that they were held up. They tried again and again to scramble on to the ridge but each time they met with accurate fire, and as dawn broke, after six hours' fighting, they dug their trenches in the gulleys and consolidated what gains they had been able to make. They lay there all day while the enemy's positions were shelled and machine-gunned; the Irish Fusiliers were firing their anti-tank guns from Gesso at Casa Spinello and at five o'clock the London Irish attacked again. Once more they tried to climb the steep ravines but the enemy, advantaged by the height, fought stubbornly and hard. After six more hours' fighting the London Irish were withdrawn.

In the meantime the Argylls' positions on Acqua Salata were in full view of the enemy on Monte Penzola and Monte Spaduro. Any movement they made was greeted with mortar fire, the regimental aid post receiving more than its share. Among the many wounded was the battalion's padre, Capt. Tyson, who had seen every action the battalion had fought for more than a year. During this period of exposure and frustration it came on to rain, and the men had to add to their discomfort by crouching in the wet sticky mud. It came as something of a relief when they were ordered forward to capture a farm, 400 yards ahead.

"Y" Company moved off in the darkness and under heavy machine-gun fire, suffering some casualties. But they were able to take the position at ten o'clock, along with half-a-dozen prisoners. It was not until dark on the following evening that the Argylls were relieved by the Royal West Kents. During the week they had lost 120 men and the survivors were weakened and battle-weary.

Yet another plan had been made for the capture of Monte Spaduro, which—it was now clear—was held much more strongly than had been originally thought. First the house, Casa di Spinello, had to be secured and then the main peak of the hill. It was to be a two-brigade attack on the night of October 23-24. The Irish Brigade on the right had as objectives: first Casa di Spinello, then Point 387, the Casa Salara ridge, and Point 362, just north of 387. 11 Brigade, the other brigade to do the attack, had as their objective the Spaduro feature (Point 396).

As a necessary preliminary to the attack the Sassatello Valley had to be occupied. The Northamptons moved forward on the night of October 21-22 and occupied Ripiano and all the farmhouses in the immediate area. It was from these houses that the Lancashire Fusiliers and the East Surreys attacked on the night of October 23.

The London Irish opened the battle with their attack on Casa di Spinello. An approach to the house had been found by a daylight patrol under Lt. Faye. This had surprised three Germans in a slit trench, killed one, wounded another, and gained invaluable information about the defences at Spinello from the third. "E" Company made the attack; they captured the house after a room-to-room battle, in which one German was even posted in the cellar to shoot up through the floorboards, and they held it against three counter-attacks. "F" Company had taken the outlying defences to the north and by 6.30 the house and twenty prisoners were in our hands.

The main attack was ordered for 10.30 that night, by which time 56 Recce, supported by fire from the Royal West Kents, had patrolled a thousand yards forward from positions south of Gesso to occupy two hills south-east of La Pieve. From here they could observe enemy positions on Monte Penzola to the south, thus exerting pressure on the enemy in a sector other than that of the main attack.

The Division's artillery was in full support. 17 Field Regiment was in action near Penzola, 132 in the hair-pin bends below Sassoleone, and 138 between the villages of Cuviolo and San Apollinare. They had the support of Sixth Army Group R.A., which included a battery of 7.2s. The German positions on Monte Spaduro had been carefully pin-pointed and registered.

The barrage came down and the Inniskillings moved down the Sassatello valley to attack from the left flank. As soon as the barrage lifted, they made their assault. "D" Company made straight for Casa Salara and took it without any trouble. "B" Company took another house on the ridge, a house called Casone, and moved on to Point 382 which was taken after a short, sharp scrap together with ten prisoners. "C" Company passed through towards 387 and met heavy opposition along the ridge. After a platoon attack lasting three-quarters of an hour this position too was in our hands and more prisoners taken. By now it was about 4 a.m. and "A" Company followed to capture Point 387. It was engaged by fire from the London Irish on Spinello, attacked by two platoons, and eventually captured with forty prisoners.

Meanwhile, at half-past ten, the Lancashire Fusiliers had begun their ascent of Spaduro. At 11.15 "D" Company assaulted and captured Point 380 and "A" and "B" passed through and attacked south along the ridge towards 396. Following close up to the artillery fire they were able to storm these positions and take ninety prisoners. By midnight "D" Company was established on Point 396 and "A" on the saddle of ground between 396 and 380. The East Surreys then came in to attack on the left of the Lancashire Fusiliers and began to clear the enemy from the north end of the mountain. "A" Company secured Point 298 against slight opposition, but "D" Company had a tough fight for Point 289 and had to attack it twice before capturing it. By 1 a.m. all the objectives on the divisional front had been taken and Monte Spaduro had fallen at last.

But there were counter-attacks during the night and the following day. The Lancashire Fusiliers were attacked, soon after taking Point 380, by four machine-gun groups supported by a number of men armed with grenades and grenade-discharging rifles. The East Surreys were counter-attacked on Point 298, but everywhere positions were firmly held and there were 155 new prisoners in the cage.

On the right 36 Brigade continued to clear the smaller hills around Acqua Salata. On the morning of October 24 the Royal West Kents pushed forward and, taking advantage of the ground mist, sent a platoon to occupy Point 410 on the high bulk of Monte Verro, which they did by midday; they then began to sweep the ridge of Monte Verro, an operation they successfully completed before midnight. But Point 410 was counter-attacked, and regained by the Germans, who were then pushed off again with casualties. The Royal West Kents took fifty prisoners that day. The Buffs immediately took up the attack and in continued heavy fighting, taking advantage of the mist, seized the second Casetta ridge, during which attack a company commander was killed. They went on to make a second attack on the next ridge, Camaggio, but although they did not manage to reach the main objective, owing to the unusually heavy going and the strong enemy opposition, they did succeed in capturing a strong point in the valley, later known as Gully House, at the cost of one officer killed and ten other casualties.

The last attack to be made during this phase of the fighting was by the Northamptons at midnight of October 24-25. Their task was to capture Point 362—the highest point on the next mountain beyond Spaduro. It was hoped that the enemy might be disorganised after the heavy defeat the previous night. The attack was preceded by an artillery and mortar concentration and the night was lit with the reflection of searchlights on the clouds. "D" Company was soon able to reach the first objective, Casa Maletto, which was ablaze. But from here on they met heavy machine-gun fire and little progress could be made. By 4.30 in the morning the ground gained was found to be untenable and the Brigade Commander ordered them to withdraw through the Lancashire Fusiliers.

That day torrential rains—ten inches in twenty-four hours—put a stop to the proposed American offensive on the left and to any further progress by the Division. It was tantalising to see, in the brief interludes of good weather, the towns and villages of the Lombardy Plain only a few miles ahead, and the flat country dotted with farms. To the troops huddled on the bare hillsides in rain and wind it was like a mirage.

It had been three weeks of some of the toughest fighting that even this division had seen, but the Divisional Commander told them:

"I want every man in the Division to understand that our achievements during the past three weeks have been by no means small.

(a) We have captured four important features:
    Point 508
    Monte Spaduro
    Monte Acqua Salata
    Monte Verro

Had the weather not broken when it did we would undoubtedly have also taken Points 448 and 362.

(b) We have captured 400 of the enemy, besides killing and wounding many more. The number of deserters who came during the days following our attacks show clearly the state to which we had reduced him.

(c) We have held the above positions against strong counter-attacks and under appalling weather conditions.

(d) We have forced the enemy to line up more than two divisions opposite us, thus making the task of the others whose turn it now is to advance so much more easy."

CHAPTER IX

WINTER IN THE MOUNTAINS

FIFTH ARMY'S offensive was suspended on October 27, and the weary troops were ordered to consolidate their positions, withdrawing their exposed units and organising reliefs and regroupments. The infantry battalions in particular now found themselves obliged, because of their recent casualties, to reorganise on the three-company basis that had been discussed while they were in Egypt.

The next three months were probably the worst period of the war for the Division—"a horrible winter", wrote Lt.-Col. Malcolm of the Argylls, "It rivalled that in Tunisia for continuous life in the open; it equalled it in the volume of rain and beat it in the amount of real cold weather. It produced no action so desperate as Green Hill or Hunt's Gap, but included many posts more uncomfortable than Cassino Castle."

It was in the second week in October that the Division's main supply route forward became too difficult for our own three-ton, two-wheel-drive vehicles and our American neighbours on the left came to the rescue with the loan of thirty-one four-wheel-drive, six-wheeled, three-tonners, each complete with its Negro driver. The only return asked for this generous gesture—which made all the difference at this moment to the maintenance of the forward troops—was a two-gallon jar of rum.

But as October ended and November began torrential rain turned the battlefields into a sea of mud. It became difficult to stand, let alone fight, in what resembled a foot or more of fluid porridge; tanks became quite useless; rivers rose at a phenomenal rate. On November 10 there was a slight fall of snow followed by sixteen days of dry, sunny weather and then the rains came again, gales of sleet making life almost unbearable. On December 23 came the first really serious fall of snow; the thermometer fell as low as fifteen degrees Fahrenheit, and even the fast mountain streams from the heights froze over. The cold, dry weather was less miserable for the men than the mud and the rain, but the mountain blizzards became a serious danger and the tracks, now sheets of glassy ice, were as difficult for vehicles as when they had been a foot deep in mud.

There had been a break-down in army supplies, and there was a shortage of socks, boots, battledress and every other kind of clothing. At one period some of the men in the front line had only one pair of socks—always wet—and cotton at that; other men were repairing roads still wearing the khaki drill trousers that were suitable only for an Egyptian summer. The men shivered in their trenches covered in wet blankets, and many, without steel helmets, were wearing balaclavas instead. Cigarettes were short—probably due to theft in the post—and the mails slow.

By mid-December, however, supplies improved. The men at the front received at least four pairs of socks each; there was an issue of "Mountain Warfare" clothing, which included windproof blouses and trousers, thick sweaters, and string vests such as are used by Arctic explorers (much appreciated, though some complained that they chafed the skin under heavy equipment). There were sleeping-bags covered with oil-silk and white snow overalls, skis, sleighs, and snowshoes. Rations fortunately, were consistently satisfactory, and the men in the forward positions received fresh rations almost every day.

A minor discomfort was the permanent smoke-screen in the San Clemente area, maintained by 53 L.A.A. Regiment, similar to the one at Cassino, which effectively concealed from the enemy the crowded river valley, with its route forward, its gun positions, and its concentrations. It was effective, though it made many of our own troops sick, and caused all of them to cough and splutter. Eventually the Americans relieved the 53 L.A.A., and used smoke generators which were just as effective tactically without being quite so offensive to our own troops.

The Division was sorry, nevertheless, to say good-bye to 53 L.A.A. Regiment, and to its commander, Lt.-Col. Bowater. Although not normally in the Division's order of battle, it had become a willing and a welcome supporter, cheerfully turning itself, as the need for anti-aircraft defence diminished, into a maid-of-all-work unit. It provided one A.A. battery, one mortar-troop (with the Irish Brigade), besides maintaining the smoke-screen, providing a stone-breaking gang for the sappers and a team of particularly gallant stretcher-bearers.

The same period saw the departure of a similar unit, 49 L.A.A. Regiment, which had also turned its hands to many jobs. Commanded throughout by Lt.-Col. Vivian Hunt, O.B.E. (after whom Hunt's Gap had been named), it had fought as infantry in North Africa, provided stretcher-bearers at Cassino and elsewhere, to say nothing of mine-lifters, road-builders, and smoke-screen operators. It had furnished diversionary fire with its Bofors guns at the Trigno crossing, and its final and crowning achievement was to build an Air O.P. landing ground near Castel del Rio in heartbreakingly difficult conditions.

The multiplicity of jobs necessarily undertaken by these units is a measure of the administrative difficulties of the period, and the strain they put on the man-power of the Division. At one time the Division's Tactical H.Q., the three Brigade H.Q.s, 56 Recce, and seven of the nine infantry battalions all had to be supplied on a "mule-and-porter" basis—supplies could be carried only so far by jeep, were then transferred to mules, and could reach the forward troops only on men's backs. Extra men were needed as porters, as traffic police, as builders of airstrips, and as stretcher-bearers. In addition to the two L.A.A. regiments, the Kensingtons and the Divisional anti-tank regiment all turned to and did whatever needed doing. So, too, did the Division's old friends of 6 Armoured Division's armoured brigade. The weather had put a good deal of armour into temporary disuse, and men of the 16/5 Lancers found themselves carrying stretchers and breaking gravel for the roads: the Lothian and Border Horse moved into the line for a time as infantry; and the Derbyshire Yeomanry built airstrips.

* * * * *

As the Germans had retreated they had been able to concentrate their guns and mortars, so the front was seldom free from harassing fire. The enemy shelled not only the front-line

Path near San Apollinare

Transport in the mountains

Making the road from Cuviolo to San Apollinare

The road to San Apollinare completed

troops in the trenches but the main roads forward, Divisional H.Q., and the supply dumps, the mule-tracks and the gun positions—and there were extensive minefields everywhere. We could not return the fire as handsomely as we had been able to in the past, for the expenditure of ammunition was cut down and controlled more and more every day. In November it was reduced to twenty rounds a gun a day for 25-pounders; by January it was down to five rounds; every round had to be counted. Visiting dignitaries from home were surprised by the complaints, the more so in view of the reassuring statements made in the House of Commons (reported in *The Times* of November 23, 1944). These assurances may have been politically necessary, but it was difficult to persuade a gunner restricted to five rounds a day that he was well-supplied with ammunition. People at home had their eyes fixed now on the sweep through France, and they did not know—nobody told them—that the successes were due partly, at least, to the expenditure of supplies that were denied to the now stationary army in Italy.

Everything possible was done to improve conditions. Such houses as still existed were patched up as much as possible; Nissen huts and shelters were put up in the most difficult places. Rest camps were organised, and it was found that it was always possible to keep a few officers and men out of battle where they would be sure of getting three hot meals a day, dry shelter, hot showers and even a chance of a day in Florence. The ancient castle at Castel del Rio, with its thick walls built to withstand cannon balls, was fitted up as a rest camp where each battalion in turn spent five days and were able to enjoy cinema shows, drink tea at Wally's Bar and go to the "Golden Chopper" Canteen run by the Council of Voluntary Women Workers. The troops remained in good heart in spite of everything, helped, no doubt, by the fact that in November the L.I.A.P. scheme for home leave was begun. True, only four or five men from each battalion could go every fortnight but it meant that there was a chance, however remote, for each man to spend Christmas at home.

Once more the main problem was one of administration. In late October the road from Castel del Rio to Sassoleone collapsed under a weight of traffic for which it had never been designed. The rain brought landslides down on it and undermined its surface. For fourteen hours this road remained impassable and the engineers strove day and night to build a new road so that the vital supplies could go forward. Thereafter traffic was strictly regulated and kept to a minimum.

Everywhere in the area roads were insufficient and a new track had to be built at great speed from Cuviolo to San Apollinare where two brigades had their headquarters and where the Division's tactical headquarters was also situated. All troops who could possibly be made available helped to build the track, especially the gunners who, with the restriction in shooting, had other activities piled on to them—road-making, tree felling and timber hauling, and stretcher bearing. They found, too, that the winter was spent in putting ammunition down and picking it up again. There was heavy dumping in November and December, whilst in January the gunners had to lift and carry back some 30,000 rounds of twenty-five pounder ammunition.

For three months 64 Anti Tank Regiment worked as makers and maintainers of roads under R.E. supervision. They had a forestry section felling trees, another laying logs as road foundations, another loading stones from the Sillaro and Santerno river-beds to spread over the logs as a new road surface. They had men digging ditches and others crushing the stones. They built one entirely new road that was opened for light traffic on November 7, and used by the Division for the rest of its stay in the sector.

Each arm of the service was faced with its own peculiar problem. The R.A.M.C., for instance, found that the downpour on October 24/25 had caused the River Sillaro to rise four feet in twelve hours and swept away all the fords that the ambulances had been using. Aerial ropeways were built by the sappers and R.E.M.E. and the wounded were passed across them in slings. All casualties had to be removed by hand, those from Ripiano and Acqua Salata being carried all the way to San Apollinare. The Division had never had so many stretcher bearers; the 460 in action included gunners and R.A.S.C. as well as all the available R.A.M.C. personnel. Major Mitchell, of 217 Field Ambulance, was awarded the M.C. for his untiring work in getting out casualties along a very exposed ridge up the forward slope of the hill. A system was evolved by which the steady flow of cases, caused by shelling and on patrols, could be directed as safely and as comfortably as possible back to the aid and dressing stations. In some cases the wounded were carried down on crib carriers by mules and others would be carried for as much as four miles by stretcher bearers, and to aid them a series of relay points were set up manned by troops of 64 Anti Tank Regiment, where the bearers were relieved and fresh porters continued the journey.

For 47 Field Hygiene Section it was a similarly busy period. On arrival in the sector the whole place was found to be in a filthy condition, littered with tins and refuse of all kinds. At first, owing to the prior claims for road maintenance and stretcher-bearing, nothing could be done, but later a small squad of Italians was made available to clear up Castel del Rio, while forward areas were cleared by the nearest unit. By the end of the year everything was much cleaner. Courses on field hygiene were given to the Italian mule-pack companies, who had little idea of hygiene or sanitation, and bath houses and drying rooms were built at Ripiano for the men of the forward battalions.

The maintenance of the San Clemente ford was a perpetual problem for the sappers. Traffic would be delayed for hours at a time at the crossing-place waiting for the waters to subside. During the thaws the work was endangered by mines laid by American troops in the river-beds upstream; when the river rose many were dislodged and carried downstream to the shallows where troops and vehicles crossed the river, and caused a number of casualties. To try to cure this the sappers built a boom upstream of the ford by driving iron stakes into the ground at intervals across the river bed.

When darkness fell the sector became a scene of activity and movement, for then began in earnest the task of supplying the forward battalion positions, which were too exposed for approach by day. From its park near the river the R.A.S.C. jeep platoon would make its way in convoy up to and along the main road, each jeep with its windscreen flat down, its loaded truck jolting over the pot-holes in the track. The jeeps would then make their way to various mule points, hidden at the foot of the hills on either flank. The troops on Monte Spaduro, for instance, were supplied by mule from Ripiano. This involved a crossing of the Sillaro at San Clemente for the jeeps—even after an hour's rain a hazardous business. Thence the track running along the southern bank of the Sillaro was a narrow one and, after snow, very dangerous. Finally, at Spaduro Corner the convoys would usually run into harassing fire, and then drive as fast as possible along the foot of Monte Spaduro, make two crossings of the bed of the Ranchi, and so to Ripiano.

At the mule points were the crews of the anti-tank guns and of some of the carriers. It was their job to accompany the mule train each night to the forward posts. The jeeps would be unloaded and the throng of mules, big strong ones from Africa, smaller but sturdy ones from India, and little ragged creatures collected from all over Italy, would be assembled into teams— the Division was employing over 1,800 mules. Then the muleteers, Sepoys or ragamuffin Italians, would load the mules with rations, water, ammunition, mail, sandbags, corrugated iron for the dugouts, cement for the three-inch mortars, and batteries for the wireless sets, and move off on their arduous journey, squelching along the familiar tracks where the engineers had laid brushwood to try to make the way easier. Sometimes they would come to shell craters which were death traps; it was common for a mule to sink into the ooze and have to be shot the next day. It was even more dangerous to leave the track because of the many minefields. One of the worst places was the causeway between Monte Pieve and Acqua Salata where even the men got bogged in the mud and shelling was more than likely. Some of the journeys, such as the one from Sassoleone, would take six hours there and back and the exhausted men would not be home till after midnight, but in other sectors the rations would be taken up by daylight under the cover of the smoke screen. To the troops near San Clemente the jeeps could bring the rations to within 1,000 yards of battalion H.Q. But it was a steep 1,000 yards, at the best a stiff pull and sometimes in wet, slippery weather completely impossible. On dark nights the supply convoys were assisted by "artificial moonlight" provided by searchlights.

While the mule convoys were arriving the infantry would be climbing out of their slit trenches and their barricaded houses to stretch their legs, to get some fresh air and to cough out the smoke that had accumulated in their lungs from the smoke-screen. Others, loaded down with equipment, weapons, great-coat, and sodden blankets would be moving back after four to six days in the line to spend a few days in one of the rest camps a mile or two back.

The front-line positions ran along a number of bald hills on which there was precious little cover of any sort. Battalion H.Q. might have found one or two rooms in a shattered building, but nine out of every ten men in the front line spent their days in the open, and under constant shell-fire. All round there was a sea of thick grey cloying mud far worse than the Division had ever known. The men would pass most of each day curled up in slit trenches or in small caves dug out of the hillside. Besides this, there would be a spell of sentry duty, a few hours' rest, an hour spent trying to clean the thick mud off the rifles or Bren guns, and periods of boiling tea over a Tommy cooker. They would sleep, covered in wet blankets, with their heads on sodden sand-bags, continually disturbed by the crump and whine of shells and mortars. At night half the men would man the forward positions while the others would be prowling out in front on patrol or trying to ambush a German patrol.

Some of the gunner regiments were luckier than the infantry in having three months' undisturbed occupation of positions which they were able in time to protect against rain and snow. But unlike the infantry they were never relieved. Even Divisional H.Q. was hardly comfortable—it had moved out of the castle at Castel del Rio at the end of October to make room for resting battalions, and lived in houses and caravans in the village. In mid-November Main H.Q. moved to Medino di Casa di Lesso, where the letter-heading "In the Field" was strictly true. But this muddy spot was safer, at any rate, than Castel del Rio and not one German shell landed in the new H.Q.

The Germans were better off: they had a good lateral road

fed by other roads from the plain and they were able to supply and reinforce their forward troops even in the worst weather. We, on the other hand, had no lateral road at all. Nevertheless, there was a steady stream of deserters from 98 Infantry Division, which was disposed on either side of the Sillaro, and in which discipline seemed to be poor and morale low—a criticism which did not apply to the other enemy formations.

At the beginning of November, XIII Corps regrouped westwards in order to relieve II (U.S.) Corps; 1 British Division relieved 88 (U.S.) Division on Monte Grande and, in the middle of the month the Divisional boundaries within the Corps were adjusted so as to even out the time spent in the line by individual battalions. The Irish Brigade relieved a brigade of 1 Division on the lower slopes of Monte Grande and established its H.Q. in San Clemente; 36 Brigade took over its positions in the centre, around Casa Salara and Spinello, while 56 Recce came temporarily under command of the Guards' Brigade of 6 Armoured Division, which took over Acqua Salata. The support of the Irish Brigade in its new positions produced a nice artillery problem for the gunners. 17 Field, its affiliated regiment, was quite out of range, so to avoid moving the guns it was arranged that the Irish Brigade should be supported by 1 Division's artillery using 17 Field's observation posts. This was further complicated by the fact that one of the two infantry brigades of 1 Division holding Monte Grande was relieved every ten days and so was its supporting regiment. But in spite of all the arrangement worked well and was an excellent example of liaison and co-operation.

This was a period of vigorous and frequent patrolling. Every night small groups of men would make their way across the muddy hills to gain information or to take prisoners. There would be frequent and bitter actions when opposing patrols clashed, prisoners would be taken from both sides, and more and more mines laid. Patrol clashes and raids were particularly frequent on the Casa Salara spur, on the Monte Spaduro front and astride the Sillaro valley.

On November 29 units of 1 Parachute Division attacked the positions held by 1 Division on Monte Castellaro, north of Monte Grande, and held on to them in spite of counter-attacks.

But Eighth Army was slowly advancing, taking Ravenna on December 5 and Faenza on December 17; the next day elements of 4 Indian Division crossed the Senio south of Highway 9, but were obliged to withdraw. Thereafter Eighth Army remained on the east side of that river until the final offensive was launched in April 1945.

Plans had been made for XIII Corps to advance as soon as the weather permitted, and it looked in early December as though the time had come. 36 Brigade was to clear the enemy from the Salara spur, with 6 Armoured Division's help on the flank; 11 Brigade was to capture Casa Ortica and Monte Merlo and Point 362 which the Northamptons had failed to take in October; the Irish Brigade with 56 Recce under command had as objectives the spurs Il Sallaro and Casa Calvana. On December 5 Monte Penzola fell to 6 Armoured Division, on the right of 78 Division, and as a preliminary to a divisional advance 36 Brigade was ordered to take Point 448 on Monte Maggiore, that steep and important hill that barred the way forward.

Monte Maggiore could be approached only from the east and from the west; in each case the approach was along a narrow ridge with a ravine on either side and a house straddled across it. On the left the approach was guarded by Camaggio house (which the Buffs had attacked in October) and on the right by a house called Figna di Sotto. The Royal West Kents were to attack Camaggio from their positions on Monte Verro and the Buffs were to attack through Figna di Sotto. The attack was to start at 11.15 on the night of December 13-14.

The fine weather that had been promised did not in fact hold—it began to rain in the afternoon—and as the two Kentish battalions began their long approach march, they found the going was as bad as ever. As they moved forward to attack, the Royal West Kents were heavily mortared and suffered casualties. Patrols had led them to believe that the enemy had thinned out at Camaggio or that they were holding the position merely as an outpost, but events proved this not to be the case. In mud waist-deep and under a downpour of rain that had persisted for the past ten hours they ploughed their way up the ridge to get to grips with the enemy securely installed on the top. The two attacking platoons carried nothing but Tommy guns, leaving the heavier loads to a third, but in spite of the lightness of their loads the men had their boots pulled off by the deep mud long before they reached the top. Halfway up the ridge they came under heavy fire again from a well concealed weapon-pit and there were more casualties, until a lance-sergeant and another man rushed the position and killed its occupants. The Royal West Kents reached the top of the ridge and had almost achieved success when the leading platoon commander was wounded. Sgt. Jones, who won the M.M. in this battle, took over the platoon pending the arrival of the C.S.M., who was evacuating casualties. The platoon then withdrew a little to reform.

The Buffs had met similar small-arms fire as they approached Figna di Sotto. The state of the approaches to the houses had been reported "fair" by Brigade H.Q. but this was far from the case; by the time the assaulting troops were near their objective they were in no physical state for the assault. But they got to within fifty yards of the house before they were held up. Ammunition for the forward platoon's P.I.A.T. got stuck in the mud, and a break-down in communication with battalion H.Q. made it impossible to call for artillery support. A counter-attack at three in the morning was thrown back, but the Buffs were withdrawn before daybreak.

At the same time as the Buffs were being counter-attacked, the Royal West Kents were attacking Camaggio again. But they met fierce resistance, the remaining officers of the leading company were wounded, the attack lost cohesion, and they too were ordered to withdraw at dawn. Both battalions fell back under a barrage, a smoke screen, and air attacks on the enemy's batteries. The Buffs had suffered over thirty and the Royal West Kents over seventy casualties in the last attempt of the winter to resume the offensive. The Division's gunners had only fired the first sixty minutes of the fire-plan for this operation, and spent the rest of the night in improvised neutralisation shoots in an attempt to extricate the infantry. In spite of the bad weather and the heavy going they fired 10,400 rounds in twelve hours and received the thanks of the Brigade commander for their support.

The ford at San Clemente

Jeep service station at Castel del Rio

Rear H.Q. 78 Division in Castel del Rio

Damaged trucks at Rear H.Q. after shelling

WINTER IN THE MOUNTAINS

Late that night Castel del Rio was shelled by a heavy gun—probably a 210 mm. that could get the range from 29,000 yards. An English illustrated weekly of November 18 had published a photograph of the village, given its name, and drawn admiring attention to the number of vehicles parked in its streets! A copy was produced by Brigadier Andrew Scott, of 1 Guards' Brigade, and the Divisional Commander, in his official protest, asked for advance copies of the future issues of the paper, so that he could make his dispositions accordingly. The shelling went on for an hour and a half and did a great deal of damage to Rear H.Q., burning transport and records. Six men were wounded.

On December 21 the Guards again assumed command of the sector around Acqua Salata and 36 Brigade was withdrawn completely from the line.

Since the attack was indefinitely postponed, the Irish Brigade had decided to make a few large-scale raids themselves. Two such raids were made on Casa Tamagnin—a group of houses on the side of a steep spur 1,000 yards from Brigade forward positions. On each side of the spur and parallel to it ran two other spurs—the one on the right was held by the enemy and the one on the left was occupied at night by a standing patrol from the Irish Brigade.

The first raid on Casa Tamagnin was made by "D" Company of the Royal Irish Fusiliers on December 18 while other troops of the battalion mounted a diversionary attack on a neighbouring position. One group of the attacking party took up a position overlooking the houses and the others made the assault. The first house was captured but we were pinned down about thirty yards from the second. A second attack was launched and some of the Fusiliers reached the second building but found it barricaded. The enemy then launched a counter-attack but was met by the fire of the assault troops and heavy mortar concentrations were brought down on him. The counter-attack was dispersed and "D" Company withdrew. The raid had been a success and the enemy casualties heavy, but among our own fourteen casualties, Lt. Parrish, a promising young officer, had been killed, and the Commanding Officer, Lt.-Col. Horsfall, again wounded.

The second raid was made by the London Irish on January 3.

For a week before the raid the area had been thoroughly patrolled and a comprehensive plan made. The raid was carried out in daylight, starting at 8.30 in the morning, and the intention was to set fire to the two houses. The assault party of seven reached the first house, found it unoccupied, and with a covered approach to the second house. The patrol commander went through this hole and from there heard a sound of stirring in the straw in the second house. Grenades were thrown into the straw which caught fire immediately and some couple of dozen Germans, mostly unarmed, jumped out of the windows and ran for cover. One was killed by the assault party, others were wounded, and the survivors were engaged by three-inch mortars. The assault party then set fire to the other house and withdrew under a smoke screen and artillery support. By 10.30 that morning all the parties had returned, their raid a complete success, and having suffered no casualties.

On the right flank, 11 Brigade's patrols were reporting that the enemy was showing increased vigilance in defence of his positions facing Monte Spaduro, but the Division kept the upper hand in the many fierce and bitter patrol activities in no-man's-land.

Christmas Day, 1944, dawned bright and sparkling, and neither side fired a shot. 36 Brigade was out of the line and was able to organise dinners in an almost traditional style. 11 Brigade did their best on the bleak hill sides of Spaduro, and the two battalions of the Irish Brigade who were in the line were promised a real Christmas dinner when they went into the reserve area at San Martino. A divisional pantomime at Castel del Rio was a great success.

36 Brigade's rest was short lived; on December 27 they were sent to relieve 2 Infantry Brigade on Monte Grande and remained under command of 1 Division until January 9 when they were relieved by 85 (U.S.) Division and reverted to the command of 78 Division. The sector they were to take over included Monte Calderaro, which projected for 1,500 yards north of the main mass of Monte Grande—a conical hill 1,875 feet high surmounted by a battered church and a few houses, and linked to the main Monte Grande position by a

ridge, shorter but more dangerous than the causeway at Acqua Salata. There was also a spur to the north-east running down to the ruins of Vezzolo within 150 yards of the enemy's positions. The whole area was under enemy observation and was constantly subjected to heavy bombardments—the Buffs suffered twenty casualties during this period, including one officer killed. The snow was two feet deep on the hills, with great drifts in the gulleys. Patrolling was limited owing to the proximity of the enemy and because of the snow and the clearness of the nights, but the signal linesmen were kept busy repairing lines cut by shell-fire, groping in the snow for broken ends and themselves shelled continuously. Gales and snowstorms blew up and the men were in constant danger of frostbite and exposure. The observations posts functioned at a height of 1,500 to 2,000 feet above the guns in the valley below.

On being relieved, 36 Brigade, less one battalion, which was placed under command of 11 Brigade, went into the divisional rest area near Florence for a week's shelter and rest, but on January 18 they were back again and from then until February 6 there were two full brigades in the line, busy with fighting patrols, and with inter-battalion reliefs carried out frequently by the battalions of the remaining brigade and 56 Recce.

One of the Division's last actions in the mountains was the result of an attack on 56 Recce's positions on Salara on February 8. That night "B" Squadron heard men approaching up the valley, one of whom shouted in good English, "'A' Company. Don't shoot!"—but the others were heard talking in German. Eleven troop opened fire and a battle of words as well as weapons broke out, the Germans telling the squadron to come out and fight. But by 2.30 in the morning the enemy was driven off, leaving behind two killed; 56 Recce had an officer and four other ranks wounded.

It was by way of being a farewell performance—farewell, at any rate, to the mountains. Eighth Army was mounting what was to be the final offensive, and the Division had first to be rested, regrouped, and trained for an attack across the plain of the Po Valley. The first half of February saw 10 Indian

Division taking over the snowy heights and the water-logged hiding-holes and gun positions, and on February 15 the last of the Division left the mountains for good. It was going back to Eighth Army's command and to V Corps, and its first stop was Forli.

CHAPTER X

SPRING IN THE VALLEY

THE plain around Forli is not so pretty as the Capuan valley in which the Division had rested in the previous April. But this Tuscan interlude in the February and March of 1945, was not unlike that other Italian springtide. There was rest and recreation as well as training—clubs and opera and concert-parties in Forli itself, and houses and green fields and vineyards instead of rocks and mud. There was spring weather, and roofs over the men's heads.

Once again, too, and most important of all, there was that keen feeling of great events to come—with the hope this time that the battle to be fought might end the war in Italy. This feeling, together with the cheerful discipline of ceremonial parades and guards under the warm spring sunshine—and notably the Irish Brigade's celebration of St. Patrick's Day—raised the Division's spirit to the highest pitch.

Just as the campaign in the mountains had reached a stalemate in the winter, so the line of battle in the Po valley had become static, with Eighth Army on the line of the Senio river. Ahead lay a maze of rivers and canals, all with high banks, right up to the river Po itself. Training, therefore, included practice in river-crossing for the infantry and in the handling of bridge-laying tanks and other devices for the sappers. The problems likely to be met in the Po Valley were so very different from those the Division had become used to in the mountains that what was needed especially was training in mobile fighting, along with armour. Moreover, new types of equipment had become available and needed getting to know.

Training began almost at once—exercises for testing communications, in river-crossings, in street fighting and, above all, in co-operation with armour. 2 Armoured Brigade, under the command of Brigadier Combe (who was later to command the Division), was affiliated to the Division for these exercises. The Bays went to the Irish Brigade, 9 Lancers to 36, and 10 Hussars to 11. It was the first time in Italy that 78 Division had lived, trained, and held the line with the armour with which it was later to carry out full-scale operations: this was the genesis of the splendid team-work between tanks and infantry soon to be shown in the final battle.

The new types of equipment were many and varied. The assault sappers produced the Arks and Avres, bridge-laying tanks; each battalion had four Wasp flame-throwers as well as Lifebuoys (portable flame-throwers carried on a man's back), and there were Crocodiles, which were Churchill tanks pulling an armoured flame-fuel container behind them. There were Weasels, Vipers, Scorpions, Buffaloes, Fantails and Platypus grousers, which were fitted to the tracks of tanks to increase their ability to get over boggy ground. Most important of all was the Kangaroo, a Sherman tank deturreted and modified to carry material or men, which had already been successfully used by V Corps in the plains. Several exercises were carried out in the Kangaroos of the 4 Hussars, who had been ordered to train many divisions in their use.

Of the normal training an exercise was held to test Brigade H.Q. signal communications: all guns were calibrated and the sappers sent two field companies to Lido di Roma to practise heavy bridging.

In the same period there was a major reorganisation of 64 Anti-Tank Regiment. Each brigade battery was converted into one self-propelled troop, one troop of towed seventeen-pounders, and one troop of six-pounders.

There had been many changes in command during the winter. Brigadier Packard, commanding 36 Brigade, had been given a staff appointment and was succeeded by Brigadier Musson, who had been in command of an infantry battalion for more than a year. Lt.-Col. Taylor of the Argylls was transferred owing to ill health, after twenty-one years with the battalion, and was succeeded by his second-in-command, Lt.-Col. Malcolm. The Buffs had had changes too; in October Lt.-Col. Tuff left for a staff appointment and in November Lt.-Col. A. J. Odling-Smee was placed in command. 11 Brigade also had a new Brigadier: in November Brigadier Thubron, who had been commanding the North Staffs in another division, took over the Brigade. In December Lt.-Col. Connolly of the Northamptons was forced to leave his battalion owing to ill health, after having commanded it throughout the campaign; his place was taken by Lt.-Col. Houchin (once of the Ox. and Bucks), who had joined the battalion in Italy. Lt.-Col. Hunter was still in command of the East Surreys. 56 Recce felt the loss deeply of Lt.-Col. Chavasse when he was promoted in March; he was succeeded by Lt.-Col. Hartland-Mahon.

In the gunners, Lt.-Col. Thomas, who had been C.O. of 17 Field Regiment during the first four months of the African campaign came back to the Division and replaced Lt.-Col. Scott Foster as C.O. of 138 Field. Lt.-Col. Baker had left 17 Field Regiment to take up an appointment at home (a great blow to the Irish Brigade) and had been replaced by Lt.-Col. Lecky; Lt.-Col. Adye was in command of 132 Field. In the sappers Lt.-Col. Denton had been promoted from 214 Field Company to be C.R.E. in place of Lt.-Col. Eking, who was sent to command "G" A.G.R.E.

On March 11, 78 Division was ordered to relieve 56 (London) Division on the banks of the Senio. Eighth Army had four corps in the Lombardy Plain following the line of the Senio. On the right was V Corps, then the Polish Corps, X Corps, and XIII Corps on the left. 78 Division was to hold the left of the V Corps' sector with 8 Indian Division on its right and 5 Kresowa (Polish) Division on its left. The Division's positions stretched for some five miles north and south-west of Cotignola, Divisional H.Q. being based on Russi. The Army policy was to maintain and locally to improve its positions, whilst plans for a major offensive were perfected.

The country around the Senio was flat and fertile, but very "close" for manoeuvre because of the thickly planted vineyards and olive-groves; in addition, visibility was limited by the embankments of roads and railways and by the tremendous floodbanks, as much as twenty-five feet high and ten feet wide at the top, which cut across the plain. The rivers between the banks varied in width and depth and were spanned by bridges going from one floodbank to the other.

MARCH, 1945

The Senio itself was a narrow stream, normally three or four feet deep, between steep muddy banks only about eighteen feet apart and six feet high. On both sides of the river bed, however, additional floodbanks had been built, each ten feet high, eighteen feet wide at the base with a flat top nine feet wide. The opposing armies faced each other across this narrowest of no-man's-lands.

The enemy held all the west bank of the river, completely controlled the river bed and had freedom of movement along it, and held several positions on the eastern floodbank as well. We, on the other hand, held only the eastern face of the eastern floodbank. The enemy had built a number of rafts and bridges across the river, so making it possible for raiding parties to cross almost anywhere—there were twenty-three footbridges in the divisional area. The Germans had prepared the banks for defence by having a strong line of machine-gun posts on the west bank, which was two feet higher than ours, and by maintaining a number of well-protected posts on the western face of the east bank. They had tunnelled into both banks in order to secure observation or the ability to fire without exposing themselves. At some points on the east bank the enemy's positions and our own were within ten yards of each other, with only the floodbank between, and close enough for the waging of verbal warfare. They held the village of Cotignola which overlooked our area.

One advantage of our positions was that supplies could be brought right up to the front line by road, and casualties could be evacuated in the same way without any difficulty. The weather, too, was perfect: it was warm and spring-like and the mud had dried leaving the grass green and fresh, not yet smothered by the dust of summer.

Facing the Division was 98 Infantry Division, composed of three Grenadier Regiments each with both its battalions in the line. This division, as we had already discovered in the mountains, was not a good one, and there were many deserters, but it was in a position to oppose vigorously any small-scale attacks and to seize any opportunity for small gains.

The conditions for the infantry on the floodbanks in some ways resembled those of the 1914-18 war. There was much

(Opposite) Left to right: Gen. Mark Clark, G.O.C. Fifth Army; Maj.-Gen. R. K. Arbuthnott; Lt.-Gen. S. C. Kirkman, G.O.C. XIII Corps.

The Senio bank

Crossing the Santerno

use of periscopes and of tunnels, a good deal of grenade-lobbing and firing of two-inch mortars and P.I.A.T. bombs. There was sniping and there were grenade battles, sudden attacks and withdrawals. Teller mines and strings of grenades were slung over the bank, and improvised bombs were made.

The Division's Intelligence section dropped propaganda leaflets and the Signals broadcast to the enemy through loudspeakers placed behind the floodbanks. It was impossible to construct a position from which a view could be obtained over the bank, and periscopes which, if not damaged by snipers, were adequate for observation by day, could not see into the river-bed. By degrees, however, we built small tunnels through the bank which gave a limited view and through which the P.I.A.T.s were able to fire direct.

The gunners, in particular, were handicapped by our lack of high ground from which to observe, and they could see only the tops of trees and houses beyond the Senio's floodbanks. Observation posts were, it is true, established in the church tower at Bagnacavallo and the sugar factory at Granarola, but we depended chiefly on the observation planes of "C" Flight, 651 Air O.P. Squadron, whose help in covering the Senio line was invaluable.

By day the tanks made minor sorties and fired point-blank into any German positions they could see from our side; one morning one of the Bays' tanks fired armour-piercing shells through the bank in order to destroy a German position on the other side.

The greatest activity on both sides was at night. A record amount of small-arms ammunition was used, especially grenade and P.I.A.T. bombs, and the night was lit with Very lights, parachute flares and rockets. The daytime, on the other hand, was comparatively quiet, except for a certain amount of sniping. The enemy did little shelling and mortaring, and it was possible for our infantry to move fairly freely behind the banks.

This was a period during which our troops learned some lessons likely to come in useful for the flat-country fighting that lay ahead. They learned not to throw grenades over the floodbanks from established posts, that the enemy snipers were busiest when the sun was setting behind them, and that the

P.I.A.T. is a useful weapon for blowing in dug-outs and breaking bridges. They learnt the use of the short-range bomb, that the enemy crossed the bridges at dusk and dawn, and that the best policy was for a Bren gunner to nip up the bank, fire at the enemy and return.

A special feature of the artillery support during this period was the placing of certain guns in positions from which they could bring enfilade fire to bear down the line of the river on the enemy's positions between the floodbanks. This entailed extreme precision of fire owing to the nearness of our own troops on the eastern bank. The early experiments were successful and there was soon a demand from the infantry for more flanking fire than the limited number of suitable gun positions could supply.

Many raids were carried out by each side using bazookas or P.I.A.T.s, grenades and light automatics. Within half-an-hour, for instance, of taking over their new positions "B" Squadron of 56 Recce was attacked. Several daring Germans rushed over the tow-path and threw grenades into their positions. Two men were buried, but a third, whose rifle was splintered to bits in his hands, tossed several grenades back and the raiding party made off. On the last morning before the squadron was relieved the enemy opened fire on the same forward positions with mortars and heavy artillery fire, so cutting all communications to Squadron H.Q. As the attack came in, the whole position was covered with a thick smoke screen. From the collapsed H.Q. where his troop-leader and the troop-sergeant were lying, badly burned by phosphorus, Sgt. Cronin managed to dig out the radio set and to re-establish communications; for his part in this action he was awarded the D.C.M. The enemy occupied the squadron's position for only half a minute before being driven off, yet in this brief space of time they killed three, wounded four, and captured five of our men.

A typical raid of ours was that made by the London Irish on a point in the floodbank known as Fritz's Bund, where the enemy—occupying both sides of the bank on our side of the river—made it virtually impossible to supply two of our posts near by. A daylight attack over the top was combined with a tunnelling operation, and the position was taken at a cost to the enemy of two killed, three wounded, and four captured. The Germans made no attempt to re-take this position.

* * * * *

During the four weeks that 78 Division occupied its positions on the floodbanks there were no important changes in the front line except that, as far as possible, the enemy was forced back from his posts on the eastern floodbank. As everyone knew this period was merely a prelude to the operations to come. Training of units and individuals continued, therefore, for all who were not actually holding the line—the brigade in reserve and even the reserve units of the forward brigades carrying out further practice with the armour and the Kangaroos.

Bright sunny days, followed by cool nights, followed in uninterrupted succession; accommodation remained excellent; and bursting into leaf of the vines and olive trees emphasised still further the denseness of the country and the limited visibility it offered.

On April 2, as a preliminary to the final offensive, 2 N.Z. Division took over the left-hand brigade sector and 11 Brigade occupied that on the right.

All this time plans and preparations for the offensive had been going ahead under a cloak of secrecy. Special roads were being made, gun areas reconnoitred and made ready, dumps of ammunition (600 rounds per gun) and all other stores prepared. Commanding officers and others, including those from the forward brigades, were assembled for sand-table exercises and discussions. Yet, up to the day before the attack, the plans had not been divulged to anybody below the rank of lieutenant-colonel.

The operation, known as "Operation Buckland", had as objective the defeat of the Germans in Italy south of the Po. (There was a stage, early in April, when the enemy intended to withdraw to the Santerno, and laid down a heavy bombardment as a preliminary. But Himself lunacy, it is said, vetoed the move—with disastrous consequences to his troops).

Five Corps' tasks was divided into three phases. First, the assault across the Senio to be made by 8 Indian and 2 New

Zealand Divisions, then the same two divisions were to establish a bridgehead across the Santerno, eight miles beyond the Senio. In the third phase 78 Division and 56 Division were to break out northwards through the bridgehead thus secured and pierce the strong enemy defences around Argenta. It was a rôle that the Division had played successfully before at the Sangro, and again in the Liri Valley. It was not surprising, therefore, that it should have been chosen for the same important task in the final, triumphant offensive.

CHAPTER XI

THE ARGENTA GAP

AS April 9 dawned, bright and warm, the Division was holding a narrow sector of the front between 8 Indian Division on the right and 2 New Zealand Division on the left. 11 Brigade, the only brigade forward, was still holding the eastern bank of the River Senio, opposite the little crossroads town of Lugo. The Brigade was almost twice its normal strength, for under command were 36 Brigade's Buffs and Royal West Kents, the Bays with their tanks, and a composite squadron of 56 Recce Regiment. The Northamptons, on the other hand, from 11 Brigade, along with 56 Recce's self-propelled 75 mm. guns, were detached to fill a gap in the Corps front far to the right. The other two infantry brigades and the 2 Armoured Brigade (under the Division's command) were thus freed to concentrate in reserve, ready for the major task ahead.

This was the day for the opening of the allies' final offensive in Italy—the offensive intended to break the enemy's defences on the Senio and to destroy his armies south of the Po. And a beautiful day it was—firm under foot for men and vehicles, cloudless overhead for our aircraft. The first punch was to be delivered by Eighth Army, more specifically by V Corps, with the New Zealanders and the Indians leading and the Division going through their bridgehead and exploiting their gains.

In the initial stage the Division had only its artillery engaged. The infantry waited, withdrawn a quarter-of-a-mile from the river to give the air forces elbow-room for their close-bombing and strafing.

The whole of the Divisional artillery, under Brigadier F. S. Reid, the C.R.A., except for 138 Field Regiment, supporting 11 Brigade, was put under command of the New Zealanders for the initial bombardment and assault. The line layout was particularly complicated: the linemen and exchange operators

—one-third Royal Artillery and two-thirds Royal Signals personnel—had 150 miles of cable out, thirty miles of which was handed over to the New Zealand artillery as it took over its sector of the front.

The Kensingtons placed two platoons of heavy mortars with each of the attacking divisions, and the Division's "Wasp" flame-throwers were strung along the whole of the Corps front.

At ten to two in the afternoon the attack began with medium and heavy bombers dropping a "carpet" of small fragmentation bombs in the enemy's rear areas. Spitfires pounced on targets chosen by the ground forces and sprayed them with machine-gun fire.

The bombardment was planned and carried out in five phases. Each phase opened with an intense gun-attack, employing every available gun and mortar on the Corps' front. Then followed a ten-minute period during which the guns were silent and fighter-bombers strafed the river banks with their cannon-fire. Next, the aircraft switched to the area behind the river, attacking it with bombs, while the guns and mortars also lifted from the floodbank and laid down concentrations beyond it.

It went on for five-and-a-half hours during which—except for the ten-minute intervals for air attack—the guns were continuously engaged. Then, at twenty past seven in the evening, the fighter-bombers came down to strafe the river bank in their turn, but this particular attack was a feint. As the aircraft swooped, "Wasp" and "Crocodile" flame-throwers all along the river bank opened their jets, and subjected the enemy to an intense and unprecedented saturation of flame. Immediately behind this came the storming infantry of the New Zealand Division and 8 Indian Division, who burst over their own floodbank, crossed the narrow river and came to grips with such enemy as still held fast on the western flood bank. At the same time the artillery support changed to a barrage, behind which the infantry began their advance westward from the captured river line.

That night and all next day the Indians and the New Zealanders continued to make substantial progress. Meanwhile, in the Division, 11 Brigade, on the evening the offensive began, reoccupied the quarter-mile strip by the river which it had evacuated before the initial air bombardment, the Lancashire

Fusiliers and a squadron of the Bays being harassed in doing so by machine-gun fire, by mines, and by Germans who had filtered forward. It was this infiltration that kept the Fusiliers— on the right of the Division's front, next to 8 Indian Division— short of the flood bank. At other parts of the front the Division was right up.

Then as the enemy withdrew in face of the main assault during the night, the brigade crossed the Senio; the East Surreys linked up with the New Zealanders in the village of Cotignola early next day. As the Division's sappers set to work on a bridge for the rest of the Division, 11 Brigade consolidated around Cotignola, while the other two brigades massed by the main road in readiness to cross.

It was these brigades—the Irish and 36—that, once across the Senio, were to link up with their armour and other arms in carefully chosen "wedding areas", to pass through the bridge-heads won by the Indians and the New Zealanders across the Santerno, and to strike for the bridge over the Reno, south of Bastia. 56 Division was advancing on Bastia itself, on the north bank of the Reno. Bastia was the hinge of the enemy's deepest defences.

Especially, though, it was the rôle of the Irish Brigade, swollen almost to the size of an armoured division, to form the break-out and the exploiting forces. The break-out force consisted of the Royal Irish Fusiliers and the Inniskillings, with two squadrons of the Bays, a squadron of 51 R.T.R.'s flame-throwing Crocodiles, a platoon of the Kensingtons' M.M.G.s, as well as a bulldozer troop, a bridge-building unit and reconnaissance parties of the Royal Engineers. Immediate support was provided by 17 Field Regiment and 11 R.H.A.

Experience had taught the Division the policy to lay down for the operations. There were to be no halts at night-fall, for instance, for we had learnt in 1944 that the enemy was often able to re-establish a line or a rearguard position during the night because of our failure to follow up with tanks or infantry during the dark hours.

Forward thrusts were to aim at important canal crossings, along the line of fewest water-obstacles: a bridge seized might well mean a day saved, or more.

And towns and villages on the main route were to be bypassed and cut off; in the previous summer the enemy had gained time by holding such strong points against our attacks.

Throughout these operations gridded air photographs proved extremely useful, both in giving the supporting artillery numbered targets and in indicating more clearly than maps the width of water-obstacles.

The exploiting force, entirely mounted on tracked vehicles, became known as "The Kangaroo Army" from the armoured troop carriers of the 4 Hussars in which the London Irish were carried. Commanded by Brigadier John Combe, commander of 2 Armoured Brigade, it included also the 9 Lancers with their Shermans, a troop of the R.H.A.'s self-propelled 25-pounders, and an assault detachment of Royal Engineers.

Each company of London Irish was allotted eight Kangaroos, ammunitioned and provisioned for forty-eight hours, and each worked with its own squadron of the Lancers' Shermans. The whole force consisted of more than a hundred tracked vehicles, linked by wireless.

In reserve were a squadron of the Bays, 254 Anti-tank Battery, a mortar platoon of the Kensingtons, 214 Field Company and an armoured troop R.E., and 152 Field Ambulance.

This phase of the campaign was to prove how effective was this complete armoured force for thrusting hard and fast against a shaken enemy defence, disgorging infantry whenever a centre of resistance was met.

But this was to look ahead. As dawn broke on April 11 the final phase was still at its beginning, and the men and guns of these follow-up brigades were moving over "Felix" Bridge—the bridge near Cotignola built by 237 Field Company—controlled by wireless from Divisional H.Q. At the same time, the Indians and New Zealanders, who had made steady progress, were crossing their second objective, the Santerno; here, in fact, the defences were cracking more easily than we had hoped—due, possibly, to the enemy's having held on too long to the untenable line of the Senio, and having suffered too much. A lot depended now on the Division's keeping up the initial pace of the Corps' attack.

The word "go" was given at two o'clock in the afternoon of April 12, when it was clear that the bridgeheads across the Santerno had merged and were firm. By early evening the Argylls, leading 36 Brigade, with two companies up, and supported by a squadron of 48 R.T.R. and by "C" Squadron of 56 Recce, were over the Santerno and a mile beyond the most forward troops of the Indian Division.

The Irish Brigade was crossing now, with its armour, but was held up by shelling of the bridge, and could not press on. But 36 Brigade did not wait for its support: the enemy was clearly disorganised, and the Argylls, riding on the accompanying tanks, and blazing away with their automatic small arms, had already penetrated three miles.

They got within a mile, in fact, of the village of Conselice that night, and the Divisional commander, anxious to exploit their swift advance, ordered the Brigade to press on. The Royal West Kents' advance was put forward so that they could go through the Argylls with a squadron of 48 R.T.R. to take Conselice.

The importance of this tiny village was that just to the west lay the last bridge over the Molini canal before this waterway joined the Reno river five miles farther north—the last way out to the west for the enemy troops still south of the Reno and east of the canal, and a way of escape that would be kept open to the last moment.

The Royal West Kents set out in the lifting darkness, supported by the tanks. In an hour their two leading companies were within 500 yards of Conselice, encountering stern opposition. One troop of the tanks knocked out two self-propelled guns, but the troop-leader was killed, his tank hit in the turret and captured. As always in his rearguard actions the enemy was making good use of his self-propelled guns. Throughout the morning they engaged the Royal West Kents and the tanks in the approaches to the town, and it was impossible for us to push on, even after intervention from our air forces.

All this, though, was to the left of the Division's main axis of attack, which lay along the road that ran due north to Bastia and Argenta. Here the Irish Brigade's advance began when the Royal Irish Fusiliers and the Inniskillings went forward in the early hours of April 13, a squadron of the Bays' Shermans and of 51 R.T.R.'s flame-throwing Churchills supporting each battalion.

It was slow and stubborn fighting between the canal on the left and the river Santerno on the right: the road ran, as it were, up the middle of a triangle the apex of which was where canal and river met, just short of Bastia. There were many enemy strong-points, which became harder to overcome as the front narrowed, and there was particularly tough fighting for both battalions in the villages of San Bernardino and La Giovecca before the order came to consolidate short of Cavamento. The left flank of this main advance was now exposed, for there was a gap between them and the Royal West Kents, in front of Conselice, but this was not the only reason for halting the Fusiliers and the Inniskillings; the thrust for Bastia was to be made by the composite Kangaroo Force.

It seemed that the enemy in front of Bastia was already shaken, for resistance to Kangaroo Force was patchy and undecided. Here and there, it is true, bazooka parties caused trouble, and one tank was lost to an anti-aircraft gun early in the battle, but it seemed, on the whole, that the enemy's grip was loosening.

By mid-afternoon the leading elements of the force were approaching the Forsotone Canal. The right flank was no longer limited by the Santerno river, and there was more room to manoeuvre. "G" Company of the London Irish dealt with the tough resistance that developed in the village of Cavamento la Frascata, near the canal, and "H" Company drove straight through in its Kangaroos, reaching the canal just in time to see the bridge blown in front of them. The infantry dismounted and, under covering fire from their tanks, crossed the canal on what was left of the road and railway bridges and rushed the houses beyond. By evening two troops of tanks had managed to get across the tumbled remains of the bridges, three companies of infantry were flushing a surprised and shaken enemy from the canal banks and the cellars of La Frascata, and the sappers were already building a new road bridge.

THE ARGENTA GAP

On the left 36 Brigade was still heavily engaged. The enemy was still firmly ensconced in Conselice, and we had not been able to make much progress there. Because of the rapid advance of the Irish Brigade on the right there was a gap on the Division's front between the brigades, and as the Royal West Kents were fully occupied in Conselice, a company of the Buffs were brought up to fill it.

The enemy was so determined to hold his ground on the left that he put in a strong counter-attack against the Royal West Kents: fighting went on until sundown, and the headquarters of the forward platoons were set ablaze by enemy shell-fire. It was decided that only a co-ordinated brigade attack would clear the flank, and the Buffs were accordingly ordered up to San Patrizio.

36 Brigade's plan was to push north-westwards to cut the road running westwards from Conselice to Chiesanova, and then to clear Conselice itself. The Argylls were to make a preliminary attack, clearing the area to the south-west of Conselice: the Buffs were then to pass through and cut the Conselice-Chiesanova road: and finally, at last light, the Royal West Kents were to clear the town.

The Argylls reached their objectives before midnight with little difficulty, taking seven prisoners at a cost of one man wounded; the Buffs went through; and the Royal West Kents, moving cautiously into Conselice, found that the enemy had withdrawn. The western flank was thus clear again, and 56 Recce Regiment pushed forward to keep it so. On the morning of April 14, therefore, the Division, the Italian Cremona Division, and 56 Division—in that order from left to right—were all converging on Bastia and Argenta.

That was the morning the London Irish reached the Reno river to find they could get across dryshod over the rubble of the bridges. Two platoons went over behind a smoke-screen, but the enemy struck back strongly; our tanks could not get over until a proper bridge was built, and the platoons had to withdraw.

But our front was forming well. The tanks had linked up with the Italians on the right and, although 56 Recce Regiment, fanning out along the line of the Sillaro river on the left, found many mines and the enemy infantry well dug-in, it was clear nevertheless that on the front as a whole the enemy's hold was loosening as he fell back on the main line of his defence based on Argenta. So it was still as important as ever to keep up the pace of our advance; somehow the whole weight of the Corps had to be brought to bear as quickly as possible against the Argenta defences; and to do this the Reno had to be bridged and crossed.

As it was, the offensive had gone according to plan for five days. The enemy had been forced back from the winter line on the Senio so quickly and positively that he had never been able to re-form and to hold a second line. The area had been cleared from the Senio to the Santerno, and from the Santerno to the Reno and the Sillaro. Argenta was only a couple of miles ahead, and away on the left Fifth Army's offensive was just beginning and Bologna was almost in sight.

* * * * *

The Argenta Gap was a narrow passage between Lake Commachio on the north-east and the Reno and its marshes on the south-west, a strip of firm land some two and three miles wide and four miles long, based on the town of Argenta itself, and carrying a main road and railway. The surrounding countryside, stretching to Lake Commachio on the east and to within ten miles of Bologna on the west, had been turned in peacetime from bog to fertile farmland by endless toil and modern machinery. Now the Germans had breached the dykes, smashed the pumping stations, and turned it back again to flood and marsh, with only the rooftops and the white streak of Route 16, on its high embankment, visible above the water. Every canal bank was dug out and fortified on its southern aspect, every culvert and bridge prepared for blowing, and the whole area turned into the most concentrated and extensive minefield the Division had come across. Fortunately, the Italian partisans knew of paths through the mines, or the Division would have suffered heavily indeed in the battles to come. The most formidable obstacles in the gap, apart from the minefields, were the floodbanks of the Reno river and the twelve-foot wide Fossa Marina, which ran diagonally across the northern end of the gap.

The enemy's defences south of the Po ran from the coast into the mountains south of Bologna. Initially they had been secured on his left by the Commachio Lake, but 56 Division and 2 Commando Brigade had forced him to fall back in this sector and his line was thus cut adrift at one end. The advance from the Senio and across the Santerno had caused the wholesale withdrawal of his front and, in order to stave off a major and strategic disaster and to get his Tenth and Fourteenth Armies across the Po, it was essential for him to find a firm pivot on which his whole line in the eastern sector of the plain could turn. This was the more urgent as the Polish Corps, south of Bologna, and the Fifth Army, further to the west, were loosening his hold on the mountains. Even if the whole front around Bologna should start to crumble, as indeed he felt it might, he still required that firmness between the mountains and the Adriatic so that an escape route might be kept open.

Eighth Army's main thrust was obviously towards Ferrara and the crossings of the Po to the north of the town; it was clear to the Germans that if they lost these they lost all their forces south of the river, and it was equally clear that Argenta was the place to stop the thrust. The motorised infantry of the excellent 29 Panzer Grenadier Division was swung out of the battles north-east of Bologna to the Argenta gap with orders to hold it as long as possible.

How long that would be depended on how quickly he could man his defences and how quickly we could rush them, and the Corps Commander decided not to wait for a bridge to be built over the Reno at Bastia. 11 Brigade, with Bays and 51 R.T.R., was sent, therefore, round our right flank to cross the river east of Bastia over a bridge belonging to 167 Brigade of 56 Division; and by the evening of April 16 the East Surreys on the right, the Northamptons on the left, and the Lancashire Fusiliers in reserve (having pushed through 167 Brigade and 56 Division near Bastia) were up to the Fossa Marina, the canal running eastward from the town of Argenta itself across the full width of the Argenta gap—the probable main line of the enemy's resistance.

Meanwhile 214 Field Company R.E. had succeeded in the not inconsiderable task of bridging the Reno at Bastia; the

APRIL 16-17, 1945

Irish Brigade had crossed to concentrate south-east of the gap, 2 Armoured Brigade had also crossed, and Divisional Headquarters followed.

Eleven Brigade's advance had been rapid and only lightly opposed, but extensive minefields had been encountered throughout, gradually thickening as the Fossa Marina was approached. On reaching the outskirts of Argenta and the line of this canal, enemy resistance became firm and a full-scale assault was clearly going to be required.

The plan evolved was that after dark, the East Surreys would move forward on the right and secure a firm base from which the Lancashire Fusiliers would assault the canal and outflank the town. Next day the Irish Brigade were to pass through the bridgehead to make room for the deployment of the Kangaroos.

The preliminary advance was successful, the Fusiliers began their assault, and within twenty minutes were fighting hand-to-hand. As their first company forced their way across the canal the waters were streaked and laced with blood, and ugly with corpses. By midnight, however, the battalion had succeeded in gaining a bridgehead on the far bank of the canal, two companies strong and 200 yards deep. Thanks to the fortitude of the sappers, working steadily under shell-fire, there was an Ark bridge behind them and three of the Bays' tanks across it.

The enemy was pounding the position with all he had. Heavy shell and mortar fire came down on the area of the crossing and along the banks of the canal. Three counter-attacks were thrown in and thrown back. The Lancashire Fusiliers did not give an inch, and their second-in-command, Major J. A. H. Saunders, won a D.S.O. that night for the way he handled the battalion after its commanding officer Lt.-Col. Pulford, M.C., had been wounded. As dawn broke our salient still pointed at the enemy's inner defences, and the German troops on its flanks were wavering.

Throughout the fighting the Divisional artillery and the heavy mortars of the Kensingtons had been laying down heavy supporting fire. It turned out that the Germans had brought across 29 Panzer Grenadier Division to the Argenta Gap in a desperate effort to hold it. This was his last reserve. The relief

THE ARGENTA GAP

was in progress on the enemy's side just as the fire-plan began and large numbers of Germans were caught in the open. Only later, as the bridgehead began to expand, did the remarkable results of the fire become apparent. Both from the barrage and from defensive fire the enemy's casualties were exceptionally heavy, and this at a time when he could ill afford to lose a single man.

From the outset, though, this attack had been chiefly a plain infantry slogging match. Its success was one of those achievements that can only be accomplished by the infantry; a bitter, painful struggle; and a solid, valuable prize, though small when measured in yards.

At first light on the morning of April 17 the East Surreys were ordered to move one company forward to protect the left flank of the Lancashire Fusiliers. After some determined resistance had been overcome this company succeeded in establishing itself in the north-east outskirts of Argenta.

The Northamptons, meanwhile, were holding a line on the edge of the town and acting as a pivot for the main weight of the Division's attack on the right.

The enemy's situation was beginning to look poor. He had failed to hold us on ground of his own choosing and he had every reason to believe that the main thrust was still to come. His forces, elements of the battered 42 Jaeger and 362 Infantry Divisions, had been bolstered up at the last moment, as we have seen, by the 29 Panzer Grenadier Division, rushed down from the north. The arrival of this formation was greeted by our own intelligence staff as a good omen. Evidently the enemy was feeling the draught in a big way; not only at Argenta, not merely in the eastern sector of the front were things beginning to crumble away, but in the whole Italian theatre. This division was the last major field formation in the Germans' Army-Group reserves.

So the enemy was preparing to make his last desperate stand at Argenta; but the crust had already been cracked by the Lancashire Fusiliers, and the Divisional Commander (Major-General Arbuthnott) was quick to realise that the strength of the whole Division would be needed to widen the crack decisively. On the morning of April 17 he ordered the Irish

APRIL 18, 1945

Brigade, with the Irish Fusiliers on the right and the Inniskillings on the left to pass through the Lancashire Fusiliers' tiny bridgehead in order to widen the gap so as to allow the armour and the Kangaroos to pass through. This was no easy operation either to plan or execute, because only one track and one bridge over the Marina Canal could be used, so that each brigade had to pass through the brigade in front. Moreover everything depended on timing. Had 2 Armoured Brigade been launched too soon its tanks and Kangaroos would have become bogged down close to the canal, blocking the only available track, and the whole momentum of the advance would have been lost. But it all went like clockwork.

Both the Irish battalions reached their objectives by the afternoon, the East Surreys pushed up on the left of the Lancashire Fusiliers on our side of the Marina, while the Northamptons set about clearing the town of Argenta itself, helped by the "Crocodile" flame-throwers of 51 R.T.R. The town was a hideous heap of rubble, the civilian dead piled in pathetic masses, and Germans still holding out in cellars and strongpoints. The Northamptons cleared it by nightfall only to be counter-attacked from the north in the early hours of April 18. The counter-attack, of company strength, with tank support, was not only beaten off but driven into the arms of the Inniskillings working round to the north of the town.

The Inniskillings, in fact, had two days and a night of heavy fighting in and around Argenta. The first two of their supporting tanks (from the Bays) were knocked out by an enemy self-propelled anti-tank gun; and enemy Tiger tanks pinned down the leading sections of infantry. In the scrappy but fierce fighting that went on from noon of April 17 to midnight of April 18/19 one company alone ("D" Company) killed eleven of the enemy, knocked out a Tiger tank and took twenty-six prisoners, among them the German battalion commander. This same company—so confused was the fighting—came under our own gunfire from the south-west, whence a Commando Brigade attack was being launched. So many guns were engaged that it was impossible to find the offenders, and the programme had to go on.

It was now possible to swing the next punch, to by-pass the

THE ARGENTA GAP

enemy still holding out just north of Argenta, and to leap-frog over the tired 11 Brigade and the Irish Brigade's break-through force. This time it was the turn of 36 Brigade and the Kangaroo Force of 2 Armoured Brigade and the London Irish. The plan was for 36 Brigade to advance as soon as possible on Boccaleone and Consandolo and then for Kangaroos to push N.N.W., towards the twin canals between San Nicolo and Portomaggiore.

At 2 a.m. on the 18th the Royal West Kents struck straight across the network of ditches, fences, wire and minefields for Boccaleone, two miles beyond Argenta on the main road through the gap. Across country, because the enemy was counter-attacking the Northamptons in Argenta and presumably had his tanks on the road to the north. The Argylls struck next—for Consandolo, the town beyond: two spearheads were driven in on the rear flank of the enemy whilst he was concentrating on an attempt to retake Argenta.

By dawn the enemy was in some natural confusion, the Royal West Kents were entering Boccaleone from the east, and the Argylls were not far from Consandolo.

Not all the enemy was fleeing, however. In addition to isolated men in scattered houses who decided to fight it out, there was a solid pocket of enemy still firmly ensconced in San Antonio, on the main road just west of Argenta. With the river to the west of them, and their enemies on the other three sides, they still fought on.

To clear this block from Route 16, which was to be the main line of communication for the whole Corps later on, 56 Recce was ordered to pass through Argenta and drive the enemy from San Antonio, but the regiment was unable to make any progress because of demolitions and bad going for vehicles.

By half past nine in the morning the Royal West Kents had done much mopping up in and around Boccaleone, and had taken thirty-eight more prisoners and a self-propelled gun. The Argylls, however, were running into the fiercest resistance they had so far encountered in the offensive. Four of their supporting tanks were knocked out in quick succession. The enemy infantry were coming to close quarters and bayonets were used. The whole battalion area was subjected to heavy fire from artillery and mortars. The closeness of the fighting was such that it was impossible for our own guns to bring any weight of fire to bear on the enemy without danger to our own troops.

But 36 Brigade was not alone in its offensive that morning. The Kangaroo army was out in the open engaging enemy tanks and self-propelled guns beyond the Irish Fusiliers on the right of the Argylls.

By mid-morning the whole front was ablaze. The Armoured Brigade, aiming at the twin canals Fosso di Porto and Scolo Bolognese, was forcing its way out into the open with the railway on the right and an unprotected flank on the left. Further west the Argylls were held up just short of Consandolo by determined enemy in strong points, and to the left again was an open flank down Route 16, until the Royal West Kents were met in Boccaleone, mopping up some difficult enemy pockets. Further south the R.A.F., at the request of 36 Brigade, was attacking San Antonio and shortly afterwards 56 Recce made a little progress up Route 16 towards this troublesome block.

Soon after midday the Argylls, still short of Consandolo, called for assistance from the air. Most of the village was razed to the ground and, beneath the piles of dust and rubbish, many bodies of German soldiers and Italian civilians were buried. Still, however, Consandolo held out and it did not fall until four in the afternoon, after a planned assault under barrage.

As darkness fell Kangeroo Force broke through the maze of canals and ditches, by the light of burning farmhouses, and past enemy guns firing over open sights. They took three bridges undemolished as they swept towards Coltra and Palazzo, an officers' mess, a battery of eighty-eights, a battery of fifteen centimetre guns, scores of single pieces and more than a couple of hundred prisoners. The enemy, having hung on as long as he could to stop the rot, was now in complete confusion, and 17 and 132 Field Regiments found themselves taking prisoners from the artillery of 42 Jaeger Division.

But there were still pockets of the enemy on the main road itself—Route 16, along which it was intended that 6 Armoured Division should strike direct at Ferrara.

A vicious little battle developed south of Boccaleone in

THE ARGENTA GAP

which almost every unit in the neighbourhood was involved. The Commando Brigade went in from the south under a heavy barrage, followed by the Inniskillings, who were involved until dawn in clearing houses and floodbanks, until the Royal West Kents came in from the north to close the circle and complete the kill.

The Buffs, meanwhile, who had followed the Argylls to Consandolo, struck out north-west in the darkness and by dawn, meeting only slight resistance, had marched eight miles to Benvigante. They had thus outstripped the farthest armour, made the longest foot-march of the operation—and brought the Division out into the open and through the Argenta gap.

In approximately sixty hours, by operations involving every battalion and armoured regiment of the Division, on ground of the enemy's own choosing, the 29 Panzer Grenadier Division, together with elements from four other enemy divisions (26 Panzer, 42 Jaeger, 98 Infantry, and 362 Infantry), had been driven from their positions and thrown back into the plain before the Po. The Division was out in the open, and 6 Armoured Division was about to pass through, striking northwest for Ferrara along Route 16; the Argenta Gap was broken and the enemy lay, straggled out along the southern bank of the Po, vulnerable at a hundred points.

CHAPTER XII

THE END IN ITALY

THE Po di Volano, although not as large as the Po itself, is a large river which runs due east from Ferrara and with the canal Diversivo di Volano, constitutes a major obstacle five miles or so short of the Po proper. It was to this water-jump, some fifteen miles ahead, that the Division was now turned, using the roads east of Route 16 by way of Portomaggiore; once over this next major obstacle we should be into the heart of the enemy's country; south of it we were on the fringe.

During the night of April 18-19 general activity continued. On the extreme right the Royal Irish Fusiliers moved forward on the east side of the railway and secured for the Division a firm right flank.

Further west the London Irish reached the twin canals Bolognese and di Porto just to the west of Portomaggiore. Here, a mile or so from the town, they found both bridges blown. In conjunction with 9 Lancers' tanks, which joined the infantry at first light, positions were established on the near bank of the double canal.

Between the London Irish and the Royal Irish Fusiliers "B" Squadron of 56 Recce, with some of the Sherman tanks of 4 Hussars, was having a confused struggle to cross the two canals in the town of Portomaggiore itself. An enemy strongpoint at Croatia, commanding the town's northern exits, was holding out with such obstinacy that no progress was possible beyond the second canal, and the squadron was confined to the difficult, rubble-strewn area of the town's western outskirts.

Patrols of 56 Recce, moving west through Consandolo, established that such enemy resistance as there was covered only the roads running northward west of Route 16, and was not a direct menace to 6 Armoured Division's main axis of advance, Route 16 itself, which was now opened for traffic.

During the morning of April 19, it had looked as if we would be able to use the route through Portomaggiore, but the enemy strong-point at Croatia was proving troublesome, and it was decided in the afternoon to cross the twin canals facing the London Irish, who were ordered to establish a small bridgehead near Porto Rotta.

11 Brigade was given the task of enlarging the Irish Brigade's bridgehead so as to cover bridging operations. In the very early hours of April 20, therefore, the Lancashire Fusiliers and the East Surreys, each with a squadron of tanks from the Bays, formed up to cross the two canals while the division's sappers set to work to make it possible for the tanks to pass over.

At two in the morning the Lancashire Fusiliers, followed by the East Surreys, began the crossing and shortly afterwards, still under mortar-fire, the sappers completed a bulldozed crossing and the tanks began to follow up. By late evening the Lancashire Fusiliers had made enough progress for the Irish Brigade to square up to their objective, and the East Surreys, on their right, had taken Gobbio. On the left the Buffs had also worked up to the canals and were in contact with the Fusiliers.

Meanwhile "B" Squadron of the Recce Regiment had failed to dislodge the enemy from Portomaggiore and Croatia on our extreme right—where it was important for 256 Field Company to build a bridge so as to open the main road north to Voghenza. One company of the Northamptons, with a Sherman squadron of 4 Hussars, had another shot at destroying the two self-propelled guns that were the kernel of the resistance. By nightfall the enemy was still in possession.

But by now 6 Armoured Division was advancing along Route 16, and the Divisional Commander decided that the Nicolo Canal would have to be attacked that night so that it could be bridged before the enemy was able to regain his balance and make it a defence line. The job was given to the Irish Brigade, with flank protection from the Northamptons and the Buffs, and armoured support from 10 Hussars.

At half past one in the morning of April 21 the Royal Irish

APRIL 21, 1945

Fusiliers and the Inniskillings moved forward under a barrage and crossed the canal by the rubble of the demolished bridges. The staging of this attack at short notice and in darkness was a particularly fine performance which could only have been achieved by very highly trained troops.

Opposition was lighter than had been expected, and by five in the morning the bridgehead was half a mile deep, taking in the village of Montesanto, and thirty prisoners had been taken, mostly from the 26 Panzer Division. Under cover of the bridgehead 237 Field Company succeeded in bulldozing a crossing of the canal which allowed 10 Hussars to begin moving across at about eight o'clock. By mid-morning most of the two squadrons had joined the infantry around Montesanto.

Meanwhile "B" Squadron of the Recce Regiment, with the tanks of 4 Hussars and the company of Northamptons, succeeded in clearing Croatia and so removed a constricting pressure from the right flank. The East Surreys, at about the same time, occupied Runco, to the north of the railway, and just short of the Nicolo canal.

In order to obtain a major break-through, however, it was necessary to unleash the Kangaroo Force as soon as possible. Before this could be done a larger bridgehead over the Nicolo canal was essential, and the Irish Brigade was ordered, therefore, to exploit its gains with all speed.

In spite of stiff opposition and some very heavy shelling, the Royal Irish Fusiliers and the Inniskillings succeeded in making a considerable enlargement of the whole bridgehead area by midday, and there was room at last for the Kangaroo Force to form up over the canal.

This time the orders to the Armoured Brigade were to advance to the Po di Volano and to seize Quartesana and Cona and the bridges over the canals at these two places. And to exploit the confusion caused by the advance of Kangaroo Force, and to protect its flanks, 56 Recce was ordered to occupy Voghenza, while 36 Brigade pressed on to the Po di Volano, west of Cona. The distance involved was about five miles from the bridgehead and it was getting late.

After an unpleasant spell in the assembly area, the force

began its advance at about three in the afternoon, creeping out into the open through the Inniskillings' positions.

As they tried to push on, both tanks and infantry came under intense fire from enemy self-propelled guns and tanks. They were frequently sited in and around the farm buildings that dotted the whole area, and every house was a potential strong point. Several times the infantry were compelled to dismount and mop up enemy posts of this kind as well as the individual soldiers with small-arms who seemed to pop up everywhere.

During the battle a number of enemy strong-points, tanks, and guns were destroyed by the R.A.F., whose fighters were at immediate call to Brigade.

Yet, as time wore on, the resistance began to stiffen more and more. Despite all that had been done by the R.A.F. and the infantry in Kangaroos, fire from enemy tanks and self-propelled guns increased. The gunners were trying to give maximum support, but it was impossible, at this late hour, for the whole divisional artillery to move forward within range of such a highly mobile force. It was the first occasion during the whole operation when the full weight of the divisional artillery was not available for each portion of the front. Even at this time the armoured force was able to call on the fire of 11 R.H.A., which was moving with the armour, on 17 Field Regiment (two batteries using super-charge), and on two medium regiments.

As darkness fell there was a growing atmosphere of suspense. The force, with its tanks and infantry and Kangaroos, was out on its own; no friendly troops were on either flank; close air support was over for the day and gunner support was limited; despite his disorganisation the enemy had plenty of men and guns in the neighbourhood.

A quick conference was held by 2 Armoured Brigade's commander: he confirmed that the bridges at Cona and Quartesana were to be seized that night.

The battle which followed was unorthodox, thrilling, and magnificently fruitful. By the light of a bright moon and of burning tanks and farm houses, the force approached the bridges simultaneously in two columns. "E" Company of the London Irish made for Quartesana and "F" Company for Cona.

Chaotic fighting ensued, with tracer flying in every direction.

Quartesana, the approaches to which were continuously under mortar fire, contained three enemy tanks, several strongpoints of bazooka men, and a number of machine-gun posts. The village and bridge beyond it were rushed, however, by the tanks and Kangaroos and, after knocking out two of the 9 Lancers' tanks, the enemy withdrew in confusion into the darkness. The bridge was taken intact.

In Cona a more complex battle developed. An enemy 15 cm. gun just beyond the river was firing over open sights into the area of the bridge and village. It was backed by strong groups of machine-gunners and bazooka-men. Two attempts were made by "F" Company, with tanks, to rush the bridge and the second was successful; a firm bridgehead was seized shortly after 11 o'clock that night and "H" Company was rushed up to reinforce "F" Company in holding the ground.

At 1 a.m. on April 22 both bridges were securely in our hands, more than five miles beyond the Nicolo Canal, which had been the front line at midday of the day before.

Meanwhile, 56 Recce Regiment had seized Voghenza, and 36 Brigade was moving up fast on the left. Far to the right the Surreys had at last seized Langirella and the road Portomaggiore–Quartesana was clear. Bailey bridges were quickly put in place and the divisional transport flooded forward.

These last few miles before Ferrara covered flat and open country, which despite the many canals and dykes proved to be favourable ground for our tanks. They made the most of it; by seven in the evening of April 21, the Argylls and the armour had reached Possessione San Antonio after encountering resistance similar to that in the Armoured Brigade's sector. Being without Kangaroo carriers, however, the infantry in this spearhead were less fortunate and suffered a number of casualties (about twenty-five wounded), between mid-afternoon and sunset.

After nightfall the Argylls, followed by the Royal West Kents, continued to push on rapidly to the line of the Po di Volano west of Cona. That this was achieved so close on the heels of the Armoured Brigade was a grand success for the pedestrian infantry. Later the Royal West Kents moved round behind the Argylls and began to clear up all the country south of the Po di Volano and as far west as the divisional boundary, just short of Route 16.

All eyes were now turned towards Polesella and Zocca—the last escape routes for the enemy across the Po which were now the Division's objectives. The next job, therefore, was to get across the Diversivo and Po di Volano. This task was given to 11 Brigade with 56 Recce.

During the afternoon, a good deal of enemy resistance was encountered in the area of Contrapo, three miles north of Quartesana on the bend of the Po di Volano, and thence northward and eastward. The Lancashire Fusiliers, who had been lorried up during the night to relieve the London Irish and 9 Lancers, were directed through the Recce Regiment's position to try and deal with some of this, and on the right the Northamptons were passed through and directed on the river to the east of the bridge by Fossalta. Resistance stiffened all along the front and it seemed that a considerable pocket of enemy was contained south of the river between Cona on the left and the Diversivo di Volano south of Fossalta, on the right, but it had, by evening, been almost entirely compressed into the river bend, or "bulge", near Contrapo.

With this exception the ground was now clear up to the Po di Volano. From the time at which 2 Armoured Brigade and 36 Brigade had broken out from the Argenta position, until 11 Brigade reached and crossed the Po di Volano, was a period of just over three days. In this time, the enemy had been relentlessly hustled along, day and night, until his whole force became compressed against the Po's south bank, as the Air Force continued to pound and slash at the crossings of this great river, and as the disorganised masses of men and transport, guns, tanks, horses, mules and all the cumbersome paraphernalia of war, grew larger and thicker in the fields and along the floodbanks. So long as the line of the Po di Volano held, there was always the chance of a "Dunkirk", but the line of the Po di Volano did not hold; someone failed effectively to blow the Sabbioncello bridge (in 56 Division's sector on the right) and in that second of time what slender chance there had been had failed.

* * * * *

By the morning of April 23 the Northamptons had a firm bridgehead over the Po di Volano and the sappers began work on the bridge at first light.

During the day the Northamptons carried out operations to extend their bridgeheads, and were supported in this by tanks of the Bays which were passed round through 56 Division's crossing at Sabbioncello and thence west along the north bank of the river. At the same time the Lancashire Fusiliers were still engaged in trying to wipe out the enemy pocket south of the river close to Baura.

By mid-morning the Northamptons succeeded in clearing Fossalta, and 11 Brigade was in process of passing the East Surreys across the river by boat and raft. Progress everywhere was slow, however, due to the open nature of the country, where wide fields of fire were available to the enemy from the innumerable little groups of farm-buildings dotted over the plain.

By evening the East Surreys were across the river and had joined the Northamptons, whilst 56 Recce with the Lancashire Fusiliers were trying to make progress into the area of the bulge and to the west of it.

At last light the Northamptons reached Giacomo, at the head of the bulge, and the East Surreys were beginning to pass through. The bridge at Fossalta was expected to be complete at any time and the Irish Brigade, with 10 Hussars, was ready to cross over in the darkness and push on.

At eleven that night the bridge was ready and the Inniskillings started to cross. The Royal Irish Fusiliers were to follow, and each battalion was supported by tanks of 10 Hussars.

Having crossed the river, the Inniskillings moved north as planned, and all went well until they began to approach Saletta in the early hours. Here, in the narrow approaches to the village, they began to run into serious trouble. The enemy's determination to stand was in no way diminished from its earlier intensity, and a fierce battle at close quarters ensued.

At this stage it was becoming glaringly apparent why the approaches to the Po just east of Ferrara were proving so troublesome. The 76 Panzer Corps, containing the 26 Panzer and the 29 Panzer Grenadier Divisions, which had been given the task of covering the withdrawal of all the other forces, had chosen as its own line of withdrawal the crossings over the Po in the area of Polesella. Thanks to the work of the R.A.F. the bulk of this Corps was still waiting to cross.

At 5 a.m. on April 24 the fighting in Saletta was over and the Inniskillings were breaking through the village and pushing north. As soon as they were clear the Irish Fusiliers followed and turned north-west towards Ruina. As morning broke both battalions were pushing out slowly but surely towards the Po.

On the left, meanwhile, 11 Brigade with the Bays had also made progress. The Northamptons advancing north-west from Giacomo were nearing Correggio at dawn, and the East Surreys, on the right, were preparing to attack a strong enemy position at Corlo, covering the bridge over the canal north-west of the village.

During the morning the break began to appear. The Northamptons attacked and captured Correggio; the East Surreys forced their way through Corlo and seized the bridge intact—a notable achievement, and one of the first importance at this stage; the R.A.F. struck at very strong enemy positions on the line of the Canale Fossetta, in front of which the Irish Brigade was held up; Kangaroo Force was passed over the river Po di Volano and prepared to strike out on its last task of destruction.

Amidst all this activity a further great work was in hand: plans were being made for crossing the Po itself and for the next stage of the pursuit. The Division had been ordered to cross the river with one brigade group as soon as could be done after reaching the south bank, but in a matter of hours the operation was cancelled. By now, the 6 Armoured, 2 New Zealand and 8 Indian Divisions were all up to the Po further to the west, and were meeting no opposition on the banks: so bridging began there, while 78 Division continued to force its way to the river through an area still strongly held by the enemy.

Soon after mid-day 2 Armoured Brigade's private army—Kangaroo Force—was launched. It was ordered to pass through 11 Infantry Brigade and sweep westward towards the main road running north from Ferrara to the Po at Pontelagoscuro. One hundred and fifty-six tracked vehicles, with some fifty thin-skinned supporting vehicles, began their sweep at 2.15 on the afternoon of April 24.

At the same time 11 Brigade was to do a similar sweep westwards and clear the ground between the Canale Fossetta and the Po di Volano.

The Irish Brigade was to continue on its original axis towards the Po, directed on Zocca and Ruina.

"Mobile battles" and "fluid situations" reigned during the afternoon. Having swept right across 11 Brigade's front, Kangaroo Force was strung out for two or three miles with an open right flank and with tank-actions in progress over the whole area; night was drawing on; the infantry, in their Kangaroos, were a wonderful target for lurking enemy tanks in the general confusion and semi-darkness. As evening approached, however, a distinct stiffening of resistance was noticeable on the Armoured Brigade's front. At 6 p.m. there were reports of many enemy tanks in the area just north of Ferrara, and shortly afterwards, as the light was failing, 9 Lancers fought an exciting tank-versus-tank battle and won its biggest regimental victory since El Alamein.

In this last flare-up of enemy resistance before the final collapse, the Lancers of Kangeroo Force destroyed the entire remaining tank strength of 26 Panzer Regiment—which had been taken by surprise, had decided to stand and fight, and had lost ten Mark IV tanks for only one of ours. The remaining crews deserted and destroyed their vehicles; and on the morning of April 25 the Kangaroo Force, which had advanced 15,000 yards in an afternoon and a night, found the triangle of country between Ferrara, Pontelagoscuro and Francolino littered with guns and equipment of all sorts, together with the **ten tanks and** four self-propelled guns they had destroyed and the thirteen tanks destroyed and abandoned by the enemy.

THE END IN ITALY

To exploit the enemy's distress, however, it had been decided on the previous night that the battle would be pressed on by moonlight. The landscape was ablaze with burning houses and vehicles; further north the R.A.F. was dropping flares and bombing the roads and railways beyond the Po; in addition to the fires caused by bombing, shelling and mortaring, a new destruction had begun—the enemy was setting light to everything he had.

At 8.30 that night V Corps telephoned to say there were strong indications that the enemy had lost control of the situation. Intelligence channels had intercepted messages from the German command that its plight was desperate, and that every man must fend for himself. It was believed that the chief confusion was centred around river-crossings north of Pescara and Francolino.

As a result, the Division Commander ordered Kangaroo Force to swing round to the north, cross the Fossa Lavezzola and make for the "disorderly enemy". This was not, however, to be done before the engagement already in progress was brought to an end.

Just before midnight Kangaroo Force, having had some four hours of intense and swift fighting, reported that things were beginning to quieten down. There had been a great deal of hostile fire from enemy tanks and self-propelled guns throughout its battle zone and the force had become widely dispersed, each portion, including Brigade Headquarters, having had its own battle to fight. The intention was to collect the bits and pieces together and move on towards the river as soon as possible.

In order to carry out this new task and switch the axis through more than ninety degrees, a deliberate advance was decided upon and a fire plan was arranged. By 1.30 a.m. the London Irish began to feel their way north, the tanks following some distance behind, ready to press through if opposition was met.

In the past few hours, however, the whole complexion of the front had changed. At sunset on April 24 there had been strong groups of enemy tanks and self-propelled guns mingled with numerous small detachments of infantry equipped with machine-guns and bazookas. These forces, although scattered and disorganised, had known their job and were determined to do it. They were to delay our advance by every means at their disposal, and especially in front of the crossings at Polesella, Zocca and Francolino. They were to fight until all their main elements had crossed the river.

As dawn approached on April 25 this proved to be no longer the case. Organised resistance was at an end.

A plan made overnight for the swift and thorough clearance of the whole divisional area was put into effect at first light. One squadron of the Recce Regiment came under the command of each of 2 Armoured, 11 and 38 Brigades, and these three formations were each given an area stretching south from a sector of the river bank for which to be responsible. On the right the Irish Brigade entered Zocca and Ruina to find an incredible scene of devastation. Packed in the fields, piled up in lanes, cast in ditches, in farmyards and woods everywhere—even in the river itself—lay the remains of the transport and equipment of the 76 Panzer Corps. Practically everything was destroyed: anything that had not been riddled with cannon-shell, or torn by bomb splinters from the air forces, had been burnt by the enemy as he fled. Abandoned horses roamed everywhere amongst the devastation.

To the west of Ruina, in 11 Brigade's sector, similar conditions prevailed, although there was less equipment than in the Irish Brigade's area. Having cleared up to the bank by mid-day the task of watching the river was handed over to its squadron of 56 Recce, and the battalions concentrated in Baura (Lancashire Fusiliers), Corlo (East Surreys), and Correggio (Northamptons).

On the left Kangaroo Force did a similar sweeping-up operation and handed over the river line to its Recce squadron by evening.

It remains to mention some of the arms whose achievements are so easily ignored.

The Kensingtons, for instance, took pride in the fact that every call received was effectively answered, that all platoons of the battalion were in continuous action, supporting every battalion in the Division in turn. They put down 12,206

4.2 inch mortar bombs and 314,750 rounds of .303 ammunition in the final offensive.

The Division's Royal Engineers were at least as ubiquitous. From April 10, when 237 Field Company built a sixty-foot Bailey bridge across which the Division crossed the Senio, to April 25, when the same company, and 214, found themselves operating an unopposed raft-ferry service across the Po, the sappers had an unusually busy and satisfying fortnight. The attack often moved so fast that minefields were over-run, and the situation became so confused that a sergeant of 256 Field Company—this is not an isolated example—removing charges from a captured bridge heard and saw a bridge blown up by the enemy only fifty yards away, and far behind the fighting. But the new system by which a sapper officer made an air reconnaissance each day did much to clarify the day's work, and 281 Field Park Company was particularly successful in moving and administering the vast, unwieldy sapper paraphernalia—bulldozers and transporters and the rest.

It has already been noted that the divisional artillery began the battle before the rest of the Division was engaged, in its support of the New Zealanders, but from the break-out onwards the artillery was back in support of the Division.

Throughout the next fortnight—a period of swift and unceasing movement—quick fire-plans and daily tactical intentions had to be issued over the telephone: there was no time to transmit written orders. On the night of April 14-15, for instance, V Corps ordered our divisional artillery to help in a barrage for 56 Division, attacking towards Bastia at six in the morning. The fire-plan was drawn from a conversation with Corps H.Q., forty-five miles away at the end of a weak telephone line, and it proved to be as well: the written orders and official trace did not arrive until the barrage had been fired.

First-class support from units of 2 A.G.R.A.; quick dumping of ammunition by the Divisional R.A.S.C.; close personal contact between the C.R.A. and the leading brigade; and the success of the new anti-tank organisation—all were leading features of the battle from the gunners' point of view.

Just as the artillery was involved in the final offensive before the Division itself, so it continued the battle for thirty-eight hours longer. By April 25, when the Division disengaged, the artillery was within four miles of the Po, and it was then switched to cover 8 Indian Division's advance along Route 16, until its own artillery was across the river.

The Divisional artillery, tired after its continuous support, finally ceased fire at eleven o'clock on the morning of April 27.

By that time the story was over. The Division had again fought a three-weeks' non-stop mobile battle, very similar to that in Sicily. What was notable about it was the continuous pressure exerted against the enemy by the G.O.C., Major-General Arbuthnott, who passed one brigade through another with unusual rapidity: it was seldom that any one brigade remained in the lead for more than twenty-four hours before it was given a mopping-up or flanking job, making way for a fresher brigade.

The close co-operation between infantry and armour (notably in Kangaroo Force), the support of R.A.F. spotters and Air O.P. aircraft, and the spirit and drive of all arms were all equally noteworthy.

The Division had played its part in fulfilling the intention of the Allied armies in Italy, and on the ground before it was the proof. Few realised yet, however, how near this was to the end of an epoch, but one who did know was Lieut.-Gen. Graf von Schwerin, commander of the 76 Panzer Corps who, with his personal staff, surrendered to the 27 Lancers on the morning of April 25. On being asked the dispositions of his Corps at that time, he is said to have replied—"You will find it south of the River Po".

On May 2 the German armies in Italy and Southern Austria surrendered.

THE OCCUPATION OF AUSTRIA

by

Maj.-Gen. R. K. ARBUTHNOTT, C.B., C.B.E., D.S.O., M.C.

APRIL 25 found the Division mopping up on the south bank of the Po. No further resistance was encountered, and the formations on the right and left moved forward across the river, leaving the Division to spend the remainder of the month in well earned rest and relaxation. A large number of German army horses had been rounded up, and a very successful gymkhana was held, as were a number of parties and celebrations. This pleasant interlude culminated on May 2 with the news of the surrender of the German armies in Italy. Apart from the fact that the Italian campaign was now finished, the news, coming as it did in advance of the general surrender, was particularly welcome to the much enduring Eighth Army, who had felt since North-West Europe's D-day that they had not got the recognition they deserved from the press and public at home.

The result of this event soon had its effect, and within twenty-four hours elements of 78 Division were moving northwards for a task with which they were to become all too familiar in the following weeks—the taking over of surrendered enemy troops. The situation in the north was reported as confused. Most Germans were readily giving themselves up. Others, covering the approach to the Austrian frontier through Tarvisio, claimed that they were not included in the surrender of Vietinghoff's Army Group. Further east large bodies of Jugoslav troops and partisans were swarming into eastern Venetia, hoping perhaps to stake a claim on this territory and anxious to get such spoils of war as were going. Italian partisans, including many women, were appearing from everywhere, some of whom were upholders of the Monarchist régime, and others who were of the "Red" variety or Garibaldini. All were heavily armed, trigger-happy, and spoiling for a fight with Germans, Jugoslavs and even among themselves. Orders for the treatment of German prisoners differed according to whether they gave themselves up before or after the surrender. In the one case they were to be treated as prisoners of war and evacuated to Italian P.O.W. camps. In the other case they were to be labelled Surrendered Enemy Personnel and treated somewhat differently.

It was accordingly something of a voyage into the unknown that began on May 3 at the river Po and which was halted for a few days in an area between Conegliano and Udine in the province of Venetia. The ultimate destination of the Division was Austria, where other and no less formidable difficulties awaited the arrival of the British Army. In addition to prisoners of war, surrendered enemy personnel and all sorts and conditions of displaced persons, there existed in the province of Carinthia two emigrant Russian formations, the Cossack and the Caucasian Divisions, which, having been used by the Germans for the purpose of holding down the Italian partisans in Northern Italy, had now retreated over the frontier and concentrated in the areas of Mauthen and Oberdrauberg. These migratory communities included about fifteen thousand troops plus their wives and families. Their transports consisted of droshkies with their characteristic wooden contraptions, packed with baggage, forage, women, children and numerous priests, and drawn by an extraordinary collection of horses and, in a few cases, dromedaries. Altogether they presented an uncouth and unmartial appearance, though there were some fine units of well-uniformed, tall and handsome men whom they called "The Guards". The officers included many ex-Tsarists who had never accepted the Soviet Régime.

The move of the Division into Carinthia began on VE day, May 8. The lovely valleys and unspoilt countryside made a refreshing contrast to the desolation of the Po valley, and the view from the top of the Croce Pass was unforgettable, with the Austrian villages looking like sparkling gems on the green landscape. 36 Brigade were directed to the Lienz-Oberdrauberg area and 11 Brigade went further east in the neighbourhood of Villach. 56 Reconnaissance Regiment

THE OCCUPATION OF AUSTRIA

travelled further north to Tamsweg in the Mur valley, while 38 Brigade passed temporarily under command of 6 Armoured Division in the area of Wolfsburg. This last was a particularly tricky assignment which involved encounters with Russians, Bulgarians, Slovaks, Croats and Jugoslavs. The adventures of 38 Brigade in this area would make a whole chapter in itself. Suffice to say that they sorted out the situation, prevented several minor wars from breaking out and held their own manfully till they were eventually relieved by 46 Division.

The period immediately following the arrival of the Division in Carinthia was hectic. To the task of collecting, checking and sorting out surrendered personnel was added the administration of thousands of displaced persons of various nationalities who had been conscripted for labour in Germany and Austria. Camps were nominated for the various types and steps were taken to move the different categories to the correct places. By May 17, 120,000 surrendered personnel were held. There were also a large number of German military hospitals to be supervised. Lists or inventories had to be made of all parts and dumps of enemy vehicles, arms, ammunition and stores. In addition, orders were received that all Hungarians in the British Zone were to be collected in 78 Division area north of Villach, while all Croat troops were to be handed over to the Jugoslavs. Trouble arose through the infiltration of Marshal Tito's troops into the southern part of Carinthia and dispositions, which fortunately turned out to be unnecessary, had to be made for their forcible ejection.

Everything seemed to come naturally to the British soldier and the work proceeded smoothly and without fuss. It soon became obvious, however, that one order of higher authority—the ban on fraternisation—was going to be difficult to enforce. The clean, well-favoured, plump Austrian girls and stolid, cheerful, inconsequent men folk were very difficult to hold at arms length. In any case, the British were supposed to be liberating the country and the locals were grateful for their protection from Russians and Jugo-Slavs, so circumstances were not favourable for an aloof attitude. The order ran:

"Troops will not make the running in any friendly

relations. Troops will not consort with civilians more than necessary. Apart from this, a correct and friendly attitude will be adopted."

Alas, the attitude soon became more friendly than correct and the order was eventually modified in recognition of the practical hardship that it sought to impose.

On May 23 it was learned that the Caucasian and Cossack Divisions, together with their families and transport, were to be handed over to the Russians. The concentration and dispatch of these unfortunate people took place early in June. It was a most distasteful task which was performed with firmness, but as humanely as possible. At first there was a good deal of resistance, but when it became apparent that the British troops were determined to execute their orders there was little further trouble, though a good many individuals escaped into the forests on the mountain sides.

The departure of the Russians was followed by a thinning out of the enemy population in the Divisional area. A scheme for the evacuation of surrendered German personnel to Germany was put into operation and a number of Austrian soldiers were discharged to civilian life. By the end of June the extra ration strength had dropped from 120,000 to 22,000. This was a merciful release and left time for other and more palatable occupations. By the energetic efforts of General McCreery a leave convoy taking some 300 officers and men of Eighth Army every second day on twenty-eight days' leave to the United Kingdom ran between Villach and Calais from the middle of June. All manner of sports were organised, such as football leagues, cricket, swimming, boating, boxing and trout fishing. A good deal of horse coping went on while units sought out likely moments for racing and show-jumping as well as for hacking. There were thousands of horses of every age, colour, size, condition and habit in the area, and units were authorised to keep a limited number to include a proportion for the use of mounted patrols. On July 14 the first Divisional Race Meeting was held. A very good course had been prepared at Spittal and several meetings were subsequently held there. These meetings were very popular and drew large crowds who patronised the

THE OCCUPATION OF AUSTRIA

Tote with perhaps more loyalty to their regimental horses than good judgment of form. There turned out to be a good number of fine performances amongst the horses and the names of The Panther, Katinka, Zonzalino and others will be remembered.

On July 6 a Divisional Ceremonial Victory Parade was held at Spittal. The large area formed by the Drau Valley in the surrounding hills made a wonderful setting. The whole Division was formed up in line and the Army Commander took the salute and afterwards rode down the line. He then took his place on the saluting base and, after two minutes silence and the playing of a lament in memory of the fallen, the whole Division marched past in column of companies or equivalent. The day was fine and a large number of spectators watched the parade. Staff officers and Battalion Commanding Officers, Seconds in Command and Adjutants were mounted and all succeeded in staying the course, thanks to much previous rehearsal. After the Divisional Staff came 56 Reconnaissance Regiment in their armoured cars; then the Artillery Field Regiments by batteries with Quads towing their guns. 64 Anti-Tank Regiment had their self-propelled guns on parade. The Engineers, being very busy, were represented by scout cars. The remainder of the Division marched on foot. It was a magnificent and moving sight watching these veterans swing past to their regimental marches played by the band of 4 Hussars and the pipes and drums of the Irish Brigade and the Argyll and Sutherland Highlanders. The standard of turn-out and drill of all units was quite remarkable. One could hardly believe that these same units only five months before had been living in mud and snow in the Central Apennines.

Thereafter changes took place both in the composition of the Division and in its commitments. The departure of 6 Armoured Division to Italy extended the divisional area to the whole of the province of Carinthia. A garrison was established in the British Section of Vienna, to which 78 Division contributed a battalion, a battery and a Reconnaissance squadron. Demobilisation made its inroads on numbers and individual units began to disappear. The 17 Field Regiment left for service in the Far East in July and later on 56 Reconnaissance Regiment and 138 City of London Field Regiment were disbanded. As the summer drew to a close thoughts were turned in the direction of securing an adequate supply of winter fuel. For various reasons there was an acute shortage of coal in Austria and the pinch was likely to be felt both in the British Zone and in Vienna. Accordingly a large programme of timber felling was started and, in addition to cutting for their own use, the troops, assisted by German S.E.P.s, set to work to provide great quantities for the Viennese. It was an arduous but healthy occupation, and work went on apace in the Unit and Brigade lumber camps until stopped by the onset of winter. In addition to this the Engineers, with German pioneers under command, were busy building hutted camps for Displaced Persons, of whom there were no less than 60,000 in the Divisional area—Poles, Jugoslavs, Balts, Reich Germans and White Russians, to mention only the larger groups.

Arrangements were made to reduce the number of horses in the Division to approximately four hundred. Difficulties of forage and stables made it impossible to keep more. However, Divisional Race Meetings were held till mid October and the season finished with a Meeting in Vienna, organised by General McCreery, which attracted horses and spectators from all over Austria and Italy.

With the approach of winter preparations were made for as many troops as possible to receive instructions in ski-ing. Expert Austrian instructors were engaged and Brigade Ski Centres arranged. The most convenient and probably the best was at Kanzal, north of the Ossiacher See, which was run by 38 Brigade. Although throughout the winter the snowfall was less than normal, all ranks who were so inclined were able to enjoy plenty of ski-ing, and many became efficient in a surprisingly short time.

Christmas brought the usual round of parties, including those given by every unit and headquarters to Austrian children. This was done at the suggestion of the Commander-in-Chief and was eagerly undertaken by all ranks. At this time there arrived the first party of married families who had travelled from home under "Operation Henpeck". A certain amount of requisitioning of accommodation and furniture was necessary to house these families but, as a considerable number of Reich

Deutsch families were being sent to Germany, no very great hardship was caused to the local Austrians.

And so came the New Year 1946. The Division was to exist for another eight months but now many of its best known personalities had gone home on release or been transferred to other parts. The New Year also saw the disbandment or transfer of many more units, and, though the spirit remained, the composition of the Division was altering rapidly. This then would seem to be the moment to bring the account of 78 Division's activities in Austria to a close. Let it suffice to mention that the summer of 1946 was passed in much the same way as that of 1945 except that most of the worries of the previous year were now well behind us and that the Divisional Commander was posted away in June and succeeded by John Combe who had commanded the 2 Armoured Brigade in the April battle in 1945.

The tale is now told, the Battleaxe laid aside and those who survived the years of campaigning are dispersed and scattered.

No one who was ever a member of that happy band can fail to look back with a certain nostalgia to the comradeship and friendship of the battle-fields and billets on the long road from Algiers to Austria.

APPENDIX A
ORDER OF BATTLE (*Major units only*)

11 INFANTRY BRIGADE
    2nd Battalion The Lancashire Fusiliers
    1st Battalion The East Surrey Regiment
    5th Battalion The Northamptonshire Regiment

36 INFANTRY BRIGADE
    5th Battalion The Buffs (Royal East Kent Regiment)
    6th Battalion The Queen's Own Royal West Kent Regiment
    8th Battalion The Argyll and Sutherland Highlanders (Princess Louise's)

1 (GUARDS) BRIGADE, *until March* 1943
    3rd Battalion Grenadier Guards
    2nd Battalion Coldstream Guards
    2nd Battalion The Royal Hampshire Regiment

38 (IRISH) BRIGADE, *from March* 1943
    6th Battalion The Royal Inniskilling Fusiliers, *until August* 1944
    2nd Battalion The Royal Inniskilling Fusiliers, *from August* 1944
    1st Battalion The Royal Irish Fusiliers (Princess Victoria's)
    2nd Battalion The London Irish Rifles

56 Reconnaissance Regiment

1st Battalion Princess Louise's Kensington Regiment

ROYAL ARTILLERY
    17 Field Regiment
    132 Field Regiment
    138 Field Regiment
    64 Anti-Tank Regiment (Queen's Own Glasgow Yeomanry)
    49 Light Anti-Aircraft Regiment, *until November* 1944

ROYAL ENGINEERS
    214 Field Company
    237 Field Company
    256 Field Company
    281 Field Park Company

ROYAL ARMY MEDICAL CORPS
    11 Field Ambulance
    152 Field Ambulance
    217 Field Ambulance
    47 Field Hygiene Section

APPENDIX B

COMMANDERS AND STAFF

These lists have been compiled from the available records, but it has not been possible to ensure their complete accuracy. In particular the decorations of officers at the time of their command are probably incomplete.

GENERAL OFFICER COMMANDING
Maj. Gen. V. Evelegh, C.B., C.B.E.   to 13.12.43
Maj. Gen. C. F. Keightley, C.B., D.S.O., O.B.E.   31. 7.44
Maj. Gen. D. C. Butterworth, D.S.O.   10.10.44
Maj. Gen. R. K. Arbuthnott, C.B., C.B.E., D.S.O., M.C.   thereafter

GENERAL STAFF OFFICER, CLASS I
Lt.-Col. A. Skeen   to 14.12.42
Lt.-Col. R. W. Hewetson   27. 8.43
Lt.-Col. R. B. James, D.S.O.   7. 1.44
Lt.-Col. D. E. P. Hodgson   29. 6.44
Lt.-Col. J. C. Preston, D.S.O.   26. 2.45
Lt.-Col. H. M. V. Nicoll   thereafter

ASSISTANT ADJUTANT AND QUARTERMASTER GENERAL
Lt.-Col. D. A. S. Browne   to 19. 1.44
Lt.-Col. C. E. Tryon   6.11.44
Lt.-Col. C. A. Chadwick-Healey   5. 3.45
Lt.-Col. R. L. Pugsley   thereafter

COMMANDER ROYAL ARTILLERY
Brig. J. Wedderburn-Maxwell, M.C.   to 12. 6.43
Brig. M. W. Denham   21. 2.44
Brig. C. D. Packard   26. 6.44
Brig. F. S. Reid, O.B.E.   thereafter

COMMANDER, ROYAL ENGINEERS
Lt.-Col. E. M. Blake, D.S.O., O.B.E.   to 14.11.43
Lt.-Col. H. C. W. Eking, D.S.O., O.B.E.   31. 3.45
Lt.-Col. R. B. Denton, M.C.   thereafter

COMMANDER, DIVISIONAL SIGNALS
Lt.-Col. J. C. Rau, O.B.E.   to 25. 1.44
Lt.-Col. W. A. Purser   11. 2.45
Lt.-Col. F. J. Shearer   thereafter

APPENDIX B

COMMANDER, ROYAL ARMY SERVICE CORPS
Lt.-Col. W. D. Hart — to 2. 6.43
Lt.-Col. A. Brown — 7. 2.44
Lt.-Col. J. F. Myddleton — 23.12.44
Lt.-Col. R. J. Wilkinson, M.B.E. — 5. 3.45
Lt.-Col. J. F. Myddleton — thereafter

ASSISTANT DIRECTOR OF MEDICAL SUPPLIES
Col. D. G. Cheyne, C.B.E., M.C. — to 27. 5.43
Col. J. C. Gilroy, O.B.E. — 16. 8.45

COMMANDER, ROYAL ARMY ORDNANCE CORPS
Lt.-Col. W. A. Kenney — to 16.12.43
Lt.-Col. F. S. R. Foster — thereafter

COMMANDER, ROYAL ELECTRICAL AND MECHANICAL ENGINEERS
Lt.-Col. T. Laird — to 5. 2.45
Lt.-Col. D. M. Aston, M.B.E. — thereafter

11 INFANTRY BRIGADE COMMANDER
Brig. E. E. E. Cass C.B.E., D.S.O. — to Oct. 43
Brig. R. K. Arbuthnott, D.S.O., M.C. — 10.10.44
Lt.-Col. J. A. Mackenzie, D.S.O., M.C. — 23.11.44
Brig. G. E. Thubron, D.S.O., O.B.E. — thereafter

2 *Lancashire Fusiliers*
Lt.-Col. L. A. Manly, M.C. — to Oct. 42
Lt.-Col. S. J. Linden Kelly, D.S.O. — June 43
Lt.-Col. J. A. Mackenzie, D.S.O., M.C. — Nov. 43
Lt.-Col. M. C. Pulford, M.C. — Feb. 44
Lt.-Col. J. A. Mackenzie, D.S.O., M.C. — Nov. 45
Lt.-Col. M. C. Pulford, M.C. — thereafter

1 *East Surreys*
Lt.-Col. W. B. S. J. A. E. Wilberforce, D.S.O. — to 6. 5.43
Lt.-Col. H. B. L. Smith, M.C. — May 44
Lt.-Col. H. M. A. Hunter, D.S.O., M.B.E. — 22. 7.45
Lt.-Col. R. D. Armstrong, C.B.E., D.S.O., M.C. — thereafter

5 *Northamptons*
Lt.-Col. A. A. Crook, D.S.O. — to 1. 5.43
Lt.-Col. T. A. Buchanan, M.C. — 8. 8.43
Lt.-Col. J. F. Connolly, D.S.O. — 18.12.44
Lt.-Col. D. J. B. Houchin, D.S.O., M.C. — 9. 5.45

36 INFANTRY BRIGADE COMMANDER
Brig. A. L. Kent-Lemon — to Dec. 42

APPENDIX B

Brig. B. Howlett, D.S.O. — to Nov. 43
Brig. Spencer — April 44
Brig. J. James — 26. 6.44
Brig. C. D. Packard — Dec. 44
Brig. G. R. D. Musson — thereafter

5 *Buffs*
Lt.-Col. T. N. Penington — to 9. 1.43
Lt.-Col. A. D. McKechnie, D.S.O. — 2.11.43
Lt.-Col. G. M. de B. Monk, M.C. — 19. 5.44
Lt.-Col. C. R. Tuff — 31.10.44
Lt.-Col. A. J. Odling-Smee — 12.11.45
Lt.-Col. D. A. Affleck-Graves — thereafter

6 *Royal West Kents*
Lt.-Col. B. Howlett, D.S.O. — to 20.12.42
Lt.-Col. H. O. Lovell — 21. 2.43
Lt.-Col. E. S. Heygate — 30. 4.43
Lt.-Col. H. O. Lovell — 10. 7.43
Lt.-Col. P. E. O. Bryan — 10. 5.44
Lt.-Col. R. A. Fyffe — 15. 6.44
Lt.-Col. E. K. Defrates — thereafter

8 *Argyll and Sutherland Highlanders*
Lt.-Col. J. G. Mackellar, D.S.O., O.B.E. — to March 43
Lt.-Col. C. Macnab — April 43
Lt.-Col. J. Scott Elliott, D.S.O. — Nov. 43
Lt.-Col. J. Taylor, M.C. — Nov. 44
Lt.-Col. A. D. Malcolm, O.B.E. — Oct. 45

1 (GUARDS) BRIGADE COMMANDER
Brig. F. A. V. Copland-Griffiths, D.S.O., M.C.

3 *Grenadiers*
Lt.-Col. A. G. W. Heber-Percy, D.S.O.

2 *Coldstream*
Lt.-Col. W. S. Stewart Brown, D.S.O.

2 *Hampshires*
Lt.-Col. J. Lee, D.S.O. — to Dec. 42
Lt.-Col. S. J. Martin — thereafter

38 (IRISH) BRIGADE COMMANDER
Brig. N. Russell, M.C. — to March 44
Brig. T. P. D. Scott, C.B.E., D.S.O. — thereafter

APPENDIX B

6 Royal Inniskilling Fusiliers
Lt.-Col. C. H. B. Allen	to April 43
Lt.-Col. T. M. Grazebrook, D.S.O.	Jan. 44
Lt.-Col. B. L. Bryar	March 44
Lt.-Col. H. E. L. Bredin, D.S.O., M.C.	June 44
Lt.-Col. J. Kerr, M.C.	Nov. 44
Lt.-Col. D. M. Shaw, D.S.O., M.C.	thereafter

1 Royal Irish Fusiliers
Lt.-Col. T. P. D. Scott, C.B.E., D.S.O.	to mid-March 43
Lt.-Col. B. H. Butler, D.S.O.	23.10.43
Lt.-Col. J. W. Dunnill, D.S.O.	June 44
Lt.-Col. J. H. Coldwell-Horsfall, D.S.O., M.C.	Dec. 44
Lt.-Col. M. J. F. Palmer, D.S.O.	Aug. 45
Lt.-Col. G. A. French, O.B.E.	till disbandment

2 London Irish Rifles
Lt.-Col. T. P. D. Scott	to 12. 7.43
Lt.-Col. M. Rogers	from 12. 7.43
Lt.-Col. I. M. Goff	19.12.43
Lt.-Col. J. H. Coldwell-Horsfall, D.S.O., M.C.	15. 5.44
Lt.-Col. H. E. L. Bredin, D.S.O., M.C.	9. 7.44

56 RECONNAISSANCE REGIMENT
Lt.-Col. K. G. F. Chavasse, D.S.O.	to 7. 3.45
Lt.-Col. R. W. M. R. Hartland-Mahon, M.C.	thereafter

1 KENSINGTONS
Lt.-Col. F. G. Parker	to 21. 3.44
Lt.-Col. B. L. Bryar	thereafter

17 Field Regiment, R.A.
Lt.-Col. R. S. Baker, D.S.O.	to 17. 2.45
Lt.-Col. R. B. Lecky, D.S.O.	9. 3.46
Lt.-Col. E. N. K. Estcourt, D.S.O., O.B.E.	thereafter

132 Field Regiment, R.A.
Lt.-Col. E. S. Herbert, D.S.O.	to 20. 6.43
Lt.-Col. J. T. G. Palmer, O.B.E.	20. 1.44
Lt.-Col. H. M. V. Nicoll, D.S.O., O.B.E.	9. 7.44
Lt.-Col. J. F. Adye, D.S.O.	8. 6.45
Lt.-Col. L. P. Twomley, D.S.O.	thereafter

138 Field Regiment, R.A.
Lt.-Col. T. C. Usher, C.B.E., D.S.O.	to 17. 7.44
Lt.-Col. K. Scott-Foster, O.B.E.	18. 2.45
Lt.-Col. G. A. Thomas, O.B.E.	thereafter

APPENDIX B

64 *Anti Tank Regiment, R.A.*
Lt.-Col. R. J. G. Temple
Lt.-Col. B. Kingsett, M.C. — to 3.10.43
Lt.-Col. J. Anderson — 31. 8.45
Lt.-Col. C. H. Drew — 12.10.45

49 *Light Anti Aircraft Regiment, R.A.*
Lt.-Col. G. V. Hunt, O.B.E., T.D. — to 8. 5.44
Lt.-Col. A. L. Mathews, O.B.E., M.C. — Disbanded 18.12.44

11 *Field Ambulance*
Lt.-Col. T. A. Butcher — to 1.12.42
Lt.-Col. R. G. M. Keeling — 8. 7.44
Lt.-Col. F. C. Mayo — 6.11.44
Lt.-Col. J. B. Barr — thereafter

152 *Field Ambulance*
Lt.-Col. W. D. F. Lytle — to 29. 6.44
Lt.-Col. F. A. Bevan — thereafter

217 *Field Ambulance*
Lt.-Col. J. C. Gilroy — to 6. 3.43
Lt.-Col. K. H. Clark — 31. 7.43
Lt.-Col. A. Crerar — thereafter

GLOSSARY

A.A. & Q.M.G., *(A.Q.)* Assistant Adjutant and Quarter Master General; senior divisional administrative staff officer.

A.D.M.S. Assistant Director of Medical Services; senior divisional Medical officer.

A.D.O.S. Assistant Director Ordnance Supply; senior divisional Ordnance officer.

A.F.V. Armoured fighting vehicle

A.G.R.A. Army Group Royal Artillery, usually heavy guns.

A.P.M. Assistant Provost Marshal; senior divisional Provost officer.

Ark. Tank without a turret, which is fitted with ramps; it is driven in to the crater or stream to be crossed, and itself acts as the bridge over which other vehicles can then pass.

A.V.R.E. Armoured Vehicle Royal Engineers; sapper armoured equipment.

Bazooka. Infantry anti-tank weapon, usually rocket propelled.

Beehive. Explosive charge primarily designed for blowing holes in rock or hard ground.

Bofors gun. Light anti-aircraft gun.

Buffalo. An amphibious troop-carrying tracked vehicle used in assaulting across water obstacles.

Carrier. Light infantry tracked vehicle.

Casa. (Italian) house.

Churchill. British heavy infantry tank.

C.L.Y. County of London Yeomanry.

C.O. Commanding Officer.

Compo Rations. Portable boxes of rations, one box containing fourteen men's rations for one day.

C.R.A. Commander Royal Artillery; senior divisional Artillery officer.

C.R.E. Commander Royal Engineers; senior divisional Engineer officer.

Djebel. (Arabic) hill.

D.U.K.W. American amphibious wheeled vehicle.

Fantail. Unofficial name for Buffalo, *q.v.*

GLOSSARY

Fire Platoon or Company. Unit which gives covering fire to other units going into the attack.

F.O.O. Forward Observation Officer.

F.W. Focke Wulf, German fighter aircraft, often used as fighter bomber.

G. Staff. General Staff, with operational responsibility.

Grant. American light tank.

G.1098. Official list of all arms and equipment which a unit is entitled to hold.

H.A.C. Honourable Artillery Company.

Honey. American light tank.

H.Q. Headquarters.

L.A.A. Light Anti Aircraft.

L.I.A.P. Leave in addition to Python. A special system of leave in U.K., in addition to the usual transfer to the home establishment after a certain period of service overseas.

Mark IV. German medium tank.

M.E.109. German fighter aircraft.

M.M.G. Medium machine gun.

M.O. Medical Officer.

M.P. Military Police.

M.T. Motor Transport.

Nebelwerfer. German multiple rocket launcher, whose projectiles were made to produce an alarming whine as they fell.

O.P. Observation Post.

Oued. (Arabic) gully.

Panther. German Mark IV tank mounted with an 88mm. gun.

P.I.A.T. Projector Infantry Anti-Tank; similar to bazooka but spring operated.

Portee. Truck built to tow or carry a light anti-tank gun.

Python. System of U.K. leave for overseas forces.

Quad. Truck used to tow 25 pounder gun.

Q.M. Quarter Master.

Q. Staff. Quartermaster Staff, with supply responsibility.

R.A. Royal Artillery.

R.A.C. Royal Armoured Corps.

R.A.M.C. Royal Army Medical Corps.

GLOSSARY

R.A.S.C. Royal Army Service Corps.

R.E.M.E. Royal Electrical & Mechanical Engineers.

R.H.A. Royal Horse Artillery, now equipped with guns mounted on tracked vehicles.

R.T.R. Royal Tank Regiment.

S.A.S. Special Air Service.

Scorpion. Tanks equipped with chain flails for detonating mines in front of them.

S.E.P. Surrendered Enemy Personnel.

Sherman. American cruiser tank.

Stuka. German dive bomber.

Supercharge. Extra charge used by artillery when it is imperative to operate at over the normal maximum range.

Tiger. German heavy tank, mounting an 88mm. gun.

Tommy Cookers. Small portable solid fuel cooker, which can be used in a trench.

Upper Register. The use of the 25 pounder gun as a howitzer rather than a field gun, *i.e.* when firing at a high trajectory, as in mountainous country.

Valentine. British light/medium tank.

Very light. Signal flare, fired by pistol.

Wadi. (Arabic) gully.

Weasel. Light armoured vehicle with wide tracks, suitable for traversing snow or mud.

W.O. Warrant Officer.

Viper. A rocket discharger which throws an explosive charge into minefield in order to detonate the mines.

INDEX

Ace Route, 126
Acqua Salata—See Monte Del Acqua Salata
Adams, R.S.M., A. H., D.C.M., 18
Adderley, Capt., 46
Adolf Hitler Line, 123, 126, 131, 133, 134, 135, 140
Adrano, 62, 63, 64, 68, 69, 71, 72, 73, 77
Adriatic Sea, 207
Adye, Lt.-Col. J. F., D.S.O., 193, 239
Affleck-Graves, Lt.-Col. D. A., 238
Alatri, 138, 140, 146
Alban Hills, 137
Aletrium—See Alatri
Alexander, Field-Marshal Viscount, v, 55, 59, 61, 64, 68, 93, 108, 124, 133, 140, 141, 160
Alexandria, 153, 154
Alexandria—Cecil Hotel, 153, Claridge's Hotel, 153
Algeria, 33
Algiers, xviii, xx, xxi, 3, 4, 5, 6, 7, 8, 17, 25, 33, 54, 59, 233
Allen, Lt.-Col. C. H. B., 239
Allfrey, Lt.-Gen. Sir Charles, K.B.E., C.B., D.S.O., M.C., xiii, 26, 31, 99, 102, 103
Allkin, L/Cpl., 128
Amalfi, 123
Anderson, Capt. (later Maj.), V.C., D.S.O., 43, 49, 50-1, 88, 130
Anderson, Capt. (later Maj.), D. J., M.C., 75, 148
Anderson, Lt.-Col. J., 240
Anderson, Gen. Sir Kenneth, K.C.B., M.C., v, 4, 5, 6, 7, 8, 26, 31, 34, 44, 47, 48
Andrews, Maj., 91
Anzio, 108, 111, 112, 124, 135, 137, 140, 156
Apennine Mountains, Central, 231
Apennine Mountains, Northern, 159, 161
Apennine Mountains, Southern, 93, 108, 155
Aquino, 123, 126, 134, 135
Arbuthnott, Maj.-Gen. R. K., C.B., C.B.E., D.S.O., M.C., vi, 157-8, 165, 209, 226, 227, 237
Arce, 135, 136, 140

Argenta, 198, 203, 205, 206, 207, 208, 209-10, 211, 219
Argenta Gap, 157, 206, 207, 208, 213
Armstrong, Lt.-Col. R. D., C.B.E., D.S.O., M.C., 237
Aurunci Mountains, 116
Ashmore, Lt.-Col. G., O.B.E., vi
Assisi, 161
Aston, Lt.-Col. D. M., M.B.E., 237
Atlantic Ocean, xix
Auchinleck Avenue, 36
Austin, A. B., vi, 33, 45
Austria, 226, 227-233
Avola, 61
Azores, xx

Badoglio, Marshal, 81
Bagnacavallo, 195
Baker, Lt.-Col. Rollo S., D.S.O., 113, 193, 239
Bald Hill (Djebel Afred), 14, 15, 24, 36, 37, 54
Baldy, Sgt., M.M., 120
Banana Ridge, 42, 48, 54
Barber, Capt., 21
Bari, 82, 83, 84, 86
Barker-Benfield, Capt., M.C., 13
Barletta, 87
Barnes, Cpl., 129
Bastia, 201, 203, 204, 205, 207, 225
Baura, 220, 224
Baxter, Lt., 127
Beja, 9, 10, 12, 24, 40, 44
Bell, Fusilier, M.M., 145
Bell, Sgt., M.M., 171
Belvedere, 112
Beni Yusef, 154
Benvigante, 213
Bernstein, Capt., D.F.C., R.A., 162
Bettiour, 52
Biferno River, 85, 86, 87, 89
Bizerta, xxi, 6, 9, 10, 14, 15, 40, 44, 48, 54
Blake, Lt.-Col. E. M., D.S.O., O.B.E., 100-1, 236
Blida, 4, 5
Boccaleone, 211, 212
Bologna, 159, 160, 163, 169, 206, 207
Bolognese Canal, 214
Bone, 7-8, 10, 17, 33, 34

R* 245

INDEX

Bou Arada, 37, 41, 43
Bougie, 5, 7, 11
Bowater, Lt.-Col., 177
Bowles, Lt. S. D., v
Bredin, Lt.-Col. H. E. L., D.S.O., M.C., 133, 156, 239
Brocklebank, Maj. G. R., D.S.O., M.C., v
Bronte, 72, 73, 74, 75
Brooke-Fox, Maj., 41
Brown, Lt.-Col. A., 237
Browne, Lt.-Col. (later Brig.), D. A. S., C.B.E., vi, 64, 236
Bryan, Lt.-Col. P. E. O., 238
Bryar, Lt.-Col. B. L., 239
Buchanan, Maj. (later Lt.-Col.) T. A., M.C., 18
Buckley, Christopher, vi
Bunting, Sgt., 92
Burrit, Sgt. S. F., M.M., 89
Burroughs, Admiral, xix
Butler, Lt.-Col. Beauchamp, D.S.O., 68, 95, 239
Butler's Hill, 53
Butterworth, Maj.-Gen., D. C., D.S.O., 157, 236

Cairo (Egypt), 153, 154
Cairo—Continental Hotel, 153
    Shepheard's Hotel, 153
    Grand Hotel, 153
    Royal Oak Hotel, 153
Cairo (Italy), 119
Calais, 330
Camaggio, 174, 185, 186
Campobasso, 85, 107
Campomarino, 90
Canale Fossetta, 221, 222
Cap Bon, 55
Cap Serrat, 40, 44
Cape Passero, 61
Capracotta, 107, 110
Capri, 93, 123
Capua, 85, 111, 122, 125
Capuan Valley, 191
Carey, Maj. D., v, 74
Carinthia, 228, 229, 231
Casablanca, xx
Casa Calvana, 185
Casa Casino, 166
Casa Di Spinello, 169, 170, 171, 172-3, 184
Casa Filetto, 166
Casa Maletto, 175
Casa Ortica, 185
Casa Salara, 172, 173, 184, 185, 189
Casa Tamagnin, 187-8
Casetta Ridge, 174

Casoli, 108
Casone, 173
Cass, Brig. E. E. E., C.B.E., D.S.O., 52, 237
Cassino, xv, 111-113, 114-121, 123-133, 134, 139, 140, 153, 156, 157, 176, 177, 178
Castel Del Rio, 161, 162, 163, 164, 178, 179, 181, 183, 187, 188
Castel Del Rio—"Golden Chopper" Canteen, 179, Wally's Bar, 179
Castel di Judica, 62
Castel Di Sangro, 108
Castellone, 112
Castel San Pietro, 169
Castiglione Del Lago, 149, 150, 151, 152
Castle Hill (Cassino), 115, 116
Catania, 62, 68, 71, 73, 75, 78
Catania Plain, 60, 61, 62
Catenanouva, 62, 63, 64, 65
Cavamento La Frascata, 204
Centuripe, 62, 63-8, 69, 71, 73, 77, 78
Ceprano, 136
Chadwick-Healey, Lt.-Col. C. A., 236
Chamberlain, Maj., 19
Chaouach, 43, 46, 47
Charters, Capt., 171
Chavasse, Lt.-Col. K. G. F., D.S.O., 83, 142, 193, 239
"Cherry Ripe"—See Centuripe
Chiesanova, 205
Cheyne, Col. D. G., C.B.E., M.C., 53, 237
Chichester, Maj. The Hon. A. P. S., 27
Chidwick, L/Cpl. D., M.M., 63
Chiusi, 148, 150
Chouigui Plain, 18
Churchill, Winston S., 55, 68, 108
Citta Della Pieve, 145
Clark, General Mark, 81, 112
Clyde River, xviii, xix,
Codronco Spur, 163
Coldwell-Horsfall, Lt.-Col. J. H., D.S.O., M.C., 156, 187, 239
Colle, The, 102
Collins, Lt.-Col. D. G., v
Coltra, 212
Combe, Brig., John, 191, 202, 233
Commachio, Lake, 206, 207
Cona, 216, 217-8, 219
Conegliano, 228
Connolly, Lt.-Col. J. F., D.S.O., 193, 237
Consandolo, 211, 212, 213, 214
Conselice, 203, 204, 205
Constantine, xxi
Contrapo, 219

INDEX

Cook, Maj. Reggie, 128
Copland-Griffiths, Brig. F. A. V., D.S.O., M.C., V, 238
Corlo, 221, 224
Correggio, 221, 224
Cortona, 152
Corunna, 93
Cotignola, 193, 194, 201, 202
Cowan, Capt., 145
Crerar, Lt.-Col., M.C., D.S.O., 89
Croatia (Italy), 214, 215, 216
Croce Pass, 228
Crocker, Maj., 144
Cronin, Sgt., D.C.M., 196
Crook, Lt.-Col. A. A., D.S.O., 237
Crotone, 83
Cupello, 95, 97
Currie, Brig. John, 83, 102
Cuviolo, 173, 180

Dakar, xviii, 6
d'Arcy-Dawson, John, vi
Darlan, Admiral, 4
Davies, Capt., 138
Davies, Sgt., John, M.M., 42
Dawnay, Lt.-Col., D.S.O., 52
Dawson, Capt. J. F., v
Dawson, Lt., M.C., 15
Deans, Gunner, M.M., 16
Defrates, Lt.-Col. E. K., 238
De Guingand, Gen., 68
Denham, Brig. M. W., 236
Denison-Pender, Maj. The Hon, R. E., v
Denton, Lt.-Col. R. B., M.C., 193, 236
Depienne, 17
Dignal, Pte., M.M., 43
Di Porto Canal, 214
Dittiano River, 62, 64
Diversivo Di Volano, 214, 219
Dixon, Maj. T., M.C., v
Djebel Abiod, xxi, 6, 8, 10-12, 13, 14, 24, 43
Djebel Afred (Bald Hill), 14
Djebel Ahmera (Longstop Hill), 25
Djebel-El-Ang, 46, 47, 52
Djebel-El-Azzag (Green Hill), 14
Djebel-El-Hamara, 18
Djebel-El-Rhar, 28, 29, 30, 51, 53
Djebel Mansour, 39
Djebel Touila, 45
Djedeida, 9, 16, 17, 18
Djidjelli, 5
Douaouda, 3
Drau Valley, 231
Drew, Lt.-Col. C. H., 240
Dryshod Drive, 36
Dudgeon, Lt.-Col. J. Hume, 31, 46

Dunkirk, 55
Dunn, Maj. 95
Dunnill, Lt.-Col. James, W., D.S.O., 148, 239
Durnford-Slater, Lt.-Col. 86

Egypt, 146, 153-7, 176
Eisenhower, Gen., 5, 8, 31, 59
Eking, Lt.-Col., H. C. W., D.S.O., O.B.E., 193, 236
El Alamein, xix, 32, 222
El Aouana (Airfield), 6
El Bathan, 20
Elliott, Lt.-Col. J. Scott, D.S.O., 88, 103, 238
Elworthy, Capt., 144, 165
Enfidaville, 48
Erskine, Capt., Barry, 15, 51
Estcourt, Lt.-Col. E. N. K., D.S.O., O.B.E., 239
Esteva, Admiral, 6
Etna, Mount, 60, 61, 62, 63, 69, 72, 75, 77
Eustace, Sgt., D.C.M., 16
Evans, Bdr., G. H., M.M., 74
Evelegh, Maj.-Gen. V., C.B., D.S.O., M.C., vi, xviii, 5, 25, 45, 54, 63, 65, 66, 67, 68, 72, 75, 78, 89, 90, 96, 99, 102, 103, 105-6, 236

Faenza, 185
Faid, 38
Fano, 160
Faye, Lt., 172
"Felix" Bridge, 202
Feltrino, 104
Ferrara, 207, 212, 213, 214, 218, 221, 222
Fewson, Maj., 96
Figline, 161
Figna Di Sotto, 185, 186
Filetto Spur, 164, 165
Filetto Torrente, 165, 168
Firenzuola, 160, 161
Fitzgerald, Maj. Peter, M.C., 71
Florence, 141, 143, 159, 161, 189
Foggia, 83, 87
Forli, 190, 191
Forman, Maj., 98
Forsotone Canal, 204
Fort Macgregor, 41, 42
Fossacesia, 103, 104
Fossalta, 219, 220
Fossa Lavezzola, 223
Fossa Marina, 206, 207, 208
Fosso Di Porto, 212
Foster, Lt., 142-3
Foster, Lt.-Col., F.S.R., 237

INDEX

France, xviii, 140, 156, 179
Franco, Gen., xvii
Francolino, 222, 223, 224
Franklyn-Vaile, Laurie, 133
Fraser, Lt., 51
Freemantle, Lt., 20
Freyberg, Gen., 99, 105
Fritz's Bund, 196
Frosinone, 112, 136, 138
Fumone, 139
Fyffe, Lt.-Col., R. A., 238

Gabes, 6
Gafsa, 39
Gaggla, 152
Gamble, Lt., 149
Gari River, 116
Garigliano River, 156
Gela, 59
George, Cpl., 171
Gerbini Airfields, 60, 71
Gesso, 163, 164, 165, 167, 168, 171, 173
Gezirah Club, 154
Gezirah Island, 154
Ghardimaou, 8
Giacomo, 220, 221
Gibraltar, xvii, 4
Gibson, Capt., 74
Gibson, Lt., 13
Gilbertson, Capt. J., M.C., 89
Gilroy, Col. J. C., O.B.E., vi, 237
Glasgow, xix
Gobbio, 215
Goff, Lt.-Col. Ion, 133
Gothic Line, 154, 159
Graham, Capt., 170
Granarola, 195
Grande, 136
Grazebrook, Lt.-Col. T. M., D.S.O., 68, 239
Green Hill (Djebel-El-Azzag), 14, 15, 24, 36, 37, 54, 84, 176
Grenadier Hill, 12, 26, 30
Grey-Turner, Lt., 29
Griffith, Lt., 19
Guglionesi, 94
Gully House, 174
Gustav Line, 123, 126, 130, 131, 133, 134, 135

Hadrian's Villa, 153
Hancock, Maj. M. S., v
"Hangman's Hill", 115
Hannibal, 146, 150, 152
Harris, Maj. D. A., M.B.E., M.C., v
Hart, Maj. V., 9
Hart, Lt.-Col. W. D., 237

Hartland-Mahon, Lt.-Col. R. W. M., R., M.C., 193, 239
Heartbreak Highway, 36
Heber-Percy, Lt.-Col. A. G. W., D.S.O., 23, 238
Hefferland, Cpl., D.C.M., 109
Heidous, 46, 47, 49, 52, 53
Heidrich, Gen., 116
Herbert, Lt.-Col. E. S., D.S.O., 239
Hewetson, Lt.-Col. R. W., 236
Heygate, Lt.-Col. E. S., 238
Highway Nine, 159, 168, 169, 185
Highway Six, 115, 123, 124, 126, 128, 131, 132, 135, 136, 137, 138, 139
Hill, Maj., 91
Hill 512, 46
Hill 667, 46, 47
Hill 622, 52, 53
Hill, "Roddy", 29
Hillian, Lt., M.C., 128
Hind, Maj. K. C., v
Hitler, Adolf, xvii, 123
Hodgson, Lt.-Col. D. E. P., 236
Hollbrook, Brigadier, M.C., 150
Horsfall, Lt.-Col.—See Coldwell-Horsfall
Houchin, Lt.-Col. D. J. B., D.S.O., M.C., 193, 237
Howlett, Brigadier B., D.S.O., 49, 51, 66, 67, 88, 89, 103, 238
Hull, Colonel, R. A., xxi
Hunt, Lt.-Col. G. Vivian, O.B.E., T.D., 178, 240
Hunter, Miss Diana, vi
Hunter, Lt.-Col. H. M. A., D.S.O., M.B.E., v, 193, 237
Hunt's Gap, 40, 43, 146, 176, 178

Il Sallaro, 185
Imola, 160, 161, 163, 164, 169
India, 182
Irwin, Capt. Roy, 147
Islay, xix
Ismailia, 153
Italy, xv, xviii, 6, 40, 55, 59, 60, 72, 75, 76, 78, 81-226
Italy, King Victor Emmanuel of, 81

Jackson, Lt., 127
James, Brigadier J., 150, 238
James, Lt.-Col. R. B., D.S.O., 236
Jefferson, Fusilier, V.C., 130
Jefna, 27
Johnson, Capt., 46
Jones, Lt. Owen, M.C., 16
Jones, Sgt., M.M., 186
Joyce, Maj., 110
Juin, General, 38

INDEX

Kairouan, 6, 45
Kaminsky, L/Cpl., M.M., 171
Kanzal, 232
Kasserine Pass, 39, 40
Kefs, The, 52, 53
Keightley, Lt.-Gen. Sir Charles, K.B.E., C.B., O.B.E., D.S.O., vi, 106, 122, 133, 139, 145, 156-7, 160, 236
Kelly, Major (later Lt.-Col.) S. J. Linden, D.S.O., 12, 237
Kemp, L/Cpl., M.M., 92
Kenny, Lt.-Col. W. A., 93, 237
Kent-Lemon, Brigadier A. L., 237
Kerr, Lt.-Col. J., M.C., 239
Kesselring, 82, 112
Kingsett, Lt.-Col. B., M.C., 240
Kintyre, Mull of, xix
Knight, Sgt., 98

La Giovecca, 204
Laird, Sgt., M.M., 36
Laird, Lt.-Col. T., 237
Lamont, Cpl., 84
La Morea, 164
Lampard, Capt., 151
Lanciano, 104
Lang, Capt., 102
Langirella, 218
Largs, xvii
Larino, 89, 91
Lecky, Lt.-Col. R. B., D.S.O., 193, 239
Lee, Capt., 118
Lee, Lt.-Col. James, D.S.O., 18, 20, 21, 22, 238
Leese, Gen. 78, 124, 133, 139
Le Patourel, Major, V.C., 20, 22, 130
Lido Di Roma, 192
Lienz, 228
Lingham, L/Cpl., M.M., 98-9
Liri River, 136
Liri Valley, 111, 112, 123, 124, 134, 135, 140, 198
Lombardy Plain, 159, 160, 161, 169, 175, 193
London, xviii, 59
London—Norfolk House, xviii,
"Longstop Gap", 25
Longstop Hill, xiv, 25, 26, 27-9, 30, 32, 37, 47, 49-51, 52, 53, 54, 69
Loveday, John, 133
Lovell, Lt.-Col. H. O., 238
Lugo, 199
Lytle, Lt.-Col., 114

McCreery, Gen. Sir Richard K.C.B., K.B.E., D.S.O., M.C., 230, 232
MacCrimmon, Sgt., 84
Macfie, Capt. Hugh, 15

McGill, Pte., 128
MacInnes, Sgt., M.M., 43
Mackay, Lt., 14
McKechnie, Lt.-Col. A. D., D.S.O., 96, 238
McKee, Capt. I., v
Mackellar, Lt.-Col. J. G., D.S.O., O.B.E., 14, 238
Mackenzie, Lt.-Col. John, D.S.O., M.C., 100, 158, 237
Mackinnon, Sgt., 14
McLeish, Lt., 51
Macnab, Lt.-Col. C., 49, 238
Madagascar, xvii,
Magione, 151
Mahdi, 45, 46, 47
Maiella, 108
Maiori, 123
Maison Blanche (Airfield), 4, 5
Majdalany, Major Fred., M.C., vi, 111, 132
Malcolm, Lt.-Col. A. D., O.B.E., vi, 176, 192, 238
Malcolm, Major, 50
Maletto, 75, 76
Manly, Lt.-Col. L. A., M.C., 12, 237
Manson, Lt., 145
Mareth, 39
Marina Canal, 210
Marrakesh, 108
Martin, Lt.-Col. S. J., 238
Massa Di Vendetti, 127
Massa Tamburrini, 127
Massa Vertechi, 126
Massicault, 26, 48, 49
Mateur, xxi, 6, 8, 14, 27, 37, 40, 54
Mathews, Lt.-Col. A. L., O.B.E., M.C., 240
Mauthen, 228
Maxwell, Brigadier, 44
Medino Di Casa Di Lesso, 183
Mediterranean, xvii, xx, 39, 59, 108, 153
Medjerda River, 12, 18, 19, 27, 42, 48
Medjez-El-Bab, xiv, 6, 9, 12, 13, 14, 15, 16, 19, 21, 22, 24, 25, 26, 28, 30, 34, 36, 40, 43, 44, 46, 47, 48, 49, 54, 76
Melfa River, 135
Merritt, Pte., M.M., 97
Messina, 60, 75, 76, 78, 83
Mignano, 111, 125
Mills-Roberts, Lt.-Col., 41
Milner, Lt., 127
Milton, Maj., M.C., 99
Mitchell, Major, M.C., 180-1
Mitchell, Lt., 71
Molini Canal, 203, 204

INDEX

Monastery Hill (Cassino), 112, 121, 139
Monk, Major (later Lt.-Col.) G. M. de B., M.C., 96, 134, 238
Montague, E. A., vi, 22, 140
Monte Battaglia, 163
Monte Cairo, 112, 116, 118, 119
Monte Calderaro, 188
Monte Capello, 163
Monte Caprara, 138
Montecassino, 118
Monte Castellaro, 184
Monte Castellone, 119
Montecilfone, 94
Monte Del Acqua Salata, 163, 164, 168, 169, 170-1, 172, 174, 175, 180, 182, 184, 187, 189
Monte De La Tombe, 164
Monte Del Verro, 168, 174, 175, 185
Monte Falchetto, 164
Monte Gabbione, 144
Monte Grande, 164, 170, 184, 188
Monte La Pieve (Point 508), 164-169, 173, 182
Monte Macherone, 74, 75
Monte Maggiore, 185
Monte Mauro, 163
Monte Merlo, 185
Montemorosino, 164
Montenero, 94
Monte Penzola, 163, 169, 172, 173, 185
Montepulciano, 150
Monte Purchio, 116
Monte Rivoglia, 74
Monte San Angelo, 138
Monte San Francisco, 138
Montesanto, 216
Monte Scalpello, 65
Monte Spaduro, 164, 168, 169, 170, 171-4, 175, 182, 184, 188
Montgomery, Field Marshal, Viscount, 37, 59, 60, 63, 68, 78, 81, 99, 103
Moodie, Major, 66
Moody, Cpl., M.M., 43
Moore, Sir John, 93
Moore, Pte. R., D.C.M., 42
Morehead, Alan, vi, 34
Moro River, 104
Morocco, 33
Mount Ausonia, 124
Mount Maio, 124
Mount Trocchio, 124
Mozzagrogna, 99, 101-2, 103
Mur Valley, 229
Mussolini, Benito, 81
Musson, Brigadier G. R. D., 192, 238
Myddleton, Lt.-Col. J. F., 237

Naceur, 43
Nave, La, 76
Naples, 81, 85, 123
Naples—San Carlo Opera House, 123
  Via Roma, 123
Newby, Major, 144
Nicholson, Brigadier, 39
Nicoll, Lt.-Col. H. M. V., D.S.O., O.B.E., 236, 239
Nicolo Canal, 215-6, 218
Nicolson, Capt. Nigel, v, 32
Nile River, xviii,
North Africa, v, xiii, xv, xx, 3-55, 59, 60, 63, 78, 82, 91, 105, 106, 120, 124, 128, 140, 155, 178
Norway, xviii

Oberdrauberg, 228
O'Connor, Major Kevin, 95
Odling-Smee, Lt.-Col. A. J., 192, 238
Oran, xx
Ortona, 105
Orvieto, 142, 144
Ossiacher See, 232
Oudna, 17
Oued Zarga, xxi, 25, 26, 34, 43, 45
Ousseltia, 38, 40

Packard, Brigadier C. D., D.S.O., O.B.E., 150, 158, 192, 236, 238
Padre Il Monelli, 152
Paglia River, 143
Palagonia, 61
Palazzo, 212
Palermo, 59, 60
Palestine, 154
Palmer, Lt.-Col. J. T. G., O.B.E., 239
Panicarola, 152
Parker, Lt.-Col. F. G., 239
Parrish, Lt., 187
Paterson, Capt. A. D., v
Patton, Cpl., 145
Patton, Lt.-Gen., 59
Payne, Capt. H. F., v
Pearce-Serocold, Capt., 19
Pearson, Major, 120
Penington, Lt.-Col. T. N., 238
Penzola, 162, 173
Perry, Lt., 11
Perugia, 150
Pesaro, 159
Pescara, 91, 138, 223
Pescia, 148
Pescia River, 148, 149
Petacciato, 94
Philippeville, xxi
Philips, Lt., 127
Piana, 152
Pianicciale, 142

INDEX

Piccolo, 136
Piedimonte, 123, 135
Pignataro, 126, 127, 128, 131
Pike, Capt. J. A., v
Pinnacles, The, 43
Piopetta River, 126, 127, 128, 131
Pisa, 141, 159
Pizzoferrato, 109
Piumarola, 131-2
Plymouth, 33
Po Di Volano, 214, 216, 218, 219, 220, 221, 222
Po River, 159, 191, 197, 199, 207, 213, 214, 219, 221, 222, 223, 225, 226, 227, 228
Po Valley, 189, 191, 228
Point 86, 127
Point 508 (Monte Pieve), 164-169, 175
Point 448, 175, 185
Point 416, 168, 169
Point 401, 166-169
Point 410, 174
Point 473, 165
Point 462, 165
Point 186, 20, 21
Point 380, 173, 174
Point 387, 169, 172, 173
Point 396, 170, 172, 173, 174
Point 362, 172, 174, 175, 185
Point 328, 166
Point 382, 163, 173
Point 289, 174
Point 298, 174
Polesella, 219, 221, 224
Poll, Pte., M.M., 97
Pollock, Major N. C., M.B.E., v
Pompeii, 123
Pont Du Fahs, 54
Pontecorvo, 135
Pontelagoscuro, 222
Pope Pius XII, 153
Porter, Capt. R. M., v
Portocannone, 85
Portomaggiore, 211, 214, 215, 218
Porto Rotta, 215
Port Said, 153
Possessione San Antonio, 218
Preston, Capt. Campbell, 15
Preston, Lt.-Col. J. C., D.S.O., 236
Pring, Capt. D. A. M., M.C., v
Proctor, Major, 95
Pucciarelli, 147, 148
Pugsley, Lt.-Col. R. L., 236
Pulford, Lt.-Col. M. C., M.C., 208, 237
Pulleyn, Lt., 144
Purser, Lt.-Col. W. F., 236
Pye, Driver, D.C.M., 77
Pyramids, The, 154

Qassasin, 153, 154
Quartesana, 216, 217-8, 219

Ramsay, Pte, M.M., 92
Ranchi River, 182
Ranciano, 148
Randazzo, 73, 74, 75, 76, 78
Rapido River, 111, 112, 113, 115, 116, 119, 123, 124, 125, 126, 128
Rau, Lt.-Col. J. C., 236
Ravello, 123
Ravenna, 185
Ravine De Madonna Del Rio, 164, 165, 168
Reggio, 78, 81, 83
Reid, Cpl., 14
Reid, Brigadier F. S., C.B.E., D.S.O., v, 199, 236
Reno River, 201, 203, 205, 206, 207
Richardson, Capt., 120
Ridley, Lt., 151
Rignano, 141
Rimini, 159, 160
Ripi, 137
Ripiano, 172, 180, 181, 182
Rivaldino, 166
Robaa, 38
Rome, 93, 108, 111, 112, 113, 115, 121, 123, 124, 125, 135, 136, 137, 138, 139, 140, 141, 143, 150, 153, 157
Rommel, Field-Marshal, 37, 38, 39, 40
Rostov, 32
Route 16, 206, 211, 212, 213, 214-15, 219, 226
Ruina, 221, 222, 224
Runco, 216
Russell, Major, 52
Russell, Brigadier Nelson, D.S.O., M.C., v, 52, 67, 102, 103, 104, 113, 114, 238
Russi, 193
Ryder, Maj.-Gen., xx

Sabbioncello Bridge, 219, 220
Sabine Hills, 153
Saletta, 220, 221
Sallustra Valley, 168
Salerno, 81, 82, 83
Salso River, 69, 70, 71, 73, 114
San Ambroglio, 124
San Angelo, 123, 126
San Antonio, 211, 212
San Apollinare ("Twin Tits"), 165, 173, 180
Sanarchangelo, 160
San Bernardino, 204
San Clemente, 177, 181, 182, 184

251

INDEX

San Fatucchio, 146-7, 148, 150
San Felice, 147
San Giorgio, 124
San Giovanni, 137
Sangro River, xv, 95, 97, 98, 101, 103, 104, 107, 108, 109, 114, 155, 159, 198
San Marino, 160
San Martino, 85, 188
San Michele, 119
San Nicolo, 211
San Patrizio, 205
San Salvo, 94, 95, 96, 97
San Servo, 84
Santa Maria, 102, 104
Santerno River, 161, 162, 163, 164, 167, 168, 169, 180, 197, 198, 201, 202, 203, 204, 206, 207
Sassatello Valley, 172, 173
Sassoleone, 163, 164, 173, 179, 182
Saunders, Major J. A. H., D.S.O., 208
Savignano, 160
Sbeitla, 39
Sbiba, 39, 40
Scolo Bolognese, 212
Scotland, xiii, xvii, 155
Scott, Brigadier Andrew, 187
Scott, Colonel (later Brigadier) T. P. D., C.B.E., D.S.O., v, 114, 156, 158, 238, 239
Scott-Foster, Lt.-Col. K., O.B.E., 193, 239
Sedjenane, 14, 44, 54
Senio River, 161, 185, 191, 193-4, 195, 197, 198, 199-201, 202, 206, 207, 229
Serracapriola, 84, 85, 90
Sfax, 6, 31, 39, 59
Shaw, Capt., 21
Shaw, Lt.-Col. D. M., D.S.O., M.C., 239
Shearer, Lt.-Col. F. J., 236
Sicily, v, xv, xviii, 6, 7, 31, 37, 40, 55, 59-78, 85, 91, 140, 153, 155, 226
Sidi Bishr, 154
Sidi Ferruch, 3
Sidi Nsir, 6, 40, 54
Sierra Nevada Mountains, xx,
Sifi, Sgt., M.M., 46
Sillaro River, 161, 163, 167, 170, 180, 182, 184, 205, 206
Simeto River, 64, 69, 70, 73, 114
Sinagoga, 128, 129
Skeen, Lt.-Col. A., 236
Sloughia, 12
Smith, Lt.-Col. H. B. L., M.C., 237
Smith, Lt. Hugh Campbell, 109
Sorrento Peninsula, 123
Souk-El-Arba, 8, 17, 34

Sousse, 6, 38, 59
Spaduro—See Monte Spaduro
Spaduro Corner, 182
Spanish Morocco, xx
Spencer, Brigadier J. L., 103, 238
Spens, Major Pat, 149
Spina River, 152
Spittal, 230
Stephan, Lt., 138, 149
Stewart, Major S., M.C., v
Stewart-Brown, Lt.-Col. W. S., D.S.O., 27, 238
Strada, 146
Strangolagalli, 136
Surkitt, R.S.M., D.C.M., 139
Syracuse, 59, 61, 83

Tabarka, 6, 8, 11
Tally Ho Corner, 42, 43
Tamera, 14
Tamsweg, 229
Tangier, xx
Tanngoucha, 46, 47, 49, 52, 53
Taormina, 78
Taranto, 83, 153, 154, 159
Tarvisio, 227
Tatham, Capt., 20
Taverna, 164
Taylor, Lt.-Col. J., M.C., 134, 138, 192, 238
Taylor, Major Hamish, 103
Tebessa, 39
Tebourba, 9, 15, 16, 17, 18, 19, 20, 21, 22, 23, 24, 25, 30, 32, 35, 36, 47
Temple, Lt.-Col. R. J. G., 240
Ten Peaks, Battle for the, 53, 54
Termoli, 85, 86, 87, 89-90, 91, 94, 95, 96, 157, 159
Terry, Lt., 144
Testour, 41
Thala, 39, 40
Thomas, Capt., 19
Thomas, Lt.-Col. G. A., O.B.E., 193, 239
Thubron, Brigadier G. E., D.S.O., O.B.E., 193, 237
Thuillier, Lt.-Col., D.S.O., 142
Tiber, 141, 142
Tito, Marshal, 229
Tivoli, 150, 153
Tossignano, 163
Toukabeur, 43, 46
Toulon, xx
Trani, 84
Trasimene, Lake, 142, 144, 146, 148-152
Trigno River, 94, 95, 96, 97, 98, 104, 114, 134, 159, 178

INDEX

Tripoli, 38
Troina, 71
Tryon, Lt.-Col. C. E., D.S.O., 120, 236
Tuff, Lt.-Col. C. R., 192, 238
Tunis, xiii, xiv, xxi, 6, 8, 9, 12, 13, 14, 15, 16, 17, 23, 26, 28, 31, 32, 35, 38, 40, 44, 48, 49, 54
Tunisia, 6, 7, 8, 24, 33, 36, 38, 39, 43, 60, 64, 68, 69, 72, 77, 107, 176
"Twin Tits"—See San Apollinare
Tyson, Capt., 172
Twomley, Lt.-Col. L. P., D.S.O., 239

Udine, 228
Usher, Lt.-Col. T. Clive, C.B.E., D.S.O., 29, 116, 239

Vaiano, 146
Valmontone, 137
Vasto, 95, 96, 97, 99
Velletri, 137
Vena Del Gesso, 163, 164, 169
Venetia, 227, 228
Veroli, 138
Vezzolo, 189
Vienna, 231, 232
Vietinghoff, 227
Villach, 228, 229, 230

Vineyard Hill, 95, 97
Voghenza, 215, 216, 218
Volturno River, 85, 87, 108
Von Arnim, General, 7, 37, 39, 40, 55
Von Schwerin, Lt.-Gen. Graf, 226

Waldron, Capt., 20
Wales, South, 13
Walke, Major Charles, 100
Webster, Major Neil, 149
Wedderburn-Maxwell, Brigadier J., D.S.O., M.C., vi, xvii, 37, 236
Weeks, Lt., 71
Whitefoord, Lt., 118
Wigram, Major Lionel, 109
Wilberforce, Lt.-Col. W. B. S. J. A. E., D.S.O., 15, 51, 237
Wilkinson, Lt.-Col. R. J., M.B.E., 237
Williams, Emlyn, 122
Williams, Capt. J. O. D., 89
Wilson, Gen. Sir Henry Maitland, v, 160
Wingfield, Capt., 20
Wolfsburg, 229
Wood, L/Cpl. L., M.M., 98
Woodhouse, Lt., M.C., 98
Wright, Lt., 19

Zocca, 219, 222, 224

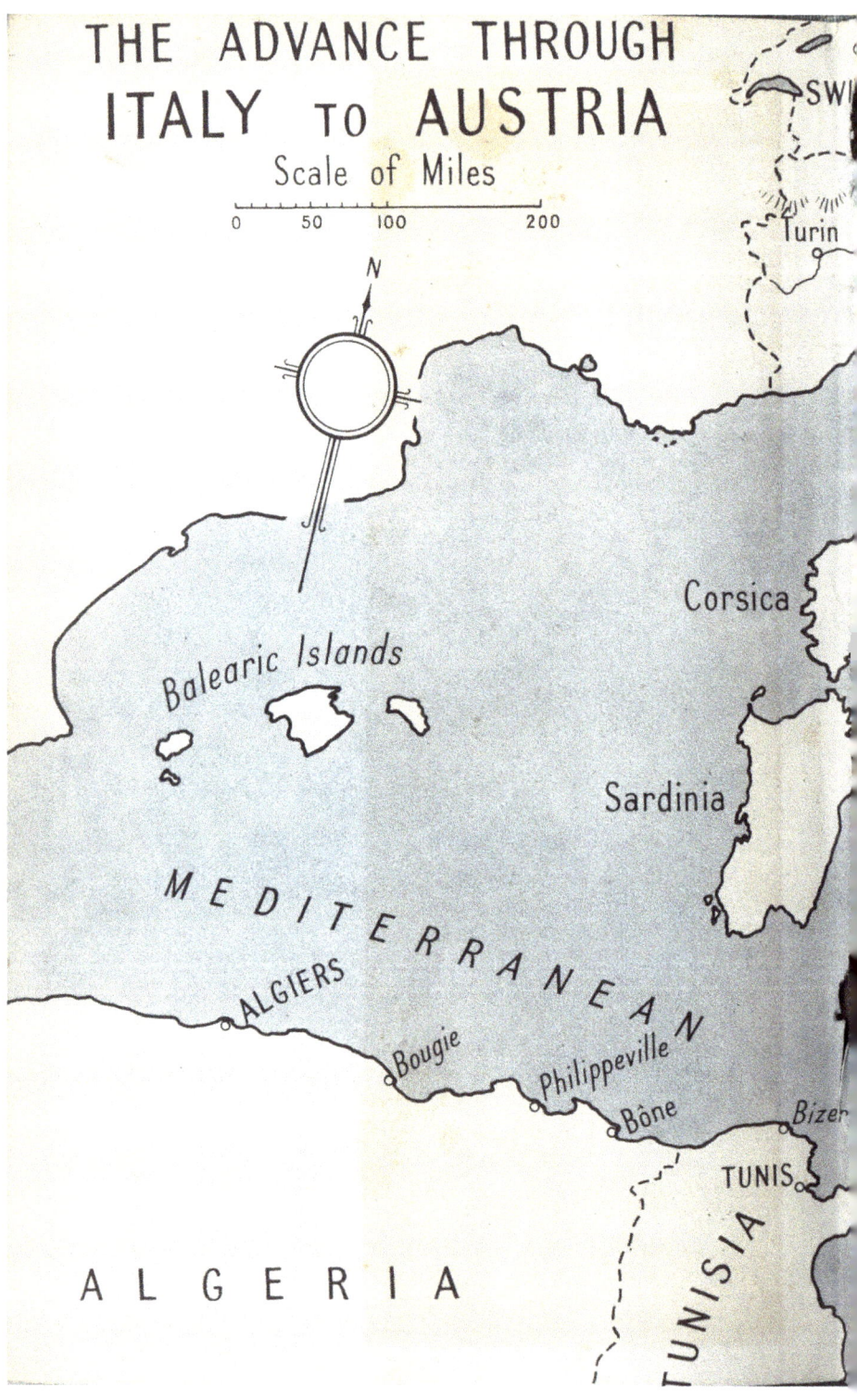

www.ingramcontent.com/pod-product-compliance
Ingram Content Group UK Ltd.
Pitfield, Milton Keynes, MK11 3LW, UK
UKHW021256180426
11947UKWH00011B/805